MW01025849

God Dwells with Us

Temple Symbolism in the Fourth Gospel

Mary L. Coloe, P.B.V.M.

A Michael Glazier Book
THE LITURGICAL PRESS
Collegeville, Minnesota
www.litpress.org

A Michael Glazier Book published by Liturgical Press

Cover design by Ann Blattner. Cover photos: Corbis Stock Photography.

Library of Congress Cataloging-in-Publication Data

Coloe, Mary L., 1949–
    God dwells with us : temple symbolism in the Fourth Gospel / Mary L. Coloe.
      p. cm.
    "A Michael Glazier book."
    Includes bibliographical references (p.) and index.
    ISBN 0-8146-5952-7 (alk. paper)
    1. Bible. N.T. John—Criticism, interpretation, etc. 2. Temples—Biblical teaching. I. Title.

BS2615.2 .C67 2001
226.5'064—dc21

                                00-049562

To the memory of my parents,
Madge and Ted Coloe.

They nurtured my faith in a loving God
and through difficult financial times
encouraged and enabled my love of learning
well beyond their own schooling opportunities.

With love and thanks.

Contents

Preface

"Make your home in me, as I make mine in you" (John 15:4).

These words have been the basis of my own ongoing spiritual journey from long before I professed religious vows. The quotation expresses for me the sense I have of the wonder and mystery of God's dwelling within me. One image that gives a tangible shape to this inner mystery is that of the Temple. As my faith journey led me to share my life with sisters of the Presentation Congregation, the Temple took on an even greater significance, as our feast day is the Presentation of Mary in the Temple. Daily I have prayed the Collect prayer of this Feast, "to be worthy, like Mary, to be presented in the Temple of God's glory." The image intrigued me. It spoke of a building, of a place of God's heavenly presence, and yet my experience, and the experience of many other Christians, has been of God's indwelling in the human heart.

When an opportunity arose to undertake research for a doctorate, immediately I knew the topic I wished to explore and the Gospel to focus on. I wanted to try to cross the centuries through this Gospel text and plunge into the experience of the Johannine community. I sought to understand what was their sense of God's indwelling, promised by Jesus, and how this might relate to the Temple which figures very strongly in the narrative. Can the Johannine text speak to the desires of Christians today who seek intimacy with God "without seeing" the Jesus of history? Can the images employed by the Gospel, that evoke such intimacy, bear the scrutiny of critical exegesis? These were my background questions as I set out on the task of a disciplined academic examination of texts that have been important over the centuries for our Christian spirituality. My faith sought further understanding.

The task involved the support and help of many people. Firstly my own religious sisters whose fidelity and love have given me so much support, and whose interest in this topic provided opportunities to share the ongoing development of this thesis. My colleagues in the school of theology at the Australian Catholic University listened to parts of this work in seminars and offered helpful criticism, encouragement and inspiration. In particular I thank Dr. Veronica Lawson, R.S.M., who read sections of the text and offered valuable suggestions to help its overall presentation and Rev. Dr. Terence Curtin, who, as the head of school, supported my applications for grants and released time to enable the work to move forward. I am grateful to Dr. Elaine Wainwright, R.S.M., from the Brisbane College of Theology, who critiqued some sections of this text and alerted me to a broader, feminist perspective. A thesis is a lonely undertaking and without the ongoing friendship and supportive encouragement from my sisters, colleagues, and friends I would have found the task beyond me. Thank you.

The most significant helper in this work has been my friend and adviser, Professor Francis Moloney, S.D.B. I attended undergraduate lectures given by Frank and was deeply moved by his sensitivity to symbol and his ability to communicate the joys and pains of the Johannine community. His lectures stimulated my academic interests and it has been a pleasure to be able to work closely with him. The encouragement from a scholar of Frank's renown and his confidence in my work enabled me to find the courage necessary to explore new paths.

Finally I express my thanks to the editors at The Liturgical Press who have taken a thesis intended for a readership of three examiners, and polished the writing to make it accessible to a wider readership.

Mary Coloe, P.B.V.M.

Abbreviations

ABD	*Anchor Bible Dictionary.* ed. D. M. Freedman. 6 vols. New York: Doubleday, 1992.
ABR	*Australian Biblical Review*
Bib	*Biblica*
BibT	*Bible Today*
BTB	*Biblical Theology Bulletin*
CBQ	*Catholic Biblical Quarterly*
EDNT	*Exegetical Dictionary of the New Testament.* eds. H. Balz and G. Schneider. 3 vols. Grand Rapids, Mich.: Eerdmans, 1990–93.
ExpT	*Expository Times*
IDB	*The Interpreter's Dictionary of the Bible.* ed. G. A. Buttrick. 5 vols. Nashville: Abingdon, 1962.
Int	*Interpretation*
JBL	*Journal of Biblical Literature*
JSNT	*Journal for the Study of the New Testament*
JSOT	*Journal for the Study of the Old Testament*
JTS	*Journal of Theological Studies*
LXX	The Septuagint
MT	Masoretic Text
NJBC	*The New Jerome Biblical Commentary,* eds. R. E. Brown, J. A. Fitzmyer, and R. E. Murphy. Englewood Cliffs, N.J.: Prentice Hall, 1989.
NRSV	New Revised Standard Version
NTS	*New Testament Studies*
NovT	*Novum Testamentum*
RB	*Revue Biblique*
RSR	*Recherche de science religieuse*

RSV	Revised Standard Version
SJT	*Scottish Journal of Theology*
TDNT	*Theological Dictionary of the New Testament*. eds. G. Kittel and G. Friedrich. 10 vols. Grand Rapids, Mich.: Eerdmans, 1964–76.
VT	*Vetus Testamentum*
Wor	*Worship*

Abbreviations of Non-Biblical Jewish Literature

Ant.	Josephus Antiquities
Jub.	Jubilees
2–3 Apoc. Bar.	Syriac, Greek Apocalypse of Baruch

Targums

Tg. Onq.	Targum Onqelos
Tg. Neof.	Targum Neofiti
Tg. Neb.	Targum of the Prophets
Tg. Ps.-J	Targum Pseudo-Jonathan
Tg. Isa	Targum of Isaiah

Dead Sea Scrolls

CD	Damascus Document
1QS	The Community Rule from Cave 1.
1QM	The War Scroll from Cave 1.
4QFlor	*Florilegium* from Cave 4.
1QpHab	*Pesher on Habakkuk* from Cave 1.
4QpGen	*Pesher on Genesis* from Cave 4.

Rabbinic Literature

m.	Mishnah
t.	Tosefta
y.	Jerusalem Talmud
Sukk.	Sukka

Introduction

In the year 70 C.E. the Temple in Jerusalem was destroyed. Two identifiable groups who had their origins in Judaism survived the devastation
of Titus' army. One group, under the leadership of the Pharisees, in particular R. Johannan ben Zakkai, set about the task of a major reinterpretation of Jewish traditions and a redefinition of its identity and cultic
practices.[1] A second group of Jews, influenced by Jesus' teaching and
under the guidance of God's Spirit, had come to believe that God's Messiah had been sent in the person of Jesus of Nazareth (John 1:41; 11:27;
20:31). This second group became known as Christians (Acts 11:26). For
both groups the destruction of Jerusalem and the loss of the Temple marked
a major turning point. At the same time as the Pharisees were engaged in
the critical task of self-definition, Christian communities were also seeking to understand the revelation of God in the life, death, and resurrection
of Jesus. Both groups therefore were engaged simultaneously in a major
religious struggle for self-identity. In this climate the two groups, who had
their origins in the one story of Israel, took separate paths.

For the people of Israel, the Jerusalem Temple had been the focal
point of their faith that God dwelt in their midst, enabling them to be a holy
people through the Temple's ongoing sacrificial cult. The rabbis sought a
theological meaning for its destruction and alternative ways of living lives
acceptable to YHWH. The rabbis found such an alternative in the Torah. The
transition from sacrifice to Torah is illustrated in this later rabbinic tale:

---

[1] A brief overview of this Jewish background can be found in W. D. Davies, "As-
pects of the Jewish Background of the Gospel of John," *Exploring the Gospel of John:
In Honour of D. Moody Smith,* ed. R. Alan Culpepper and C. Clifton Black (Louisville:
Westminster John Knox Press, 1996) 46–52.

1

Once, as Rabban Yohanan be Zakkai was coming forth from Jerusalem, Rabbi Joshua followed him and beheld the Temple in ruins.

"Woe unto us," Rabbi Joshua cried, "that this, the place where the iniquities of Israel were atoned for, is laid waste!"

"My son," Rabban Yohanan said to him, "be not grieved. We have another atonement as effective as this. And what is it? It is acts of loving kindness, as it is said, *For I desire mercy and not sacrifice*" (Hos 6:6) (Avot de Rabbi Natan, ch. 6).[2]

Members of a Christian community found themselves in conflict with post-70 Judaism and sought answers for their situation. They had been proclaiming Jesus as the Messiah for many years, even while the Jewish members of the community continued to join in synagogue prayers and Temple worship.[3] When they found they were no longer accepted within the synagogue, when those who professed Jesus as the Christ were being rejected from Judaism (John 9:22; 12:42; 16:2), they faced a painful question— **how could they maintain their Jewish traditions, especially their rich cultic traditions, and maintain their new faith in Jesus?**[4]

The Fourth Gospel is the written record of one Christian community's response to this question. How could this community tell the story of Jesus in a way that gave full value to Israel's historical and cultic traditions? When the rabbis were proclaiming that they had the Torah which could replace the Temple as a means of sanctification of the people, so that God could still dwell with them, what could a small, recently formed, Christian community offer to counter the Mosaic Torah? Even if the community turned to Jesus as the one who fulfilled Israel's hopes, what could such faith mean so many years after the experience of his historical ministry? When their Jewish neighbors gathered to pray and celebrate the great festivals of their faith and history, what did the Johannine Jewish-Christian group have to celebrate? Where could they gather for prayer, with the Temple gone and the local synagogues no longer tolerating unorthodox views?

---

[2] Quoted in J. Neusner, "Judaism in a Time of Crisis: Four Responses to the Destruction of the Second Temple," *Judaism* 21 (1972) 324.

[3] Although part of the theological agenda of Luke-Acts, see the way Acts records the continued contact with Temple and synagogue (e.g., Acts 2:46; 3:3; 5:12; 6:9; 21:26).

[4] On the break with the Synagogue indicated in 9:22; 12:42; 16:2, see F. Manns, *John and Jamnia: How the Break Occurred between Jews and Christians c. 80–100 A.D.* (Jerusalem: Franciscan Printing Press, 1988) and *idem, L'Evangile de Jean à la lumière du Judaïsme,* Studium Biblicum Franciscanum Analecta 33 (Jerusalem: Franciscan Printing Press, 1991) 470–509. This issue will be discussed further below.

In this book I examine the creative theological insight that drew on the great cultic traditions and meaning of Israel's Temple to answer such questions by presenting Jesus as the Temple. Through a detailed analysis of relevant passages from the Fourth Gospel, I will show that the Temple is not just one symbol among many, used by the community to express who Jesus is for them; for the Johannine community the Temple is the *major* symbol that functions in two ways:

i. The Temple, as the dwelling place of God, points to the identity and role of Jesus.

ii. The imagery of the Temple is transferred from Jesus to the Christian community, indicating its identity and role.

In other words, I propose to show that the Temple functions in the narrative as the major christological symbol that gradually shifts its symbolic meaning from the person of Jesus to the Johannine community in the post-resurrection era. In the time of Jesus' ministry, he is the focus of the cultic imagery of Temple and Tabernacle. Within the Jewish feasts of Passover, Tabernacles, and Dedication, Jesus appropriates to himself the cultic symbols—bread (6:35, 48, 51), water (7:37-39), light (8:12), sacred place (10:36). Within the narrative there are indications that what is said of Jesus, will, in a future time, apply to the community of believers (4:23; 7:38, 39; 14:2). These proleptic comments are associated with the future gift of the Spirit.

The Temple, therefore, is not a peripheral image. It is used consistently throughout the text and moves beyond the life of Jesus into the life of the community, giving the community a clear sense of identity and a way of sustaining faith in the absence of Jesus. Furthermore, I will show that the actual plot of this Gospel is announced as the destruction and raising of a Temple (2:19) and only when this is achieved does Jesus announce, "It is finished" (19:30).

The Temple in Contemporary Scholarship

While some scholars have studied the significance of the Temple in the New Testament, and even devoted entire books to particular Johannine passages, none to date have traced the Temple symbolism across the Gospel or shown how the actual narrative presents the destruction and raising of the Temple prophesied in John 2:21.[5] While the commentaries

[5] Y. Congar, *The Mystery of the Temple: The Manner of God's Presence to His Creatures from Genesis to the Apocalypse*, trans. R. Trevett (London: Burns & Oates,

discuss Jesus' words about destroying and raising the Temple (2:19), along with the narrator's explanation that he spoke of his body (2:21), this verse has not been given due weight in interpreting other Temple passages. Its significance for the rest of the Gospel narrative has not been explored, nor has there been an analysis of what is meant by destroying and raising the Temple within the Johannine narrative. How does the narrative show this destruction and rebuilding? This is the task I set myself. I will explore what the Temple means as a symbol of Jesus' identity and then look at the way the Temple symbolism is transferred from the person of Jesus to the Christian community. I will show first that the Temple is a christological symbol and second that it becomes a symbol of the Christian community for this particular group of believers.

Symbol

In speaking of the Temple as a symbol, it is important to clarify some of the terms used. Symbol (Σύμβολον)—as the word itself suggests—is the throwing together, the joining together of two otherwise dissimilar realities.[6] The Fourth Gospel displays a self-conscious use of symbolism and its religious function to bring together the divine reality, the world "above," with the human reality, the world "below."[7] At a literal level these

---

1962); J. Daniélou, *The Presence of God,* trans. W. Roberts (London: A. R. Mowbray & Co., 1958); J. McKelvey, *The New Temple: The Church in the New Testament,* Oxford Theological Monographs (Oxford: Oxford University Press, 1969); P. Walker, *Jesus and the Holy City: New Testament Perspectives on Jerusalem* (Grand Rapids, Mich.: Eerdmans, 1996); M. Barker, *The Gate of Heaven: The History and Symbolism of the Temple in Jerusalem* (London: SPCK, 1991); M. Barker, *On Earth as it is in Heaven: Temple Symbolism in the New Testament* (Edinburgh: T & T Clark, 1995); J. McCaffrey, *The House With Many Rooms: The Temple Theme of Jn 14, 2–3* (Rome: Biblical Institute Press, 1988); L. Nereparampil, *Destroy this Temple: An Exegetico-Theological study on the meaning of Jesus' Temple-Logion in Jn 2:19* (Bangalore: Dharmaram College, 1978).

[6] R. A. Culpepper, *Anatomy of the Fourth Gospel: A Study in Literary Design* (Philadelphia: Fortress, 1983) 182. Sandra Schneiders gives a fivefold definition of a symbol as "(1) a sensible reality (2) which renders present to and (3) involves a person subjectively in (4) a transforming experience (5) of the mystery of the Transcendent." See S. Schneiders, "Symbolism and the sacramental principle in the Fourth Gospel," *Segni E Sacramenti Nel Vangelo Di Giovanni,* ed. Pius-Ramon Tragan, Studia Anselmiana 67 (Rome: Editrice Anselmiana, 1977) 223.

[7] Throughout the Gospel Jesus uses symbolic language to disclose something of his own person—"I am the bread of life" (6:35); "I am the light of the world" (8:12); "I am the vine" (15:1). As Schneiders states, "Jesus himself is presented as the unique and totally adequate symbol of God. The exclusive centrality of the person of Jesus in the

two worlds are incongruous and mutually exclusive. Symbolism allows the incongruity to be displaced as the human mind is stretched to transcend the literal meaning of the words and glimpse a further level of possible meanings. The literal meaning is nonsense forcing the hearer/reader to look for a "surplus of meaning." So Nicodemus is asked to go beyond the literal meaning of "birth" to a deeper meaning (3:3-5); the Samaritan Woman is required to understand a further level of meaning in the phrase "living water" (4:11). Basic to religious symbolism is a belief that creation has come from God, and therefore things of the created world have the potential to reveal God.[8] "What has been created can become a symbolic bearer of the revelation."[9] The Johannine Gospel makes this explicit with the statement, "the Word became flesh" (1:14); that which is of the Divinity becomes human.

A metaphor names two apparently dissimilar realities. According to Ricoeur, a good metaphor "implies an intuitive perception of the similarity . . . in dissimilars."[10] In the example "I am the vine," two things are linked—"I" and "vine." The reader is challenged to find the points of connection. In what way is Jesus like a vine, or like bread, or light? In the language of semantics the "I" is the "tenor" and the "vine" is the "vehicle."[11] When the narrator makes the comment, "But he spoke of the temple of his body" (2:21), this is a metaphor, where "Temple" is the vehicle, and "body" is the tenor. Two different types of realities are brought together, a building and a human person. At a literal level the words are nonsense. The readers, if they are to enter into the narrative world, are required to puzzle out how the notion of "Templeness" could relate to the body of Jesus, and conversely, what is it of Jesus that can be called "Temple."

Fourth Gospel . . . is due precisely to John's reflectively explicit consciousness of Jesus as the symbol of God. . . ." See S. Schneiders, "History and Symbolism in the Fourth Gospel," *L'Évangile de Jean: Sources, rédaction, théologie,* ed. M de Jonge, Bibliotheca Ephemeridum Theologicae Lovaniensis 44 (Louvain: Louvain University Press, 1977) 373. Technically, the "I am *X*" statements are metaphors, two realities are spoken of, a human person "I" and something of nature "bread," "light," "vine." For more detailed analysis of terms such as metaphor and symbol see Culpepper *Anatomy,* 181–98 and C. Koester, *Symbolism in the Fourth Gospel: Meaning, Mystery, Community* (Minneapolis: Fortress, 1995) 1–31.

[8] Koester, *Symbolism,* 2.

[9] J. Painter, "Johannine symbols: A Case Study in Epistemology," *Journal of Theology for Southern Africa* 27 (1979) 33.

[10] P. Ricoeur, *The Rule of Metaphor: Multidisciplinary studies of the creation of meaning in language* (London: Routledge & Kegan Paul, 1977) 23.

[11] Culpepper, *Anatomy,* 181.

A symbol, as distinct from a metaphor, only presents the vehicle and the reader is required to supply the tenor. If the readers do not recognize that a symbol is being given, they are left with only a literal level. So Jesus accuses the crowd of seeking him because "you ate your fill of the loaves" (6:26). The deeper symbolism of the feeding, the links with Moses and the Passover, they have missed. The failure to recognize a symbol can also lead to misunderstandings, such as those displayed by characters in the Gospel, Nicodemus, (ch. 3) and the Samaritan Woman (ch. 4).[12] Symbols can be missed, and they can be misunderstood. "The potential symbols can also fail to become vehicles of the revelation."[13]

In my reading of the Fourth Gospel, the Temple functions as a symbol. In the Prologue, and in chapter 2, the reader is given two metaphors that identify Jesus in terms of Israel's cultic system. Jesus is the tabernacling presence of the divine Word (1:14). Jesus is the Temple (2:21). In these metaphors the reader has both the tenor (flesh, body of Jesus) and the vehicle (Tabernacle, Temple). The symbolism is explicit even if the full meaning of the symbol remains unclear.[14] Having given the Temple the quality of a symbol whose meaning transcends a literal building, the discerning reader will carry this transcending impetus into the rest of the reading experience. The Temple will not be just a neutral setting within which Jesus and other characters interact. The Gospel has created a narrative world where the Temple and Jesus are intrinsically linked. The Temple, in one sense, is like a voiceless character or spectator in the narrative whose presence and significance must never be taken for granted. It looms large on the Johannine stage. My aim is to analyze how the Temple functions within the symbolic world created by the narrative. Just as characters can have a particular function within a plot, so also, I contend, does the Temple.

The historical and religious context may explain why the Temple captured the imagination of this community as a means of expressing who Jesus was, and what it, the community, is. The stark fact that the Temple no longer existed, except in memory, meant that Judaism was transferring the meaning of the Temple's destruction and sacrificial imagery into daily living. The Johannine community, in the midst of a Torah-centered Jewish community, also needed to reinterpret the meaning of the Temple's destruction. In this historical situation, the Johannine community transferred the meaning of the Temple to the person of Jesus. But this could be only a partial solution. For if the image of the Temple applied only to Jesus, then

[12] Culpepper provides a list of Johannine misunderstandings, *Anatomy*, 161–62.

[13] Painter, *Johannine symbols,* 33.

[14] Culpepper, *Anatomy,* 183, quotes William Tindall and speaks of a symbol containing a "residual mystery that escapes our intellect."

the Johannine community would be in exactly the same situation as Israel without their Temple, for Jesus is now absent. Whatever one makes of his post-Easter presence, the physical body of Jesus is absent. The creativity of the community, or perhaps its leader, is shown in the way it transfers the symbol of the Temple from the body of Jesus to the community of believers.[15] As the meaning of the Temple lives on in rabbinic Judaism through Torah, the meaning of the Temple lives on within the Christian community in the ongoing presence of Jesus in the lives of the believers through the power of the Spirit-Paraclete (14:17, 26; 16:14).

A second reason why the Temple may have been chosen as such a major symbol is because of cultic considerations. It was precisely within the cult that the Johannine community was feeling the pain of its separation from Judaism, in no longer having access to the praying community of Israel in the synagogue. Since worship was such a critical point of division, the community needed a means of reinterpreting Israel's cult so that the Jewish members of the Johannine community, in their radical decision to accept Jesus, would not feel they were entirely cut off from their traditional roots.

Methodology

To describe the methodology I have used, Sandra Schneiders' comment is appropriate, "Rather than starting with a method or even an established methodology . . . the interpreter starts with the questions that he or she wants to answer."[16] My initial questions could be stated as:

- in what way does the Temple, as it is presented in the Fourth Gospel, reveal the identity and mission of Jesus?

- in the absence of the historical Jesus of Nazareth, what is the significance of the Temple for the Christian community?

My approach is text focused. The text creates a particular narrative world, employs language and symbols, depicts characters and events in an attempt to engage a reader. But the text is not a closed system. The Gospel emerged within a particular historical, religious, and cultural milieu and is self-consciously in dialogue with readers who are part of that milieu.[17] The narrative, through the world it creates, has an explicit aim to

---

[15] I will argue that this transferal is most clearly indicated in John 14 through the use of the image "My Father's House" (14:2). See chapter 8 below.

[16] S. M. Schneiders, *The Revelatory Text: Interpreting the New Testament as Sacred Scripture* (San Francisco: Harper Collins, 1991) 111.

[17] On two occasions the reader is deliberately addressed, "that you may believe" (19:35; 20:31). Apart from these explicit comments to the reader, other narrative techniques,

bring a reader to faith (19:35; 20:31). There is a dialogue between the text
and the historical/social/religious world of the first century. My approach attempts to take seriously both parties in the dialogue and to hear their voices
resonating through the Gospel. With these questions as my starting point and
a dialogical approach the investigation used the following methods:

- For each chosen pericope I established a structure that gave a literary
  and logical coherence to the entire passage. I am unable to accept "displacement" theories, such as those proposed by Bultmann, as an explanation of the tensions which appear in the Johannine narrative.

- I investigated the religious and cultural background to:
  —any scriptural allusions, both explicit and implicit
  —any relevant first-century customs
  —any liturgical practices indicated by the text.

This involved a study of various Jewish texts, primarily the M.T., the
LXX, the Targums, with some reference to the Apocrypha and Pseudepigrapha, the Dead Sea Scrolls, and rabbinic writings.

- I sought any inter-textual allusions where the Gospel had pre-
  established a particular significance for a word or phrase. By such
  inter-text the evangelist creates his own system of meaning that may
  confirm or critique Jewish traditions.

- I maintained a distinction between the *characters within the narrative*
  and the *readers of the narrative*.[18] Characters in the narrative are limited in what they know. They have access only to specific pieces of information and react to Jesus and each other on the basis of this. Readers
  of the narrative have far greater information. They have access to the
  entire Gospel as it has so far unfolded. In addition to the words and actions of *all* the characters, they have the information given in the Prologue, the narrative asides (e.g., 1:38; 2:21; 4:2; 3:24; 7:50) and the
  enlightened point of view of the post-Easter author (e.g., 2:22; 12:33).[19]

---

such as asides and irony, are used to involve the reader in the unfolding of the narrative.
"Irony is a kind of fellowship into which the author and sound reader and spectator
enter in silence." See P. Duke, *Irony in the Fourth Gospel* (Atlanta: John Knox Press,
1985) 29. Duke's examination of Johannine irony is but one of a growing number of
books examining what is called "the implicit commentary" in the Gospel which addresses and directs the reader.

[18] For greater descriptions of the function of Johannine characterization and the Johannine implied reader, see Culpepper, *Anatomy,* 101–48; 205–27.

[19] Stibbe claims that there are approximately sixty of these asides informing and
educating the reader. See M. Stibbe, *John as storyteller: Narrative criticism and the*

Of particular importance in this approach is the possible first-time or implied reader who has a general knowledge of the Christian story but is gradually educated, through the reading process, in the particular Johannine meaning of this Christian story.[20]

These methods, partly literary critical, partly historical critical, are a means of entering the world or system of meaning created by the text. How is the Temple incorporated into the world as it is constituted by a first century author and theologian for a first century audience? What meaning is the Temple given in a text which took its final form some twenty to thirty years after Jerusalem's destruction? By examining the text, the context, and inter-text, I hope to provide some answers to these questions.

Presuppositions

i. The Text

I accept the text as a unified whole, allowing for the probable stages of a first writing and then a later writing or writings, by the same author.[21] Along with most scholars I accept that chapter 21 is from a later editor, who may have also either rearranged or made additions to the Last Discourse.[22] In my reading, the Gospel displays a consistency of language, emphases, symbols, theological purpose, and design that leads me to presume its author is a first-century writer of great theological insight, gifted also with artistic and literary skill. I presume therefore, that the text as we have it made good sense to this author for his particular purposes and his community. If I, as twenty-first century reader, cannot see the sense of the

---

fourth gospel, Society for New Testament Studies Monograph Series 73 (Cambridge: Cambridge University Press, 1992) 20.

[20] Stibbe, *John as storyteller* 11–12, comments on the importance of the awareness of the first-century audience and the historical dimension of the Gospel—"biblical narrative is a functional structure; it is social discourse oriented to an historical audience." For further description of the role of the "implied" reader and this reader's relationship to the real reader, see F. J. Moloney, "Who is 'The Reader' in/of the Fourth Gospel," *The Interpretation of John,* ed. John Ashton (Edinburg: T & T Clark, 1997) 219–33.

[21] Most commentaries discuss questions of authorship and composition. Raymond Brown suggests the Gospel went through five editorial stages. See R. E. Brown, *The Gospel According to John.* 2 vols. Anchor Bible 29–29a. (New York: Doubleday, 1966 and 1970) 1:XXIV–XXXIX.

[22] A brief introduction to the complexities of the composition of the final discourse can be found in F. F. Segovia, *The Farewell of the Word: The Johannine Call to Abide* (Minneapolis: Fortress, 1991) 24–47.

Gospel's design, or language, or symbolic system, it is not doing justice to the text to presume a multiplicity of non-authorial sources, or a later reshuffling and addition of sections, or to suppose that the bulk of the text is the work of a later "clumsy" hand.[23]

In taking this approach I draw upon traditional historical-critical methodologies in combination with more recent narrative approaches. By taking this synthetic approach, I hope to allow the text to speak for itself, and through the text, to allow a first-century author to disclose his intentions.[24]

ii. The Locale [25]

The Gospel is written in a situation of conflict.[26] The consistent conflict Jesus experiences with some of the Jewish leaders, the strong rhetoric that emerges in these conflicts, the three instances of the term ἀποσυνάγωγος (John 9:22; 12:42; 16:2), suggests a community in conflict with at least the local synagogue, if not the wider post-70 Jewish community. The importance of the synagogue in comprehending the milieu of the Gospel is well argued by Craig Evans. He cites as evidence for the synagogue background the following five points each of which he then develops:[27]

1) There is expression given to certain rabbinic terms and methods;
2) There are important parallels with specific targumic traditions and rabbinic midrashim;

[23] In the words of C. H. Dodd, "I shall assume as a provisional working hypothesis that the present order is not fortuitous, but deliberately devised by somebody—even if he were only a scribe doing his best—and that the person in question. . . had some design in mind, and was not necessarily irresponsible or unintelligent." See C. H. Dodd, *The Interpretation of the Fourth Gospel* (Cambridge: Cambridge University Press, 1953) 290.

[24] See the comments by P. S. Minear on the relationship between the author's intentions and the first readers of the text, "The audience of the Fourth Gospel," *Int* 31 (1977) 340.

[25] The work of J. L. Martyn on the historical context of the Johannine Gospel has been widely accepted among scholars, at least in its general outline. See J. L. Martyn, "Glimpses into the History of the Johannine Community," In *L'Évangile de Jean* ed. M. de Jonge, 149–75; and *idem, History and Theology in the Fourth Gospel.* 2nd ed. (Nashville: Abingdon, 1979). A summary of his reconstruction of the community's origin and development can be found in R. E. Brown, "Johannine Ecclesiology—the Community's Origins," *Int* 31 (1977) 381–83.

[26] There is much dispute on how widespread this conflict was. See F. J. Moloney, *John,* Sacra Pagina 4. (Collegeville: The Liturgical Press, 1998) for further references to this scholarly discussion.

[27] C. Evans, *Word and Glory: On the Exegetical and Theological Background of John's Gospel.* Journal for the Study of the New Testament Supplement Series 89 (Sheffield: JSOT Press, 1993) 146–86.

3) Explicit reference is made to the expulsion of Christians from the synagogue;
4) The use of the Old Testament appears to reflect an apologetic designed to present Jesus as Israel's Messiah and to deflect skepticism and criticism arising from the synagogue;
5) There are also important parallels with Qumran which suggest that portions of the Johannine tradition had their origin in Palestine.[28]

Outline of the Argument

I begin by examining the Prologue and situating the issue of God's dwelling within the historical context of Jewish and Christian conflict in the years after the destruction of the Temple. The question for rabbinic Judaism, and the nascent Christian community is—Where is God, and where is God's revelation accessible? The Prologue provides the readers of this Gospel with the first clue to the unique symbolic system that will permeate the text of the narrative; Jesus is introduced in cultic terms as the tabernacling presence of God's glory now visible within the human story (1:14).

The following chapter examines the various traditions that may lie behind the choice of the word ἐσκήνωσεν, to describe the flesh-taking of the Divine *logos* (1:14). This chapter traces the development of Israel's cultic traditions from the Tabernacle to the Solomonic Temple, and the various reactions to Israel's cult. This long and detailed chapter is crucial for a full appreciation of all that is involved in the brief statement of 1:14. Through the analysis of Israel's cultic traditions, I seek to establish what was Israel's sense of God's dwelling in their midst, how this was expressed in the institution of the Temple, and how this expression changed due to changing historical and religious circumstances. I examine the attempts made in the prophetic, Deuteronomic, wisdom and apocalyptic traditions (including Qumran) to reform or "spiritualize" the cult. In this survey of Israel's history, I discuss some of the terms found in the Targums (מימרא *Memra*, שכינה *Shekinah* and יקר *Yichra*) that may provide a liturgical insight into Jewish worship contemporary with the Johannine community.[29] This chapter provides evidence that traditions of God's presence in Israel

---

[28] The geographical location of the Johannine Community is much disputed. Wayne Meeks discusses three possibilities Galilee, Batanaea, and a small *polis* such as Ephesus in the Diaspora. See W. Meeks, "Breaking Away: Three New Testament Pictures of Christianity's Separation from the Jewish Communities," *"To See Ourselves As Others See Us": Christians, Jews, "Others" in Late Antiquity,* ed. Jacob Neusner and Ernest Frerichs (Chico, Calif.: Scholars Press, 1985) 93–115.

[29] מימרא is usually translated as *word,* שכינה as *presence* and יקר as *glory.* These terms will be treated more fully within ch. 3.

were not static but underwent frequent reinterpretations in response to different historical needs and religious sensitivities.

The fourth chapter begins the formal exegesis of Johannine texts explicitly concerned with issues of Temple worship. Before examining the Johannine approach to the Temple, I briefly describe the various presentations of the Temple within the Synoptic Gospels. The Fourth Gospel in its use of Temple imagery is taking a motif already present within the Christian tradition but developing this motif into a christological symbol of Jesus' identity and mission. The so-called "Cleansing of the Temple" provides a major hermeneutical key to understanding the symbolism of the Temple in later passages, "But he spoke of the temple of his body" (2:21). I argue that this scene goes far beyond a "cleansing" of Israel's cultic practices; rather, Jesus' actions and words declare the Jerusalem Temple as void. Jesus is the new Temple, the new dwelling place of God in human history.

The dialogue with the Samaritan Woman (4:1-26) raises the issue of the place and manner of worship. While the Temple is not named explicitly, the discussion of a sacred *topos* (4:21), of future worship in spirit and truth (4:23) and Jesus' relationship to the Samaritan traditions is highly relevant to this analysis.

In chapters 6 and 7 two Jewish festivals are examined, Tabernacles (7:1-10:21) and Dedication (10:22-40). An important movement begins in the feast of Tabernacles when there is a proleptic interruption of the narrative to speak of a future gift of the Spirit (7:37-39). While this is not the first reference to the Spirit (cf. 3:5, 6, 8, 34), this prolepsis begins the transferal of the Temple symbolism from the person of Jesus to the future community of believers. The Feast of Dedication not only concludes the series of "the feasts of the Jews" (chs. 5 to 10) but also brings to a climax Jesus' revelation of his intimate identity with the Father (10:30, 38).[30] Jesus is the consecrated dwelling place of God (10:36).

---

[30] I will follow the convention of the text in its naming of God as "Father." It is worth noting however, that this Gospel contextualizes the "father" image in such a way that it in fact subverts it as an image of a patriarchal father-figure. An excellent article by D. Lee examines the image of "the Father" in the Fourth Gospel and details a number of ways in which the Gospel departs from a contemporary father-rule image. This article gives numerous references to similar approaches by prominent feminist biblical scholars. See D. A. Lee, "Beyond Suspicion? The Fatherhood of God in the Fourth Gospel," *Pacifica* 8 (1995) 140–54. See also Lee's more recent article raising a similar theme in *idem*, "Abiding in the Fourth Gospel: A Case-study in Feminist Biblical Theology," *Pacifica* 10 (1997) 122–36.

In chapter 8 I examine the image of "My Father's House" (14:2). In this examination I show how the image of Temple-as-building undergoes a shift in meaning to Temple-as-community. This shift in meaning is part of the process of transferring the symbolism of the Temple, as applied to Jesus during his ministry, to a future post-resurrection time when it will apply to the believers.

The final chapter examining the Johannine text involves a study of "the Hour" (John 18–19). This chapter brings many of the preceding arguments to their conclusion. I place particular emphasis on Jesus' role as the builder of the new Temple and what this building process involves. I show how the Johannine narrative depicts the destruction and raising of the Temple. The chapter leads into a summary and conclusion.

The Rationale for Scenes Chosen

I have chosen those pericopes where I believe there is a relationship between the words of Jesus and the physical setting: the Temple Act and *Logion* (2:13-25) within the Jerusalem Temple; the discussion of worship situated at Jacob's well near the site of the ruins of the Samaritan Temple (4:1-45); Jesus' claims to be water, light and ἐγώ εἰμι set within the Temple during the rituals of Tabernacles (7:1–8:59); Jesus' self-description as the "Consecrated-one" situated in the Temple during the Feast of Dedication (10:22-42); Jesus' words which reinterpret the meaning of the Temple in terms of a community (14:1-31), set within his farewell discourse surrounded by his disciples; Jesus' words on the cross as the Temple is destroyed and rebuilt (18:1–19:42). These scenes allow for an interplay between the words used and the physical setting, adding thereby a dramatic emphasis to the meaning of the words.

The dramatic emphasis serves a theological purpose. The Fourth Gospel asserts that the divine glory is now accessible to human sensory experience in the flesh of Jesus (cf. 1:14). Physical reality is the means by which God can be revealed. Geography, time and place create both a narrative world in which events take place, and a symbolic world where God's presence and purpose are revealed:

> Les images concrètes et les scènes se succèdent dans une sorte de <<métaphorisation>> progressive. On peut même dire que l'ensemble de l'évangile, narrations et discours, est unifié par un réseau de symboles pour constituer un univers où les objets et les événements concourent à signifier le rayonnement de Dieu en ce monde.[31]

[31] R. Kieffer, *Le Monde Symbolique de Saint Jean*. Lectio Divina 137 (Paris: Cerf, 1989) 101.

The scenes chosen show the narrative skill and theological insight of the author who designs his scenes to convey his christological perspective that Jesus, and later the community, displaces the Temple as the *locus* of the divine dwelling.

In many ways the approach taken in these pages has grown out of my own ongoing spiritual journey that has come to know an indwelling God. Christians of many centuries have found in the Fourth Gospel words that speak to their experience of God's closeness. Who has not been moved by the images in chapter 15?—"Abide in me, and I in you" (15:4); "I am the vine, you are the branches" (15:5)? Can the words of this Gospel still speak to men and women of the twenty-first century who seek intimacy with God "without seeing" the Jesus of history? Are these images just words, or do they name a reality that Christians of all ages can experience? Can we still see in our world a God who dwells with us? These types of questions and an intuitive "yes" born of hope and experience led me into the task of a disciplined academic examination of texts that have been important over the centuries for Christian spirituality.

The Prologue

JOHN 1:1-18

Within the first eighteen verses of the Gospel, the reader is drawn into the tension between Jesus and the Law. The Prologue not only identifies two different divine gifts—the Law, and Jesus Christ (v. 17) but makes the claim that it is the Christian community which now possesses the fullness of God's revelation, because of its relationship with Jesus and his unique relationship with God. This assertion has its context in the historical conflict between Judaism and Christianity in their claims to be true recipients of divine revelation, embodied for Judaism in the Torah, and enfleshed for Christianity in Jesus. The essence of Christianity's claim is expressed in terms of Israel's cultic traditions when in verse 14, the flesh-taking of the divine *logos* is described as a "tabernacling" (ἐσκήνωσεν) among us. Because the Prologue introduces the major themes of the Gospel, I will present an analysis of its structure and purpose in some detail before moving to a more focused examination of verse 14.

The Structure of the Prologue

Many commentators have analyzed the poetic structure and language of the Prologue in search of an original source which was used and adapted by the Evangelist. Some supposed it was a pre-Christian Gnostic hymn.[1]

---

[1] C. A. Evans, "On the Prologue of John and the *Trimorphic Protennoia*," *NTS* 27 (1981) 395–401. This article discusses the relationship between the Prologue and the Gnostic document most frequently cited as its source. A more recent publication sets out in columns the parallels between the two documents and argues convincingly that the Gnostic document may be dependent on the Johannine writings rather than the reverse. See *idem, Word and Glory*, 49–67.

Bultmann attributed it to a *logos* hymn created by the disciples of John the Baptist and used by the Evangelist in a polemical way to counter claims that the Baptist could be the Messiah.[2] Others draw parallels with early Christian hymns found in the epistles and present it originating as a hymn within an early Christian (Johannine) community.[3] This type of analysis looks to Hellenistic, Hebrew, and even Aramaic poetic rhythms to explain why some verses can be attributed to the source and others to the redaction of the Evangelist.[4] To date, no one theory has been generally accepted, and there is the danger that this approach ends up presenting the Prologue as a complex jigsaw puzzle, where there is not even agreement about what shape the pieces have.[5]

The search for an original source can sidetrack us from the real task—making sense of the Prologue as we now have it and its relationship to the rest of the Gospel. Instead of searching for an original source, the approach taken here accepts that the text we now have comes from the hand of an author who is selecting and probably creating material to express his particular purpose,[6] which he states as "that you may believe that Jesus is the Christ, the Son of God, and that believing you may have life in his name" (John 20:31). Since authors choose their words and manner of presentation in order to communicate with the reader, then I would expect that by adopting a more literary analysis, it should be possible to grasp what the Evangelist was wanting to say to his readers.

In looking at how the Prologue is structured, there are basically two approaches. One approach shows the Prologue developing as a succession

[2] R. Bultmann, *The Gospel of John: A Commentary,* trans. G. R. Beasley Murray et al. (Oxford: Blackwell, 1971) 17–18.

[3] R. Schnackenburg, *The Gospel according to St. John,* trans. K. Smyth et al. 3 vols. Herder's Theological Commentary on the New Testament (London: Burns & Oates, 1968–1982) 1:225–31; Brown, *Gospel,* 1:20.

[4] Brown, *Gospel,* 1:22, gives a summary in table form of the verses accepted as original by a number of major scholars.

[5] On this I agree with Barrett who sees the Prologue as "one piece of solid theological writing . . . necessary to the Gospel as the Gospel is necessary to the Prologue." See C. K. Barrett, *New Testament Essays* (London: SPCK, 1971) 48.

[6] I take the view that the Prologue and Gospel were written by the same author. Carter analyzes four major themes within the Prologue and shows that these are also the major concerns of the Gospel. See W. Carter, "The Prologue and John's Gospel: Function, Symbol and the Definitive Word," *JSNT* 39 (1990) 35–58. Carson also presents a number of parallels before concluding that "the tightness of the connections between the Prologue and the Gospel render unlikely the view that the Prologue was composed by someone other than the Evangelist." See D. A. Carson, *The Gospel According to John* (Grand Rapids, Mich.: Eerdmans, 1991) 111.

of ideas in a linear or chronological manner. The following chart shows the way three commentators structure the Prologue along these lines.

BROWN (1966)[7]	BARRETT (1978)[8]	BEASLEY-MURRAY (1987)[9]
1-2 Word with God	1-5 Cosmological	1-5 Word and creation
3-5 Word and Creation	6-8 John's witness	6-8 Witness to the Word
*6-9 addition		
10-12b Word in World	9-13 Coming of Light and failure to accept it	9-13 Reactions to the Word in the World
*12c-13 added		
14 and 16 Community's share in the Word	14-18 Economy of Salvation	14-18 Confession of the Word by the Church
*15 added		
*17-18 added		

The major problem which this type of structure must address is the double presentation of John's witness. For Brown, as for many others, these Baptist verses are later additions into a Johannine hymn, written in for polemical reasons.[10] But this still leaves unanswered the question—why place these additions where they are and draw attention to the Baptist twice?

The second method is to structure the Prologue using literary models such as chiasms (Culpepper)[11] or parallelisms (de la Potterie, Moloney).[12] Such methods establish a structural balance in the double mention of John the Baptist.[13] The structure discussed below falls into this category, even though differing from the authors mentioned.

[7] R. E. Brown, *Gospel,* 1:22.

[8] C. K. Barrett, *The Gospel According to St. John.* 2nd ed. (London: SPCK, 1978) 149–50.

[9] G. R. Beasley-Murray, *John.* Word Biblical Commentary 36 (Waco: Word Books, 1987) 5.

[10] Brown, *Gospel,* 1:22.

[11] R. A. Culpepper, "The Pivot of John's Prologue," *NTS* 27 (1980–1981) 16. See also M.-É. Boismard, *St. John's Prologue* (London: Blackfriars, 1957) 80.

[12] I. de la Potterie, "Structure du Prologue de saint Jean," *NTS* 30 (1984) 354–81. See also F. J. Moloney, *The Word Became Flesh.* Theology Today Series 14 (Dublin/ Cork: Mercier Press, 1977) 35–39; *idem, Belief in the Word: Reading John 1–4* (Minneapolis: Fortress, 1993) 25–27.

[13] For a detailed explanation and critique of the structures proposed by Culpepper, de la Potterie and Moloney see M. Coloe "The Structure of the Johannine Prologue and Genesis 1," *ABR* 45 (1997) 41–44.

A new proposal

The structure I propose follows the idea of parallel themes but has a bi-partite form within an introduction (vv. 1-2), and a conclusion (v. 18), where the conclusion recapitulates and develops the opening verses and the process of this development is shown in the intervening verses (vv. 3-17). Each of the two major sections tells the story of the Word's coming into the world. Each part has three strophes that trace the historical development of the Word's presence in the world (vv. 3-5; 14), the witness of John the Baptist (vv. 6-8; 15), then the arrival and responses to the enfleshed Word (vv. 9-13; 16-17). The first part **reports** the stages of this story in the third person, while the second part **announces** it as personal testimony, using first person verb forms and pronouns—us (v. 14b), we (vv. 14c, 16b), I (v. 15c), me (vv. 15c, d, e). This structure can be shown schematically:

Bi-Partite Structure

Introduction (1-2)   *logos/theos* in eternity

Part 1 (story)   **Part 2 (testimony)**

A (3-5)   have seen   **A'** (14)
B (6-8)   have heard   **B'** (15)
C (9-13)   have experienced   **C'** (16-17)

Conclusion (18)   *Son/Father* in history

The three-fold development within each section has strong echoes with the introduction to the first Johannine epistle where there is a similar emphasis on seeing, hearing, and experiencing:

1:1 That which was from the beginning
which we have **heard,**
which we have **seen** with our eyes,
which we have **looked upon** and **touched** with our hands . . .
1:2 we proclaim to you the eternal life
which was with the Father and was made manifest to us.
1:3 That which we have **seen** and **heard**
we proclaim also to you.

Both the Prologue and the introduction to the epistle emphasize the sensory nature of the community's experience. The pre-existent Word of God has become flesh and so is accessible to ordinary human experience; it has been seen, it has been heard, it has been touched.

The Prologue

Introduction. 1. In the beginning was the Word, and the Word was with God and what God was, the Word was.
2. He was in the beginning with God.

Story	Testimony
of the Word in creation and coming into history	to the Word's presence and revelation in history

S 3. Everything became through him E and without him became nothing E 4. In him was life N and the life was the light of men 5. The light shines in the darkness and the darkness has not overcome it.	14. And the Word become flesh and dwelt among **us** and **we** saw his glory, glory as of the only son of the Father the fullness of a gift which is true.

John The Baptist

H 6. There was a man sent from God E whose name was John. A 7. He came as witness R to bear witness to the light, D that all might believe through him. 8. He was not the light but came to bear witness to the light.	15. John witnessed concerning him and cried out saying, "This man was the one of whom **I** said,— He who comes after **me** came before **me** for he was before **me**."

Two Responses To The Word

E 9. The true light that enlightens
X   everyone was coming into the
P   world
E 10. He was in the world and the
R   world was made through him
I   and the world knew him not.
E 11. He came to his own and his own
N   did not receive him.
C 12. But those who did receive him
E   he gave them the power to become
 	
D   children of God those believing in his name.
    13. Those born not of blood, nor the will of the flesh, nor the will of a man, but of God.
	16. From his fullness
	
	    we have all received a gift in place of a gift.
	17. For the Law was given through Moses,
	the true gift came through Jesus Christ.

Conclusion. 18. No one has ever seen God; the only Son who is in the bosom of the Father, that one has made him known.

The Prologue and Wisdom

According to Warren Carter, one of the issues facing both the Christian community and post-70 Judaism was, where wisdom is to be found, "where God in God's knowability, visibility and audibility was to be encountered."[14] The Wisdom literature of Judaism had identified Wisdom and Torah. According to one tradition Wisdom found a dwelling place in Jerusalem and was embodied in the Mosaic Torah:[15]

Then the Creator of all things gave me a command. . .
Make your dwelling in Jacob. . .
Thus in the beloved city he gave me a resting place,
and in Jerusalem was my domain. . .
All this is the book of the covenant of the Most High God,
the law that Moses commanded us
as an inheritance for the congregations of Jacob (Sir 24:8, 11, 23).

He found the whole way to knowledge,
and gave her to his servant Jacob
and to Israel whom he loved.
Afterward she appeared on earth and lived with humankind.
She is the book of the commandments of God,
the law that endures forever (Bar 3:36–4:1).

The identification between Wisdom and Torah became crucial in the restructuring of Judaism following the destruction of the Temple. In discussing the various responses to the events of 70, Jacob Neusner identifies four different trajectories: an apocalyptic movement, the Qumran community, Christianity, and Pharisaic Judaism.[16] Of these responses only Christianity and Pharisaic Judaism proved formative in history.

In answer to the questions—where can God be encountered, how can humans have access to the divine mysteries?—the Pharisees at Yavneh turned to the Torah while the Christian community looked to Jesus. Where Jewish texts, roughly contemporary with the Fourth Gospel, described vi-

---

[14] Carter, *Prologue*, 47.

[15] John Ashton describes an alternative Wisdom tradition where Wisdom and Torah are rival claimants to revelation, and Wisdom does not find a home within human history. "Wisdom went out in order to dwell among the sons of men, but did not find a dwelling, wisdom returned to her place and took her seat in the midst of the angels" (1 Enoch 42:1-2). J. Ashton, "The Transformation of Wisdom: A Study of the Prologue of John's Gospel," *NTS* 32 (1986) 168–69.

[16] J. Neusner, "Judaism in a Time of Crisis: Four Responses to the Destruction of the Second Temple," *Judaism* 21 (1972) 313–27.

sions, journeys, and ascents as a means of acquiring true revelation,[17] the Johannine community proclaimed that in the life of Jesus, revelation is accessible to human sensory experience. The very structure of the Prologue with its emphasis on seeing, hearing, and experiencing affirms the accessibility of the divine Word.

The Prologue and Creation

The bi-partite form outlined above, framed by an introduction and conclusion, is found in the first creation account in Gen 1:1-2:4a:

Johannine Prologue		Genesis	
Introduction (1-2)		Introduction (1-2)	
A (3-5)	A' (14)	A (3-5) light/darkness	A' (14-19)
B (6-8)	B' (15)	B (6-8) heaven/earth	B' (20-23)
C (9-13)	C' (16-17)	C (9-13) land/waters	C' (24-31)
		Climax: The Sabbath (2:1-3)	
Conclusion (18)		Conclusion (2:4a)	

The Fourth Gospel begins with the first words of Genesis "In the beginning" and follows a similar structure of three strophes set out in parallel between an introduction and a conclusion.[18] The first of the three strophes in Genesis and in the Prologue develops the theme of light. Genesis has one significant difference in that the six days of creation in this narrative from the priestly tradition lead to the seventh day climax. This climax has no structural parallel with the Prologue for reasons I will take up later.

In the Targums there is further evidence for linking the Prologue with the Genesis creation story.[19] In Targum Neofiti, God creates through the *Memra*—a term, usually translated as "word." *Memra* is used in the Targums to represent God's self-manifestation in the world. "From the

[17] See for example, 1, 2, and 3 Enoch; Book of Jubilees; Testament of Moses.

[18] Evans, (*Word and Glory,* 77–78) notes that the conceptual parallels between Genesis and the Prologue are "obvious and quite significant." He does not consider any structural parallels.

[19] Dating of the Targums is problematic. The text of the Targums may be later than the New Testament era, but the text reflects a liturgical origin making it possible that the targumic traditions pre-date the Johannine text. See the discussion in G. Vermes, *Jesus and the World of Judaism* (London: SCM, 1983) 74–88, especially his conclusion on 85. Manns makes use of Qumran material to show that the term *Memra* was being used in a Jewish milieu in the first century. See Manns, *L'Evangile,* 41–42.

beginning *with wisdom, the Memra of the Lord* created *and perfected* the heavens and the earth" (*Tg. Neof.* Gen 1:1).[20]

The Targums, Aramaic translations of the Hebrew Scriptures used in the Liturgy, show significant differences from the Hebrew Text. The *Memra* or Word is added, as is wisdom. These additions reflect later wisdom theology already found in the books of Proverbs (8:22-30) and Sirach (22:1-12). In Neofiti, it is the *Memra,* not God who gives the command, "Let there be light" (Gen 1:3). In the Targum to Exodus 12:42, we read "The first night: when the Lord was revealed over the world to create it. The world was without form and void, and darkness was spread over the face of the abyss, and the Memra of the Lord was the Light, and it shone" (Tg. Neof.).[21]

If these targumic traditions were familiar to the Johannine community from their synagogue liturgy, then these Jewish liturgical texts provided a likely basis for the Johannine concept of the *logos,* and the first creation account provided the Johannine author with the structure for his introduction to the story of the *logos* in creation. This same conclusion is reached by Evans.

> In sum, virtually every element of the Johannine Prologue is paralleled in targumic and midrashic materials. Moreover, there are many significant parallels between the targumic *memra* and the Johannine *logos*. It appears that every assertion regarding the *asarkos logos* in the Prologue's opening five verses is true of the targumic *memra*.[22]

In the new structure presented above, the Prologue has six strophes in parallel array, whereas the first creation account in Genesis has six strophes leading into a seventh-day climax. The Prologue has no equivalent to the "seventh day climax" in its structure. The seventh day, in the Genesis narrative, brings creation to its completion in the institution of the Sabbath. The priestly authors saw in the institution of the Sabbath the fulfillment of God's creative activity, for creation had been finished. "Thus

---

[20] For a brief summary of the finding and history of Neofiti 1, see M. McNamara, *Targum and Testament: Aramaic Paraphrases of the Hebrew Bible: A Light on the New Testament* (Grand Rapids, Mich.: Eerdmans, 1972) 183–89. A more detailed introduction to the Palestinian Targums can be found in *idem, Targum Neofiti 1: Genesis,* The Aramaic Bible 1A (Edinburgh: T & T Clark, 1992) 1–46.

[21] M. McNamara and M. Maher, *Targum Neofiti 1: Exodus; Targum Pseudo-Jonathan: Exodus.* The Aramaic Bible 2 (Edinburgh: T & T Clark, 1994). Evans' work sets out many more parallels between the Targums and the Prologue. See C. Evans, *Word and Glory,* 114–20.

[22] Evans, *Word and Glory,* 120.

the heavens and earth were finished and all their multitude. And on the seventh day God finished the work that he had done. . ." (Gen 2:1-2a). Targum Neofiti draws on this theology when it adds the words "the Lord created *and perfected* the heavens and the earth."

The Fourth Gospel maintains that such fulfillment was not possible within Israel, that Israel's "seventh" day of perfection was illusory; the creative work of God had not been completed "in the beginning." Jesus was sent to finish the Father's work (John 4:34). In the conflict on the Sabbath Jesus states, "My Father is working still and I am working" (5:17). Real fulfillment comes about only through the life and death of Jesus. Jesus' dying word, "It is finished" (τετέλεσται) announces the true completion of God's work and echoes the use of the same verb (τελέω) used in the LXX version of Genesis to announce the finish of God's work in creation (Gen 2:1 cf. John 19:30). In the death of Jesus, the Scriptures which opened with the words Ἐν αρχῆ (Gen 1:1; John 1:1) have been brought to fulfillment. "The work is now finished, and the Sabbath that begins after Jesus' death (xix 31) is the Sabbath of eternal rest."[23]

The six strophe structure of the Prologue, like the six days of creation in Genesis 1, requires one final act to bring it to completion. This act begins in verse 19 as the Gospel narrative of God's final work, to be accomplished in the life and death of Jesus, now begins. Until the story of this final work has been told, there can be no "seventh day." By utilizing the structure of Genesis, but breaking from its pattern, the very structure of the Prologue asserts that something more is still to come. God's creative activity is still unfolding, and the final creative word has not yet been spoken. Israel's past history and traditions are part of this unfolding activity which is now being brought to fulfillment when the Word is spoken in a new way within human history. In its themes and in its structure, the Prologue refutes the claims of Israel to possess already the fullness of revelation. By extension, the cultic traditions of Israel have also been brought to perfection when the divine Word establishes his tabernacle in human flesh. Israel's cultic traditions will be the focus of the next chapter.

The Dwelling of the Word (John 1:14)

In the structure presented above, verse 14 marks the start of a new section of the Prologue, and the use of the word σκηνόω draws attention to many older traditions of God's presence dwelling in Israel.[24] The story

---

[23] Brown, *Gospel,* 2:908; 1:217.

[24] It is my contention that this verse is critical in any investigation of the Temple theme within the Gospel since the Temple was one of the major symbols of God's presence in

related in verses 3-13 is now retold from the stance of first person testimony. Writers vary in their evaluation of the significance of verse 14 within the Prologue. For Bultmann it is a solemn "turning point;"[25] Schnackenburg calls it "the climax;"[26] Moloney regards it as a "synthesis" of all that has preceded;[27] Käsemann places greater emphasis on 14c as the proclamation of salvation,[28] while Beasley-Murray calls 14a "the controlling utterance of the sentence."[29] In what follows I will argue that verse 14 in its entirety, is the basic credal statement of the Johannine community. It expresses the Johannine insight into the identity of Jesus as the enfleshed *logos* (14a, b), the nature of the community as witnesses (14c) and the mission of the *logos* as bearer of a true gift (14d, e). There is an essential unity between these three realities, nature, witness, and mission, so they are expressed in one succinct verse.

The Nature of the Enfleshed Logos

Verse 14a recalls the language in verse 1 when it reintroduces the term *logos*. Reading verse 14 a and b in the light of verse 1 there is a very clear reversal:

1.a Ἐν ἀρχῇ ἦν ὁ λόγος,   14.a Καὶ ὁ λόγος σὰρξ ἐγένετο
     καὶ ὁ λόγος ἦν **πρὸς τὸν θεόν**,   καὶ ἐσκήνωσεν **ἐν ἡμῖν**,
     καὶ θεὸς ἦν ὁ λόγος.

14a and b express the polar opposite of 1a and b.
   in time -   a - From a state of infinity to a state of finitude.
   in place -   b - From being πρὸς τὸν θεόν, to ἐν ἡμῖν.

IN TIME
   One of the many ways καί is used in the New Testament is in expressions where the second καί introduces a contrast of terms. Expressions such as κάι . . . κάι . . . carry the sense of "on the one hand . . . on the other hand / and yet."[30] The use of καί to reintroduce the *logos* has this sense—"In the beginning was the Word . . ." and yet "the Word be-

---

the midst of Israel. See ch. 3 following for a discussion of the various traditions and cult objects that could provide the background for the Johannine term σκηνόω.

   [25] Bultmann, *Gospel*, 60.

   [26] Schnackenburg, *Gospel*, 1:266.

   [27] Moloney, *Belief*, 40.

   [28] E. Käsemann, *New Testament Questions of Today*. New Testament Library 41 (London: SCM, 1969) 164–65.

   [29] Beasley-Murray, *John*, 13.

   [30] K.-H. Pridik, "καί," *EDNT* 2 (1990–1993) 228.

came flesh." In v. 1 the *logos* was described using the indefinite ἦν, thus placing the *logos* in an indistinct time "in the beginning," whenever that may have been, whereas in verse 14a the *logos* is placed in a definite historical past using the aorist ἐγένετο and the word σάρξ. While 1a is the language of mythology, 14a is the language of history.

The word σάρξ emphasizes the temporality of the Word. In this context there is not a contrast between flesh and spirit, nor is there any moral sense of "sinful" flesh. Flesh is the term used to designate the human state of mortal finitude. Flesh is bound by time and destined to die. There is a possible allusion to Isa 40:7-8 which also emphasizes the finitude of flesh in contrast with the eternal existence of the Word of God.

Isaiah 40:7-8 (LXX)

πᾶσα **σὰρξ** χορτὸς,	All flesh is grass
καὶ πᾶσα **δόξα ἀνθρώπου**	and all the glory of man
ὡς ἄνθος χόρτου	as the flower of grass.
Ἐξηράνθη ὁ χόρτος	The grass withers
καὶ τὸ ἄνθος ἐξέπεσε·	and the flower fades
τὸ δὲ **ῥῆμα** τοῦ Θεοῦ ἡμῶν	but the Word of our God
μένει εἰς τὸν αἰῶνα	abides forever.

The LXX refers to the δόξα ἀνθρώπου ὡς ἄνθος χόρτου which contrasts with the Prologue's δόξαν ὡς μονογενοῦς παρὰ πατρός. The proximity of the word ἐσκήνωσεν to the word σάρξ in 14b supports this interpretation that the emphasis is on the mortality of flesh.

Since the flesh referred to in verse 14a is the flesh of the incarnate Word, it is necessary to see if the emphasis on mortality continues in the Gospel when it speaks of Jesus' flesh. All references to the flesh of Jesus occur within the Bread of Life discourse in chapter 6. The first is in 6:51c, "The bread that I will give for the life of the world is my flesh." The reference to a future time when flesh is given for the life of the world clearly indicates the future death of Jesus. The separation of flesh and blood in 6:52, 53, 54, 55, 56 continues to draw attention to Jesus' death.[31] We have here an example of Johannine irony in that the flesh-leading-to-death for Jesus, is the bread-leading-to-life for the world. By using the word σάρξ in the Prologue's statement—"the Word became flesh," the death of Jesus is already intimated.

The structure and language of 14a, in comparison with 1a expresses a real change of state. The affirmation, ὁ λόγος σὰρξ ἐγένετο is not a

---

[31] F. J. Moloney, *The Johannine Son of Man.* 2nd ed., Biblioteca di Scienze Religiose 14 (Rome: LAS, 1978) 87–123.

mere appearance, a putting on of flesh as one puts on clothes. "The ἐγένετο announces a change in the mode of being of the Logos."[32] While agreeing with Käsemann that the *logos* does not cease to exist as a divine being, there can be no doubt that there is a transformation that makes the incarnation more than a divine epiphany.[33] In the schema given above I noted that while 14a and b present the antithesis of 1a and b, there is no corresponding antithesis for 1c. The statement καὶ θεὸς ἦν ὁ λόγος remains operative. By the careful use of articles in verses 1a and b and by placing the complement θεός before the verb "to be" without the article, the author indicates oneness in nature, not identity in being.[34] In becoming flesh the *logos* does not lose his divinity, which means that the Johannine incarnation is not an experience of humiliation or *kenosis*. There is no attempt to explain how this mystery could occur. There is just the bold statement of a profound paradox, supported by primary witnesses—the divine Word became human flesh and we saw his glory. As Bultmann rightly comments,

> . . . this is the paradox which runs through the whole Gospel: the δόξα is not to be seen alongside the σάρξ, nor through the σάρξ as through a window; it is to be seen in the σάρξ and nowhere else.[35]

[margin handwritten note: The glory of God is only seen in the flesh.]

Because verse 14a and b hold the divine and human polarities in paradoxical tension, 14c is possible. The glory of the *logos* is accessible to human sensory experience. If either polarity was denied, there could be no true revelation.

IN PLACE

As 14a asserts a change in the temporal mode of the *logos*, 14b asserts a change in location from being πρὸς τὸν θεόν, to ἐσκήνωσεν ἐν ἡμῖν. The verb σκηνόω has the meaning of "to dwell in a tent" and is derived from the word for tent σκηνή.[36] There are several possible sources for the background of this verb: the Sinai/Mosaic Covenant and Wilderness traditions of the Ark and Tent, the Priestly cult associated with the

[32] Schnackenburg, *Gospel*, 1:267.

[33] Käsemann, *New Testament Questions*, 160–61.

[34] Harner suggests that this verse be translated, "The Word had the same nature as God." See P. B. Harner, "Qualitative Anarthrous Predicate Nouns: Mark 15,39 and John 1,1," *JBL* 92 (1973) 87. The New English Bible translates this verse: "What God was, the Word was also."

[35] Bultmann, *Gospel*, 63.

[36] The LXX uses the term σκηνή to translate both the Tent of Meeting (e.g., Exod 27:21; 28:39; Lev 1:5) and the Tabernacle (e.g., Exod 25:9; Num 9:20; 1 Chr 6:48) housing the Ark associated with the Sinai covenant.

ancient Tabernacle and Temple, the Wisdom literature and the rabbinic term *Shekinah*. In examining the possible sources it is necessary to examine not only the traditio-historical precedents, but also the first century milieu of the Johannine community. Finally, the Prologue itself may provide literary clues to favor a particular background. The examination of the background to verse 14 within Israel's cultic traditions is the task of the next chapter.

The Prologue has already established a number of contrasting themes such as light and darkness (v. 5), those who receive the Word and those who do not (vv. 11, 12). This contrast continues in 14c and the rest of the Prologue where a contrast is set up between Israel's Law and the identity and role of Jesus. In 14c, the claim is made that "we saw his glory," a vision Moses desired (Exod 33:18) but was not permitted (Exod 33:20-23). The community of those who received the Word (John 1:12) are able to see what Israel could not. In the Gospel this pattern continues. Many in Israel see Jesus but their lack of receptivity blinds them to the deeper perception of his glory (9:40-41).

The nature of the Word's "glory" is explained in 14d in terms of a filial relationship. The intimacy between the *logos* and *theos* introduced in verse 1 is now expressed in the human relationship that exists between a father and son. Once the *logos* enters history, the human metaphor is appropriate to tell his story. In 14d the contrast with the Mosaic Law continues in describing the relationship between the Father and Son "as the fullness of a gift that is truth."[37] The word πλήρης is indeclinable so it is necessary to elicit from the context what it refers to—the *logos,* the *doxa* or the nature of this glory, i.e., the filial relationship just described in 14c. Earlier in the Prologue a gift had been described, a gift given to those who received the Word and believed in his name; this gift was the power to become children of God (v. 12). This verse establishes a precedent for understanding the gift referred to in 14d as a filial relationship. The gift promised to believers in verse 12 is fully expressed in the Father-Son relationship of the enfleshed *logos*. It is this filial intimacy that is described as the fullness of a true gift.[38]

---

[37] In this translation I am following the grammatical arguments of Bultmann, *Gospel,* 73–74, and F. J. Moloney, "The Fulness of a Gift which is Truth," *Catholic Theological Review* 1 (1978) 31. For further discussion on the Johannine use of the term χάρις in verse 14 and 17, see I. de la Potterie, *La Vérité dans Saint Jean,* Analecta Biblica 73 (Rome: Biblical Institute Press, 1977) 129–50.

[38] In ch. 9 I will show how the gift of divine filiation is intrinsically linked to the theme of the Temple. In verse 14 this link is suggested and the narrative will establish the truth of this claim.

The Gift of the Law—The Gift of Jesus

The concept of *gift* is taken up in verse 16, where once again a contrast is made with Israel's gift of the Law by use of the expression χάριν ἀντι χάριτος.[39] The following verse makes explicit the nature of both gifts, and again there is the claim that the true gift has come through Jesus Christ. "For the Law was given through Moses, the gift that is truth came through Jesus Christ." The polemical tone continues in verse 18 with the clear statement **no-one** has ever seen God; no-one therefore, can lay claim to be the revealer of heavenly wisdom; no-one except the only begotten one, whose intimacy with the Father enables him to be the true revealer and revelation of God. In the person of Jesus, the divine presence which Israel sought to see, to hear and to experience, came and dwelt in the midst of humanity. For the Johannine community, the key institutions of Israel, her Law and her Temple, have now fulfilled their promise.

Conclusion

D. A. Carson calls the Prologue a "foyer," "simultaneously drawing the reader in and introducing the major themes."[40] As a foyer, the Prologue is incomplete in itself and requires the rest of the Gospel to explain the story it has sketched, and to resolve the questions it leaves unanswered. The Prologue is unfinished and requires the "seventh day" of the Gospel narrative to bring it to a conclusion. In its structure the Prologue sets up a balance between the story told in verses 3-13, and then the story retold from the perspective of first person witness, a witness that has seen and heard and experienced the Word in the person of Jesus (vv. 14-17)—a witness therefore that is reliable. Since this story focuses on the *logos,* who entered history in the person of Jesus, the introduction and conclusion show that the revelation offered by the *logos* is true, because of the intimate relationship between the *logos-theos* in eternity, and the Son-Father in history. There is a progression of witnesses to the revelation of

---

[39] ἀντί is usually translated as "upon" or "in addition to" giving the sense "grace upon grace?" Such translations impose the Pauline sense of χάρις in the Johannine text. χαρις in ordinary Greek usage usually means *gift* and ἀντί means "instead of," "in place of." See R. Edwards, "XAPIN ANTI XAPITOΣ (John 1:16): Grace and the Law in the Johannine Prologue," *JSNT* 32 (1988) 3–6; also Moloney, *Belief,* 46–47.

[40] Carson, *Gospel,* 111. The actual term πρόλογος suggests it is an announcement made beforehand of things that will later be developed in the narrative. For a background on the literary genre see ch. 1 of Elizabeth Harris's work *Prologue and Gospel: The Theology of the Fourth Evangelist,* Journal for the Study of the New Testament Supplement Series 107 (Sheffield: JSOT Press, 1994) 1–25.

God, firstly the *logos*/Son/Jesus, then the Baptist, followed by the Johannine community present in the use of the first-person pronouns, and finally, as the author announces, "these things have been written" (20:31)—there is the witness of the Gospel itself.

God's Dwelling Place in Israel

The Ark and Tent of Meeting

There are three objects associated with the Exodus-Sinai experience, the Ark, the Tent, and the Tabernacle. These are treated quite differently within the Pentateuchal traditions and the distinctions can reveal differing perceptions of the divine presence. Koester makes the point that first-century Judaism and Christianity did not read these traditions in isolation but within the single text they had received.[1] While this is true, these communities were recipients, not only of a text, but also of a living tradition that had undergone many changes; Israel under the monarchy and worshipping in the Solomonic Temple had a different perception of God's presence than earlier in the tribal confederacy or later in the experience of Exile. Each new situation called for a reclaiming and a reinterpretation of the past. By examining the objects associated with God's presence within particular traditions, I hope to determine the way Israel received and reshaped its tradition during major crises.

The Yahwist[2]

The Yahwist tradition first mentions the Ark in the passage called "The Song of the Ark":

---

[1] C. Koester, *The Dwelling of God: The Tabernacle in the Old Testament, Intertestamental Jewish Literature, and the New Testament.* Catholic Biblical Quarterly Monograph Series 22. (Washington, D.C.: Catholic Biblical Association of America, 1989) 6.

[2] The classic form of the documentary hypothesis and its chronology J-E-D-P is currently much debated and as yet no alternative hypothesis has achieved scholarly

> Whenever the Ark set out, Moses would say, "Arise O Lord, (יהוה) let your enemies be scattered and your foes flee before you." And whenever it came to rest, he would say, "Return O Lord of the ten thousand thousands of Israel" (Num 10:35-36).

In these verses the Ark is addressed as YHWH, as the leader of Israel's army. A second reference from this tradition is found later in Numbers where once again the Ark is associated with Moses and is presented in a military context (14:44). When the Ark is present, the Israelites experience victory and the enemies of YHWH are scattered; when the Ark is absent their forays are defeated (Num 14:44-45). As in the Song of the Ark, the Ark signifies the Lord's presence, for without the Ark, Moses warns the people, "the Lord is not among you" (14:42).

In this early tradition, the Ark is presented as a type of military standard, a palladium, signifying YHWH's leadership over Israel's army host.[3] The Ark continues the experience of YHWH fighting on the side of Israel as he had fought with them in the crossing of the Sea and in the defeat of Pharaoh's armies (Exod 14:14-31). The very name Israel means "El fights" and points to a very early understanding of Israel's God as a mighty warrior, a "man of war" (Exod 15:3) who fights for his people and is responsible for their victories. The cloud theophany that was with them at the sea (Exod 13:21; 14:24) accompanies them in their journey from Sinai and is closely linked to the Ark (Num 10:33-35) which comes to be seen and hailed as an extension of YHWH's presence.[4]

---

consensus. I am following the recent analysis by Campbell and O'Brien of Martin Noth's book, *A History of Pentateuchal Traditions* (Englewood Cliffs, N.J.: Prentice-Hall, 1972). Campbell and O'Brien present the four source texts and provide a synopsis of the history of Pentateuchal studies and the current debate. See A. F. Campbell and M. A. O'Brien, *Sources of the Pentateuch: Texts, Introductions, Annotations* (Minneapolis: Fortress, 1993), especially 1–20. Unless otherwise stated, the assigning of specific verses to a particular tradition will follow this text.

[3] J. H. Jones argues against the concept of the Ark as a war palladium and refers to the incident in 1 Sam 4:2-4 when the Ark remained at Shiloh while the Israelites went out to battle the Philistines. See G. H. Jones, "The concept of holy war," *The World of Ancient Israel: Sociological, Anthropological and Political Perspectives*, ed. R. E. Clements (Cambridge: Cambridge University Press, 1989) 310.

[4] R. E. Clements discusses a further development in which the Ark may have drawn to it an idea of being a Throne for the Divine Presence who was invisibly seated upon it. Such ideas may have been borrowed from the Canaanite religions and were most likely to have been acquired when the Ark was at Shiloh some time before 1050 B.C.E. R. E. Clements, *God and Temple*, 28–35.

The Elohist and Deuteronomist[5]

In the Elohist and the later Deuteronomic traditions, there are two objects associated with the experience at Sinai—the Ark and a Tent called the Tent of meeting (Exod 33:7-11 [E]; Num 11:16, 24; 12:4-5, 10 [JE]; Deut 31:14 [D]).[6] It is unclear whether the Ark of E was thought to be a container since there is no description of it. It was likely to be a simple, unadorned wooden chest such as the Ark described in the D account.[7]

> So I made an ark of acacia wood, and hewed two tables of stone like the first, and went up the mountain. . . And He wrote on the tables. . . and the LORD gave them to me. Then I turned and came down from the mountain, and put the tables in the ark which I had made (Deut 10:3-5).

The Tent of Meeting lay outside the camp and was a simple structure that Moses could pitch unaided (Exod 33:7). This Tent was the place where the people went to seek guidance from the Lord who came in a Theophany as at Sinai.[8] The Lord did not enter the Tent but appeared outside, at the door of the Tent.

> Now Moses used to take the tent and pitch it outside the camp, far off from the camp; he called it the tent of meeting. And everyone who sought the LORD would go out to the tent of meeting which was outside the camp. . . When Moses entered the tent, the pillar of cloud would descend and stand at the entrance of the tent, and the LORD would speak to Moses (Exod 33:7, 9).

[5] A more detailed analysis of the Deuteronomic tradition will follow the discussion of the Solomonic Temple. At this stage I link the E and D traditions in their description of the Tent of Meeting.

[6] The LXX uses the term σκηνὴ τοῦ μαρτυρίου (Tent of testimony) to translate the Hebrew אהל מוצד. Thus in the LXX there is not the clear distinction between the Tent and the Tabernacle. This may reflect the translator's association of the letters *skn* with both the Tent and the Hebrew form of the word "Tabernacle" משׁכן. See W. Michaelis, "σκηνή," *TDNT* 7 (1971) 371. Campbell and O'Brien note the difficulties in clearly distinguishing the sources in Exodus 33, Numbers 11 and 12. See *Sources of the Pentateuch*, 199 n. 39, 151 n. 153, 152 n. 155. For further comments on the designation of Elohist and Deuteronomist to these passages see R. J. Clifford, "Exodus," *NJBC* (1989) 59; C. E. L'Heureux, "Numbers," *NJBC* (1989) 85; and J. Blenkinsopp, "Deuteronomy," *NJBC* (1989) 107.

[7] M. Haran, *Temples and Temple Service in Ancient Israel: An Inquiry into the Character of Cult Phenomena and the Historical Setting of the Priestly School* (Oxford: Clarendon, 1978) 263–64.

[8] Although the text says, "everyone who sought the LORD would go out to the tent of meeting which was outside the camp" (Exod 33:7), the Tent is primarily linked with Moses. Later, Moses is called to bring seventy elders to the tent (Num 11:16) and Aaron and Miriam (Num 12:4).

Joshua remained as the attendant in the Tent (Exod 33:11).

In the D and E traditions, the Tent of Meeting was not a cultic institution housing a deity; the interior of the Tent was empty and it was simply a place where Moses went to prepare himself for a moment of revelation, a fleeting prophetic glimpse of God.[9] As such this Tent carried the Sinai experience with the people throughout their desert wanderings. It offered the possibility of prophetic revelation when Israel had departed the mountain. Both at Sinai and at this Tent, Moses had to leave the camp to receive the revelation and there is no suggestion, in these traditions, that this tent was linked with sacrifice, with priests or with any type of ritual. It was a place of revelation, not a dwelling of YHWH.

Canaanite Influences on the Ark and Tent Traditions.

Behind the traditions of the Ark and Tent of Meeting lie older myths of the Canaanite pantheon. In the mythology of Canaan, 'El is the supreme deity who may be likened to a great Patriarch/Creator:

> Unlike the great gods who represent the powers behind the phenomena of nature, 'El is in the first instance a social god. . . He is at once father and ruler of the family of gods, functions brought together in the human sphere only in those societies which are organised in tribal leagues or in kingdoms where kinship survives as an organising power in the society.[10]

The social nature of 'El is indicated in the various covenant accounts wherein Israel's ancestors enter into binding agreements with a particular deity bearing an 'El epithet (Gen 14:22, El Elyon; 16:13, El-Roi; 17:1, El Shaddai). Through various covenants 'El, or the god linked with a specific patriarch, enters into a kinship bond with the individual and clan, binding himself to guide and protect this group. Canaanite 'El dwells in his heavenly court where his tent is stretched out across the skies in the manner of a nomadic patriarch.[11] El's mode of self-manifestation is by visions or auditions, frequently in dreams or visitations.[12]

---

[9] M. Haran, *Temples and Temple Service,* 266.

[10] F. M. Cross, *Canaanite Myth and Hebrew Epic: Essays in the History of the Religion of Israel* (Cambridge: Harvard University Press, 1973) 42–43. More recently John Scullion examined the numerous 'El epithets used in the ancestral stories and in Israel's worship and poetry. He argued that 'El used in Israel's traditions was not the Canaanite 'El but simply a term to designate "God" the supreme being. See J. Scullion, "The God of the Patriarchs," *Pacifica* 1 (1988) 150.

[11] Cross, *Canaanite Myth,* 43

[12] Cross, *Canaanite Myth,* 43 and 177–85.

The Canaanite deity who deals most directly with the people and the land is Baal, the powerful storm god of Ugaritic mythology. It is Baal who comes as a mighty warrior to do battle with the forces of chaos, Yamm, the primeval Sea. It is Baal who then returns to the heavens to be enthroned as King at 'El's right hand, and whose Temple is built to acknowledge his victory and sovereignty. Baal's mode of self-manifestation is in the storm theophany. He rides to conquest with the storm clouds as his chariot, and with weapons of thunder and lightning; before his wrath nature quakes and declines; with his triumphant return Baal's voice thunders from his cosmic temple calling nature to respond in exuberant joy and fertility.[13]

In his examination of early Israelite poetry, Cross detects elements of 'El and Baal myths impinging upon and providing the images to express Israel's historical experience in the Exodus/Sinai event. In the cultic covenant-renewal festival, the Ark is the symbolic presence of YHWH. The tribes reenact YHWH's march of conquest, telling the story, not in terms of a cosmic battle with the Sea, but of YHWH's defeat of Israel's enemies at the sea. A number of mythic elements are conflated in the presentation of YHWH Sabaoth (1 Sam 1:3, 11), who is both the divine Kinsman bonded by covenant with Israel, as well as the mighty Creator and leader of cosmic armies, who leads his people in Holy Wars of conquest, then reigns from his cherubim throne (1 Sam 4:4).

What is significant to note for the purpose of this study is that the Ark, within the Epic (JE) tradition, and the later Deuteronomic tradition, is not considered to be a place wherein YHWH dwells. While it represents YHWH's presence in the midst of his covenanted people, and is a rallying point of the tribal league for military and cultic purposes,[14] YHWH is still the transcendent Lord who comes to the people in their times of need; nor is the Tent of Meeting considered to be YHWH's earthly dwelling place. It is possible that the Tent was meant to correspond with a cosmic tent-dwelling, as in the 'El mythology, for the Tent tradition has similarities with the perception of 'El as the divine patriarch offering counsel and judgements. The Tent acquired the theophanic mode of the deity's presence, more readily associated with Baal of the storm cloud than 'El (Exod 33:9).[15]

While these traditions do not describe a tent covering the Ark, it is hard to imagine such a sacred object simply resting in the camp without being covered by a tent. So in these traditions there are probably two

[13] This description summarizes the comparison Cross makes between YHWH and Baal, *Canaanite Myth,* 147–94.
[14] G. H. Davies. "Ark of the Covenant," *IDB* 1 (1962) 223.
[15] The cloud at the entrance to the Tent is the mode of Baal's revelatory presence.

tents, one in the midst of the people to shelter the Ark when they are at rest, and a second tent, called the Tent of Meeting, pitched outside the camp as a place of prophetic revelation.

The JE traditions do not continue the story of the Ark into the land of Canaan. The history of its journeys is taken up in the D tradition which culminates in the Ark being installed in the newly built Temple in Jerusalem (1 Kgs 8).

Jerusalem—The Dwelling Place of YHWH

When David captured the Jebusite city of Jerusalem and established it as the capital of a united nation, one of his first acts was to bring the Ark from Baale-judah to Jerusalem (2 Sam 6). At first it was placed in a tent but then David planned to build a Temple to house the Ark.[16] His desire was refused, but in this context he was given the promise of a dynasty, and told that his son would be the one to build a Temple (2 Sam 7). In the changes brought about through the transition from tribal association to nation, there were shifts in Israel's perception of God's presence and dwelling place. According to Clements, the Psalms dating back to this early monarchic period provide the clearest insight into Israel's religious consciousness at this time.[17] The narratives of the monarchy, found in the Deuteronomic history and the books of Chronicles, come from later periods, and show evidence of later theological interpretation. The early Psalms point to a borrowing of Canaanite mythological concepts and their incorporation into Israel's worship of YHWH. The victories of Israel's armies testify to the victory of YHWH over other gods. Psalm 68 combines historical and mythical elements in its acclamation of YHWH as savior.[18] The god of Sinai (vv. 7, 8, 17) who delivered his people from Egypt, is also the cosmic warrior vanquishing the Serpent and the Deep Sea (v. 22).[19] A fur-

---

[16] Cross notes a warning of the difficulty of being sure about David's intentions—in spite of the tradition. The plan to build a Temple may have been attributed to David by Solomon to support his own designs, *Canaanite Myth,* 231.

[17] Clements, *God and Temple,* 40–62.

[18] Various dates are given for Psalm 68. According to Dahood, the Psalm has elements that date back to Solomon's time and the ninth century. See M. Dahood, *Psalms 11:51-100.* Anchor Bible 17. (New York: Doubleday & Company, 1968) 133. Similarly Mowinckel places it within the Jerusalem Temple, later than David. See S. Mowinckel, *The Psalms in Israel's Worship.* 2 vols. (Oxford: Basil Blackwell, 1967) 1:153. Kraus gives it a much earlier date within the cult at Mt. Tabor during the time of Saul. See H.-J. Kraus, *Psalms 60–150: A Commentary* (Minneapolis: Augsburg, 1989) 49–51.

[19] On the mythologizing of Israel's Exodus experience see Barker, *Gate of Heaven,* 66.

ther aspect of Canaanite religion that was assimilated into Yahwism was the relationship between the gods and the land.

Prior to David's time, the chief god of Jerusalem was El-'Elyon, "Lord of sky and land" (Gen 14:19).[20] Later El-'Elyon is identified with YHWH (Gen 14:22). In the Jebusite cult of El-'Elyon, Mount Zion was regarded as his abode and in accordance with Canaanite mythology, his lordship gave him ownership of the land of Canaan.[21] Those who acknowledged El-'Elyon's sovereignty in worship received the right to live in his land and receive his blessings of fertility. David's victory over the Jebusites and the installation of the Ark of YHWH into Jerusalem gave YHWH a claim on Zion as his home and the right to assume El-'Elyon's lordship over earth and sky. In Psalm 48, Zion is likened to the Canaanite Mount Zaphon (vv. 2-3), which was hailed as the dwelling place of Baal and later assimilated into the El-'Elyon cult and identified with Zion.[22] Mount Zaphon is a "world mountain" whose base is on the earth and whose heights reach up to the heavens, thus the mountain links earth to heaven.[23] It is within this mythological understanding of Zaphon/Zion as the dwelling place of God that some of the titles of YHWH must be understood. In Psalm 110, dated in the tenth century, God is entitled YHWH of Zion, "he has forged your victorious mace, YHWH of Zion has hammered it" (Ps 110:2).[24] Other Psalms whose dating cannot be as definite give YHWH other divine epithets linking him with Zion; YHWH is called "Resident of Jerusalem" (Ps 135:21), the "Enthroned of Jerusalem" (125:1), and "King of Zion" (9:12).[25]

Israel's Ark had its roots in history, in the Exodus-Sinai traditions wherein God did not have an abiding presence with them. With the

[20] Clements, *God and Temple*, 43.

[21] Clements, *God and Temple*, 53.

[22] Clements, *God and Temple*, 47. Dahood sees in the identification of Zaphon and Zion an allusion to the theme of Jerusalem as the navel of the earth. See M. Dahood, *Psalms 1:1-50*. Anchor Bible 16 (New York: Doubleday, 1966) 290; also H.-J. Kraus, *Theology of the Psalms* (Minneapolis: Augsburg, 1979) 79. For a discussion on the *foundation stone,* see Barker, *Gate of Heaven,* 18–19.

[23] For a discussion of the notion of 'world mountain' within Near Eastern Mythology see Clements, *God and Temple,* 1–16; Dahood, *Psalms* 2:21; Barker, *Gate of Heaven,* 63–64.

[24] The translation follows Dahood who translates יהוה מציון as a construct. See M. Dahood, *Psalms 111:101-150*. Anchor Bible 17A. (New York: Doubleday, 1970) 115. See also Ps 128:5 and 134:3 for other references to YHWH of Zion.

[25] These titles of YHWH follow Dahood's translations. Kraus, *Psalms 60–150*, 349, makes a strong link between YHWH and Zion but he does not favor the translations as constructs so gives more cautious translations; cf. Ps 110:2, "Yahweh from Zion"; Ps 135:21, "who dwells in Jerusalem,"; also Ps 9:12 "enthroned on Zion," *idem, Psalms 1–59: A Commentary* (Minneapolis: Augsburg, 1988) 189.

settlement in Canaan and the capture of Jerusalem, Israel's historical tradition encountered a mythology that perceived a permanent relationship
between the god and an earthly abode. To reconcile their history with
Canaanite mythology Israel expressed the theology of YHWH's dwelling
in Jerusalem in terms of election.[26] As YHWH chose David to be King, so
YHWH chose Zion as his dwelling:

> The LORD swore to David a sure oath
> from which he will not turn back:
> "One of the sons of your body
> I will set on your throne.
> If your sons keep my covenant
> and my testimonies which I shall teach them,
> their sons also for ever
> shall sit upon your throne."
> For the LORD has chosen Zion;
> he has desired it for his habitation:
> "This is my resting place forever;
> Here I will dwell, for I have desired it.
> I will abundantly bless her provisions;
> I will satisfy her poor with bread" (Ps 132:11-15).[27]

Within the mythology of Canaan, the land which the god possessed
as his abode was given over to the god's worshippers as their inheritance.
Since Zion was chosen as YHWH's dwelling place, the people of Israel
who worshipped YHWH were entitled to the land by divine inheritance (Ps
78:54, 68). Worship of YHWH secured Israel's right to possess YHWH's
land, and his blessing of fertility in the land. In the ancestral narratives of
the Yahwist tradition there is a strong theme of the land being promised to
Israel, a promise seen to be fulfilled when YHWH leads Israel to Canaan
and gives victory into their hands. Possession of the land is divinely sanc-
tioned because YHWH has chosen them as his people, and chosen Zion as
his dwelling place:[28]

> Thou hast led in thy steadfast love the people whom thou hast redeemed,
> Thou hast guided them by thy strength to thy holy abode. . . Thou wilt

[26] Clements, *God and Temple*, 48.

[27] Dahood, *Psalms,* 3:241, classifies this as a royal psalm dating to the tenth century probably during the reign of Solomon; Kraus, *Psalms 60–150,* 477, dates it earlier
to the time of David within a "royal festival of Zion" celebrating the choice of Zion as
the central sanctuary, and David as YHWH's chosen. David's act of bringing the Ark to
Jerusalem would have provided the origin for such as royal Zion Feast.

[28] Clements, *God and Temple,* 50–54.

bring them in and plant them on thy own mountain, the place, O LORD, which thou hast made for thy abode, the sanctuary, O LORD, which thy hands have established (Exod 15:13, 17).

The mythological themes of Canaan, when coupled with the historical theme of Israel's election, provide the basis for a new conceptualization of YHWH's presence and dwelling. Throughout the Old Testament there is a constant refrain that Zion is the holy mountain of YHWH, and this is the only place designated as his dwelling, with the exception of two minor references to Shiloh (Ps 78:60; Jer 7:12). Zion is looked upon as the city YHWH founded (Ps 87:1-2); from Zion YHWH will come forth with deliverance (Pss 14:7; 20:2; 50:2-3; 53:6).

From his examination of Canaanite mythology, as it is reflected in the Psalms, Clements concludes that Zion did not become YHWH's dwelling place because the Temple was built there, rather, the Temple was built there because Zion had become YHWH's abode by right of conquest.[29] Prior to the building of the Temple, Israel did not have a theology of God's continual presence dwelling in their midst. Neither the Tent of Meeting nor the Ark within the JED traditions were conceptualized as God's dwelling place.[30] When Israel required God's power or guidance the Tent and Ark functioned as symbols of YHWH's gratuitous presence. In all God's dealings with Israel, God was free to come and go as God desired, for a movable tent shrine and Ark maintained God's sovereign transcendence. With the capture of Jerusalem and the building of the Temple, a new religious situation was created. The very structure and position of the Temple invited a redefining of Israel, a retheologizing of YHWH's relationship with Israel and a reinterpretation of Israel's history.

God's Presence within the Solomonic Temple

During the period of the tribal league, the cultic celebrations were primarily focused on a celebration of YHWH's action in history. Canaanite

---

[29] Clements, *God and Temple*, 55.

[30] Within the D tradition there is just one possible reference to a tabernacle within the Oracle of Nathan. "I have not dwelt in a house since the day I brought up the people of Israel from Egypt to this day, but I have been moving about in a tent for my dwelling" (2 Sam 7:6). The expression באהל ובמשכן is sometimes read "in a tent and in a tabernacle." McCarter argues from textual evidence that במשכן arose as a gloss or variant on אהל. See P. K. McCarter Jr. *II Samuel: A New Translation with Introduction, Notes and Commentary*, Anchor Bible 9 (New York: Doubleday, 1984) 192. Anderson reads the expression as a hendiadys or an instance of Hebraic doubling. See A. A. Anderson, *2 Samuel*. Word Biblical Commentary 11 (Dallas: Word Books, 1989) 111. I would also add the evidence that there is no other reference to a tabernacle within the D tradition.

cosmic mythology was in the background as YHWH's conquests were grounded in Israel's own triumphs over earthly foes. With the institutions of Kingship and Temple, both derived from Canaanite practice, the mythic element moved into the foreground in a national theology and cult, and an ideology of Kingship.[31] In its origins Israel's Kingship developed from the charismatic leadership of judges to a conditional and non-dynastic Kingship of Saul. The concept of a conditional covenant fits well with the non-permanent Tent-shrine which David first built in Jerusalem to house the Ark of the Covenant.[32] Cross sees evidence of a conditional covenant ideology in Psalm 132, which he argues must be placed early in the Jerusalem cult.[33] Following the opening verses, recalling David's oath to find a dwelling place for the Lord, and the bringing of the Ark to Jerusalem, there is the oath sworn by the Lord to David:

> The LORD swore to David a sure oath from which he will not turn back:
> "One of the sons of your body I will set on your throne.
> If your sons keep my covenant and my testimonies which I shall teach them,
> their sons also for ever shall sit upon your throne" (Ps 132:11-12).

The conditional nature of this covenant with the Davidic House is changed under Solomon, when a Judean royal ideology develops, symbolized in a dynastic Temple, representing the eternal dwelling of the deity and the unconditional choice of the Davidic House. The former language of a conditional covenant, or kinship bond, is changed into a permanent relationship, expressed now in the language of David as the *adopted son* of YHWH:[34]

> I have found David, my servant;
> with my holy oil I have anointed him . . .
> He shall cry to me, "Thou art my Father,
> my God, and the Rock of my salvation."
> And I will make him the first-born,
> the highest of the kings of the earth.
> My steadfast love I will keep for him for ever,
> and my covenant will stand firm for him.

[31] Cross, *Canaanite Myth*, 144.

[32] Cross, *Canaanite Myth*, 233. For further discussion on the Oracle of Nathan and the opposition to a permanent Temple, see 241–61.

[33] Cross, *Canaanite Myth*, 233.

[34] "The covenant relation is properly described as a substitute kinship relation. Conceptually, they differed in that the father-son relationship was inherently permanent, "eternal," while the covenant relationship was conditional in time and scope, qualified by stipulations." See Cross, *Canaanite Myth*, 257–58.

I will establish his line for ever
and his throne as the days of the heavens (Ps 89:20, 26-29).

The Judean royal ideology expressed above is closely bound up with the Temple and its cult. In the enthronement Psalms of YHWH, Temple and Kingship are celebrated as divinely ordained. The Kingship of David and his House is seen as an earthly type of the Kingship of YHWH.[35] The House of the Lord in Jerusalem replicates his cosmic Temple, giving YHWH a permanent place to dwell in the midst of his chosen. The shift from Tent-shrine to Temple reflects an enormous theological shift from YHWH's transcendent Lordship to his immanence and permanence. In the Jerusalem cult, YHWH is present to hear the people's supplications, and to receive their homage. Because of God's presence, the Temple is a source of blessing and fertility (Pss 84; 128:5; 134:3); from Jerusalem, YHWH's dwelling place, YHWH's word and judgments are sent out to the earth (Ps 147:15, 18).

During the era of the Tribal League, the major festival was the Covenant-renewal ceremony. In Solomon's time the cultic highpoint shifted to the fall New Year Festival, celebrating the founding of the Temple and the Davidic House.[36] Mythological elements borrowed from the cult of Baal's enthronement erupted in a celebration of Kingship and YHWH's taking residence in the Temple, as a sign of his sovereign rule. This celebration, commonly known as "Tabernacles," is simply called "the Feast" (1 Kgs 8:2, 65; 2 Chron 7:8; Neh 8:14; Isa 30:29; Ezek 45:23, 25); elsewhere it has other names, "ingathering" (Exod 23:16) and "the Feast of the Lord" (Lev 23:39; Judg 21:19).

Of the three pilgrim festivals, Tabernacles ranks as the original pilgrimage festival, developing from a harvest celebration, then taking on theological meaning to recall Israel's wilderness times.[37] Given the mythological borrowings, and the reinterpretation of Israel's history, this wilderness time was readily celebrated as the conquest march of YHWH, the warrior who had defeated Israel's enemies at the Sea, to take up residence and be enthroned in Zion. Harvest booths, nomadic tents in the wilderness

[35] Cross, *Canaanite Myth,* 239.

[36] Cross, *Canaanite Myth,* 123 n. 37, argues that there were two New Year festivals in the early cult of Israel, both of which were covenant renewal festivals. The autumn festival coincided with the New Year festivals of Canaan and Egypt. This became the great festival of the era of the kingship in Jerusalem and Bethel. The spring New Year festival had Mesopotamian links and was the major festival of the old league sanctuaries of Gilgal and Shiloh which fell from use in the development of a national cult centered on Jerusalem.

[37] J. C. Rylaarsdam, "Booths, Feast of," *IDB* 1 (1962) 455.

journey, traditions of the Ark and the Tent of meeting, David's Tent and the glorious Temple came together in the polyvalent title "Tabernacles."

The primary conception of God's presence was in a theophany, when God came to Israel amidst signs of cloud, smoke, fire, thunder, and earthquake. In the cultic reenactment of the Exodus event, the Ark was the prime symbol of YHWH leading Israel's hosts to victory. Within the Temple worship, the Ark continued to be the primary cult object and was housed within the inner sanctuary; in addition to the Ark, the sights and sounds of Israel's worship duplicated aspects of YHWH's theophanic presence—the fire from lamps illuminating the Temple courts, the clouds of incense and smoke rising from sacrifices, the blasts of the *shofar* and shouts of acclamation.[38] YHWH's presence was manifest in the cult in signs perceptible to the senses. In the liturgical celebrations the line between symbol and reality, myth and history, was blurred. In the Temple, YHWH found a place to dwell and his presence was manifest in Israel's worship, guaranteeing for them salvation and prosperity.

The royal ideology expressed in Israel's Temple and the Davidic dynasty came to a highpoint in the time of Solomon. Over the following centuries it is possible to see a steady reaction against this too literal and simplistic sense of YHWH's presence and the syncretism of Canaanite mythology and worship that it was based on. The reforms of the prophets, as well as the Deuteronomic and Priestly traditions, correct and refute ideological claims that ran counter to Israel's older, covenant faith. In these reforms there is a movement from a literal sense of YHWH's presence dwelling in the Temple to a more spiritual conception of this presence. The later apocalyptic movements, including Qumran, are an extension of this same "spiritualizing" movement away from an earthly, national Temple to a spiritual sense of God's presence dwelling in the midst of the people.

The Spiritualization of the Temple Cult[39]

The Deuteronomist[40]

The reforms undertaken in the reign of Josiah (640–609), were given a theological expression in the rewriting of Israel's traditions. In the books

---

[38] A more detailed discussion of the Temple rituals will follow in examining the festivals of Passover, Tabernacles, and Dedication in the Johannine narrative.

[39] I use the term "spiritualization" to describe a movement away from associating God's presence with the externals of cultic requirements, to an internal religious and ethical response.

[40] I am following the view that the Deuteronomic history grew out of a number of sources and redactions. The basic history was written in the time of Josiah to support

of Deuteronomy, Joshua, Judges, 1 and 2 Samuel, and 1 and 2 Kings, the seventh-century Deuteronomist recalled the conditional nature of early covenant traditions. Blessings were guaranteed only if Israel kept covenant faith:

> **If** you heed these ordinances, by diligently observing them, the LORD your God will maintain with you the covenant loyalty that he swore to your ancestors; he will love you, bless you, and multiply you; he will bless the fruit of your womb and the fruit of your ground, your grain and your wine and your oil (Deut 7:12-13 NRSV).

> And **if** you forget the LORD your God and go after other Gods and serve them and worship them, I solemnly warn you this day that you shall surely perish (Deut 8:19).

The conditional nature of the promised blessing was expressed in the heartfelt cry "And if you will obey my commandments. . . " "For if you will be careful to do all this commandment. . . " (Deut 11:13, 22). The twofold possibilities were clearly stated, "Behold, I set before you this day a blessing and a curse: the blessing, if you obey the commandments of the LORD your God, . . . and the curse, if you do not obey. . . " (Deut 11:26-28). In the era of covenant fidelity, the theme of judgment was set over and against the theme of the promise to David.[41] The Deuteronomist named David the servant of God rather than son, a term which better expressed a conditional covenant, and the necessity of obedience (cf. 2 Sam 3:18; 7:5, 8; 1 Kgs 3:8; 8:24, 25, 26, 66; 11:13, 32, 34, 36).

As Kingship was reinterpreted in the light of a conditional covenant, so to, the Temple was described, not as a dwelling place for God, but as a house for the **name** of God (1 Kgs 5:5). Central to Deuteronomic theology was the notion that God could not be contained, for God's true dwelling place was in the heavens (1 Kgs 8:27, 30, 39, 43):

> But there can be a presence without containment, and Deuteronomic theology expressed that presence of God as the presence of God's name. So the temple is that place of which God has said: "My name shall be there" (1 Kgs 8:29).[42]

---

his reforms and the final redaction took place early in the post-Exilic period. See a clear summary of various positions in A. F. Campbell, *The Study Companion To Old Testament Literature: An Approach to the Writings of Pre-Exilic and Exilic Israel.* Old Testament Studies 2 (Wilmington, Del.: Michael Glazier, 1989) 232–48.

[41] Cross, *Canaanite Myth,* 278–85.

[42] Campbell, *Study Companion,* 159–60.

The literal and theophanic mode of presence was refuted in the reinterpretation of the Temple as a house of prayer rather than as God's dwelling place:

> If there is famine in the land, if there is a plague, blight, mildew, locust, or caterpillar; if their enemy besieges them in any of their cities; whatever plague, whatever sickness there is; whatever prayer, whatever plea there is from any individual or from all your people Israel, all knowing the afflictions of their own hearts so that they stretch out their hands towards this house; then hear in heaven your dwelling place, forgive, act and render to all whose hearts you know. . . so that they may fear you all the days that they live in the land you gave to our ancestors (1 Kgs 8:37-40 NRSV).

In this dedicatory prayer of Solomon, the Temple is demythologized as the immediate link between the natural and supernatural worlds, through which God's blessings can be poured out on the people and the land:

> There is no natural link between God and his world, made effective by the temple and its symbolism; instead the link is a spiritual one, made effective by the sincere cry of humble men [sic], who turn to Yahweh.[43]

The Ark was the central symbol of God's presence in Israel, and its function in the D narrative was to show the transition from the institution of the Judges to that of the monarchy.[44] The Ark also maintained a focus on the covenant ideology, so central to the Deuteronomic historian, for the Ark was clearly and simply described as the container to hold and protect the tablets of the Law (Deut 10:1, 3). There is no mention here of a cherubim-throne or a mythological sense of God's presence. For the Deuteronomist the relationship between God and Israel was based on the Law.[45] When the Temple was complete and the Ark placed within it, the promise made to David of an eternal Kingdom (2 Sam 7:13, 16) was renewed with Solomon, but unlike the promise to David, this was a conditional promise, in keeping with a covenant ideology:

> I have consecrated this house which you have built and put my name there forever; my eyes and my heart will be there for all time. And as for you, **if** you will walk before me as David your father walked, with integrity of heart and uprightness, doing according to all that I have commanded you, and keeping my statutes and my ordinances, **then** I will establish your royal throne over Israel for ever, as I promised David your Father (1 Kgs 9:3d-5a).

---

[43] Clements, *God and Temple,* 91–92.
[44] Campbell, *Study Companion,* 200.

The warning was also given that if Solomon or his children turned aside from following God, then "the house which I have consecrated for my name I will cast out of my sight (1 Kgs 9:7).

Even with the problems of a royal ideology, for the Deuteronomist the Temple was still a primary symbol of unity in faith and worship. The palace (היכל) of the King and the Temple (היכל) of God stood side by side in Jerusalem. The building of this richly decorated structure established a powerful visible symbol at the center of Israel:

> Just as the Shema . . . is an extraordinary unification of all human life, providing a centre and a core that radiates out upon the whole, so too the deuteronomic insistence on the centrality of the temple in Jerusalem is a re-markable endeavour to duplicate this spiritual unity in physical terms.[46]

While the Jerusalem Temple was central to single-hearted worship of God, the Deuteronomist broke sharply from any magico-religious under-standing of the link between the natural and supernatural worlds. God transcends the world of nature. The basis for God's blessing lay in cove-nant fidelity, for Israel's relationship to God "was not something perma-nently rooted in the natural order, but rather an ethical and spiritual relationship grounded in a covenant of grace."[47] The Deuteronomist re-minds Israel that their existence as a people came about through the gra-tuitous initiative of God. Unlike the mythology of the Canaanites, their relationship with God was not established in the order of creation, but was based on a covenant which was conditional upon Israel's living as God's people.

The Pre-Exilic Prophets

The prophets move away from a sense of the immanence of God's presence, and draw their imagery primarily from Canaanite El mythology rather than Baal and his storm theophany. The prophet stands as messen-ger in the heavenly court and so hears God's judgments and can therefore be sent as messenger of the Divine Council to proclaim, "Thus says the LORD . . . "[48] The movement from the theophanic mode of presence as-sociated with Baal is illustrated with profound clarity in the story of Elijah.[49] After his conflict with the priests of Baal (1 Kgs 18:20-40) where God

---

[45] Clements, *God and Temple*, 96.

[46] Campbell, *Study Companion*, 246.

[47] Clements, *God and Temple*, 99.

[48] The role of the prophet as messenger to the Divine Council is brought out strongly in the call of Isaiah (Isa 6:1-8).

[49] Cross, *Canaanite Myth*, 191–94.

achieves victory, Elijah returns to Sinai, and like Moses, he experiences God's presence. But God does not come in the wind, or the earthquake, or fire; Elijah experiences the presence of God in silence (1 Kgs 19:11-12). Theophany has been replaced by silence, and it is the role of the prophet to interpret the mysterious ways of God.

Amos and Hosea both prophesy in the Northern Kingdom and both are highly critical of the cult (Amos 2:6-8; 5:21-23; Hos 2:11) as they call for a return to covenant fidelity and morality (Amos 5:24; Hos 12:66). Both prophets offer hope that God will still be present in their midst, but this is conditional on covenant morality,

"Seek good and not evil that you may live;
and so that the LORD, the God of Hosts will be with you" (Amos 5:14; cf. Hos 11:9).

A further element of the *spiritualization* of the cult is the early expression of eschatological hope—an expression Cross calls "proto-apocalyptic".[50] In some of the oracles of Isaiah, prophecy is directed to a future divine intervention, when God will once again vindicate Zion by executing vengeance on the nations, then recreate Zion in abundant fertility and joy (Isa 34, 35). In the "Apocalypse" of Isaiah (2:2-4), the House of God will be clearly revealed as the great cosmic mountain where God dwells. The nations will gather to the Temple, and Zion will be a source of universal judgment and peace. In the present time, the Lord will protect Jerusalem (Isa 31:4), but the fullest expression of God's blessings are no longer located solely in the historical Temple and its cult; true peace (שלם) lies in the future.

For Micah and Jeremiah, later prophets to Jerusalem, God's presence in the Temple is going to be a source of judgment, not blessing. The people have false hope when they say, "Surely the LORD is with us! No harm shall come upon us" (Mic 3:11). Jeremiah is even more scathing:

Do not trust in these deceptive words: 'This is the temple of the LORD, the temple of the LORD, the temple of the LORD.' Has this house, which is called by my name, become a den of robbers in your sight? Therefore will I do to the house that is called by my name, in which you trust, and to the place that I gave to you and your ancestors, just what I did to Shiloh (Jer 7:4, 11, 14 NRSV).

The Temple no longer guarantees God's favor; God, the Holy One of Israel, cannot dwell in the midst of a people whose lives are no longer holy.

[50] Cross, *Canaanite Myth,* 135, 137, 169, 171, 174, 324, 343–46.

Ezekiel depicts in graphic manner the departure of God's glory from the Temple (Ezek 10:18-19) and then from Jerusalem (11:23). His description portrays the plaintive words of Jeremiah, "I have forsaken my house, I have abandoned my heritage; I have given the beloved of my soul into the hands of her enemies" (Jer 12:7). The departure of God's glory foreshadows the destruction of Jerusalem and its Temple (Ezek 33:21). With the end of the earthly Temple, Ezekiel begins a series of oracles of hope, when the exiles will be restored to life (37:1-14) and will be reunited under a future Davidic King (37:15-25). When Israel has been reconstituted as one nation then God will once again dwell in the midst of a covenant people:

> I will make a covenant of peace with them; it shall be an everlasting covenant with them; and I will bless them and multiply them, and will set my sanctuary in the midst of them for evermore. My dwelling place shall be with them; and I will be their God, and they shall be my people (Ezek 37:26-27).

In these later chapters, 37–40, Ezekiel's oracles exhibit elements of a new form of prophecy—apocalypticism. The oracles against Gog and Magog recall the mythological places at the dawn of creation.[51] Time is expressed in phrases that have an eschatological sense, "After many days . . ." (37:8a); "in the latter years. . . " (v. 8b); "on that day. . . " (v. 10). According to Cross, in the catastrophe of the Exile, the old forms of faith and tradition collapsed or were transformed.[52] The Epic traditions, which had their focus in history, were silenced in the mystery of history's flux. A new expression of faith was formed, drawing together elements of myth, history, prophecy, and wisdom. The old myths of creation, Exodus, conquest, enthronement were given an eschatological function. The myths of primeval creation, and the apocalyptic visions of a future creation, frame Israel's history, giving history a transcendent significance, "significance not apparent in the ordinary events of horizontal history."[53]

Part of Ezekiel's eschatological program is his vision of a future Temple as the first gift in the new eschatological age (Ezekiel 40–47). This Temple, though highly idealized, is similar to Solomon's Temple.[54] The glory of God that had abandoned the Solomonic Temple, returns and

---

[51] Magog, Meshech, Gomer, Tubal (Gen 10:2), Beth-togarmah (Gen 10:3), Tarshish (Gen 10:4).

[52] Cross, *Canaanite Myth,* 342–46. In these pages Cross briefly discusses the origins of sixth-century apocalypticism which found expression in Deutero-Isaiah and Ezekiel.

[53] Cross, *Canaanite Myth,* 346.

[54] Barker believes Ezekiel's description of the eschatological Temple is based on his memory of the Jerusalem Temple prior to its destruction. See Barker, *Gate of Heaven,* 69.

reconsecrates the building as God's dwelling (43:5). "Son of man, this is the place of my throne and the place of the soles of my feet, where I will dwell (שכן) in the midst of the people of Israel for ever" (43:7). The Temple is the source of life, healing and fertility for the New Israel. Water flows from under the sanctuary to cleanse and fructify the whole land (47:1-12). This chapter recalls the creation myths of Canaan and Israel where waters well up from the cosmic rivers of paradise to provide life (Gen 2:6, 10-14).[55] Once the land has been restored to life by the waters flowing from the side of the Temple, the land is divided among the twelve tribes of a restored Israel, with the sanctuary of the Lord in the middle of it.

The vision of the Temple belongs to the future and is intrinsically linked to a new covenant (Ezek 37:26). In the experience of the Exile, Jeremiah and Ezekiel look beyond the former covenants with Moses and David, and their cultic expressions symbolized in the Ark and Temple. For both prophets, the new covenant is symbolized, not by a cult-object, but by the human heart. The law will be written on the heart (Jer 31:31-33); the heart of stone will be replaced by the gift of God's spirit and a heart of flesh (Ezek 11:19; 36:26; 37:12). These verses portray a movement towards a more personal spirituality of the heart and they fit in well with Ezekiel's call to personal moral responsibility and conversion (chs. 18, 33).[56] The new covenant, to be made in the future, is in terms of personal repentance and the gift of God's spirit. The covenant people will be led by an ideal shepherd/king, David, and will be made holy by the action of God in establishing his sanctuary in their midst (Ezek 37:28).[57]

[55] See Barker, *Gate of Heaven,* 75–82, for a discussion on the Temple as a source of fertility for the earth. The description of waters flowing from beneath the Temple may well have a basis in history, apart from the mythical significance. The non-biblical text "The Letter of Aristeas," dated some time in the second century B.C.E., describes "an endless supply of water" as well as reservoirs and deep channels under the foundations of the Temple (Aristeas 89–91). See C. T. R. Haywood, *The Jewish Temple: A non-biblical sourcebook* (London: Routledge, 1996) 26–37.

[56] The book of Deuteronomy resonates with a similar *heart spirituality* which is at the essence of the *Shema* (Deut 6:4-6). Moses' final words invoke this heart spirituality, "The word is very near to you; it is in your mouth and in your heart, so that you can do it" (Deut 30:14).

[57] David epitomizes these two aspects of the new covenant in his humble act of repentance (2 Sam 12:13) and because he was endowed with God's spirit (1 Sam 16:13). There is nothing in the new covenant and Temple that suggests a nationalistic ideology of Kingship and Temple which was associated with the Temple cult in the time of Solomon.

The Priestly Tradition and the Tabernacle

In this section I have been examining a movement away from an emphasis on the cultic presence of God. This presence reached its fullest expression in the era of Solomon, when the Temple was understood to provide a divine guarantee of God's presence in Jerusalem, and a permanent covenant with the Davidic House. In the Deuteronomic reform and the prophets, I have traced a reaction to such a naive view of God's presence and the underlying mythology it expressed. The Deuteronomists and the prophets recalled the covenant obligations and the conditional nature of God's promises. With the destruction of Jerusalem, and with it the collapse of an historic royal ideology, one response was to look to the creation of a new covenant in the future. In Jeremiah and Ezekiel this new covenant was not expressed in a national ideology but in a personal spirituality of the heart.

In looking to a future covenant how are the past historical traditions to be interpreted? What is the place of the cult in the vision of a new restored Israel? During the Exile a theology emerged, designated "the Priestly" (P) tradition, that reformulated Israel's historical origins and gave a new understanding of Israel's cult, and the mode of God's presence.[58]

In the P tradition, the dimensions of time and space are ordered so that what is sacred is clearly defined and separated from that which is secular. By such separations holy space and holy time are established which make possible the presence of the utterly holy and transcendent God. Without this separation, the pervasive sinfulness of humanity would create an unbridgeable gap between God and Israel. To bridge this gulf, God gave creation the gift of the Sabbath, and it is the Sabbath that is the particular sign of the Sinai covenant in the P tradition.[59] "You shall keep my sabbaths, for this is a sign between me and you throughout your generations, that you may know that I, the LORD, sanctify you" (Exod 31:13). The Sabbath and the festivals of Israel ensured sacred times. The Tabernacle was the gift that created in Israel a sacred space. Through these two gifts of a sacred time and a sacred space God could be present in the midst of the people.

> I will set my tabernacle (משכן) in your midst, and my spirit shall not despise you. I will walk about (הלך) among you and will become your God and you shall become my people (Lev 26:11-12 [my translation]).

---

[58] There are divergent views on the Priestly tradition regarding whether it was a narrative tradition in its own right, or whether it was simply an editorial framework incorporating the older JE traditions. Cross, *Canaanite Myth*, 30–21, argues that it was not a narrative; against this see the recent arguments and narrative outline of Campbell, *Study Companion*, 62–91. The issue does not affect my argument.

[59] Cross, *Canaanite Myth*, 298.

Sabbath and Tabernacle express the paradox of the immanence of the Holy One.

Within the P tradition, two terms take on a technical sense in describing the presence of God, שׁכן and כבד. The earlier traditions used both ישׁב, to sit or dwell, and שׁכן, to dwell, with the connotation of dwell in a tent, (משׁכן).[60] Both terms were used of the deity and of human agents. In the P tradition שׁכן is used exclusively of the presence of the transcendent God in the sanctuary.[61] In describing this presence, P uses a further term in a deliberate, technical manner כבד, glory. So it is not God who dwells in the tabernacle, rather it is God's glory which is present. "The glory of the LORD filled the tabernacle" (Exod 40:34b, 35c). In P, the cloud theophany is quite different from God's glory, they are two distinct realities. "Behold the glory of the LORD appeared in the cloud" (Exod 16:10).[62] By means of such technical expressions, P avoids a literal, anthropomorphic sense of the deity sitting (ישׁב) on the cherubim throne within the sanctuary (1 Sam 4:4; 2 Sam 6:2; 2 Kgs 19:15; Ps 80:1). God is the transcendent Holy One, and not even Moses is permitted to see God directly (Exod 33:18-23).

The P tradition, developed within the Exile,[63] looked back to a time when Israel did not have a Temple, and it reformulated the older Sinai traditions. Features of the Solomonic Temple were retrojected onto the wilderness Tabernacle, whose origins may have been a more simple Tent around the Ark—as distinct from the Tent of Meeting that Moses pitched outside the camp. The Solomonic Temple was thus presented as the legitimate successor to the Tabernacle; but even as it makes this link, the P tradition also offers a critique of the Solomonic Temple—perhaps suggesting why it ultimately was rejected by God:

---

[60] Abram dwelt (שׁכן) near the oaks of Mamre (Gen 14:13). Abram moved his tent and dwelt (ישׁב) by the oaks of Mamre (Gen 13:18).

[61] As well as immanence, the Tabernacle also suggests impermanence. The experience of the Exile created a gap in the history of God's presence in Israel. To show that God was not permanently bound to one place—and had never been—the authors used the verb form "to tabernacle." See Clements, *God and Temple*, 117.

[62] Cross examines two possible origins for the use of the term כבד. One possibility is that it derives from the term for the storm cloud, ענן כבד (Exod 19:16). The second possibility, which Cross favors, is that it is a concretization of the abstract "majesty" of the deity—the aureole which accompanies his sovereign presence. See *Canaanite Myth*, 135 n. 30; 164-67.

[63] Campbell, *Study Companion*, 63: "The most commonly held view puts the composition of the Priestly Document during the Exile or the immediate post-Exilic period." Haran, *Temples and Temple-Service*, 5–12, is a notable exception in dating P as a pre-Exilic document, belonging to the Jerusalemite priesthood of the First Temple.

- The Tabernacle was constructed according to a divine pattern (Exod 25:9) and its builder was specially selected by God and filled with God's spirit, with abilities, knowledge and skills (Exod 31:1-6). Solomon's architect was a Phoenician, who was full of skill, intelligence and knowledge (1 Kgs 7:14) but without the spirit of God.
- The Tabernacle was made from the free will offerings of the people (Exod 35:20-29). The Temple was built from conscript labour (1 Kgs 5:13-14).

It is the view of the P tradition that the cult, with all its paraphernalia, is not the creation of Israel, to manipulate divine power, nor is it forced on the people by a demanding God. It is the free gift of a sovereign Lord who desires to dwell with Israel, and the free response from the hearts of a less than perfect Israel. The Tabernacle creates space within the midst of a sinful people, wherein God's glory, the earthly manifestation of the Divinity, can reside.

The theology of the Priestly tradition had profound consequences on post-Exilic Israel. When Persia defeated Babylon the exiles were permitted to return and rebuild. Some chose to do this and a Second Temple was built. But some exiles chose to remain in Babylon, as others remained in Egypt. The theological thought that developed during the Exile gave Israel the freedom to retain their religious identity away from the land, the Temple or national ideologies.

This theology may be summarized thus:

- God's sovereignty was not co-extensive with national boundaries. God was Lord of the whole earth and God's presence could be known anywhere.

- In emphasizing the Sabbath, the priests gave Israel a festival, built into the order of creation, which could be celebrated apart from a Temple. Each family home became a center for worship.

- Just as the Tabernacle had clearly defined zones of holiness, so in the pattern of daily living, Israel could establish ways of being a separate, holy people. The principle of holiness by separation was established.

The Second Temple

In the period of the Second Temple, Israel's faith found expression in two new forms—Apocalypticism and Wisdom. Both emerged from the Exile experience and both struggled with the issue of God's Presence.[64]

---

[64] The beginnings of Apocalypticism can be seen in Israelite prophecy. Passages such as Isa 2:2-4 and Ezekiel 38, have been discussed above. There is no firm consensus

Deutero-Isaiah had promised a glorious return of God to Zion (Isa 43:14-21; 44:24-28; 45:13-14; 49), but even when the Temple was finally rebuilt in 516 B.C.E., God's triumphant return was delayed. In the Apocalyptic tradition, the unfulfilled hopes of the post-Exilic community were shifted to a future time, when the world would undergo a cataclysmic transformation and so become a suitable place for God to dwell. Apocalypticism therefore, stressed the transcendence of God, and looked to a future time when Israel would once again experience God's presence in its midst.

Alongside this was the sense of God's closeness, expressed in ways other than Temple rituals.[65] The Exile had shown that God was not confined to Zion, and the Temple was not essential for worship. The theological perspective of the Priestly tradition, with its emphasis on separating the "sacred" from the "profane," not only in the cult but in all aspects of life, enabled the people to take on an identity as a cultic community,[66] a holy people set in the midst of the nations. In the P theology creation came about when God's word imposed order on primal chaos (Gen 1:1–2:4a). The Wisdom tradition developed this outlook further, with its emphasis on order and time, and its concern for how to live in this world.[67] As Apocalypticism emphasized God's transcendence, the Wisdom tradition emphasized God's immanence, for Wisdom is of God and Wisdom has come to dwell in Israel (Sir 24:10; Bar 3:36-37). I will examine the two forms of post-Exilic literature for the light they can shed on Israel's developing sense of God's presence dwelling in their midst and on the way the Temple functions as an image of this divine dwelling in the world.

Wisdom Dwelling in Israel

The Wisdom mentality is essentially a contemplative attitude, able to see God at the heart of the world. Though this contemplative vision may eventually be refined and expressed in dry, pithy sayings, it calls for a

---

as to the origins of Israel's Wisdom tradition. Some scholars favor the clan and family in which lessons would have been transmitted, others favor a school associated with the royal court. According to R. E. Murphy, "Introduction to Wisdom Literature," *NJBC* (1990) 448, whatever its origins, "the wisdom literature in its present form was edited and written in the post Exilic period."

[65] Clements, *God and Temple*, 127.

[66] Clements, *God and Temple*, 120.

[67] In tracing the steps in the development of the Wisdom tradition, von Rad identifies order as the starting point. "The order which was formerly perceived in a vague and unthinking way and as existing in many different forms must itself have more and more become the object of thought. It was objectified as something which was uniform and which could be perceived in every separate experience, and it was conceptually determined (as 'wisdom')." See G. von Rad, *Wisdom in Israel* (London: SCM, 1972) 171.

profound awareness that all of life's experiences are transparent to the activity of God:

> It was perhaps her [Israel's] greatness that she did not keep faith and knowledge apart. The experiences of the world were for her always divine experiences as well, and the experiences of God were for her experiences of the world.[68]

While expressed in forms different from the earlier traditions, with their definite historical contexts, Wisdom literature is rooted in history, not history on the scale of the grand epic or national event, but history in the details of daily life:

> The sages penetrated into the divine mystery in a manner that even the prophets never equalled. God drew the people, through their daily experience of themselves and creation, into the mystery of God's dealings with each individual human being.[69]

According to von Rad, God's active ordering of the whole of creation was conceptualized as Wisdom. This Wisdom, although immanent in creation, was differentiated from creation itself in the great poems of Job 28, Proverbs 8, and Sirach 24.[70] In these poems, Wisdom is personified and allowed to speak directly, in the manner of a "Divine Speech" in the prophetic literature. Only here, it is Wisdom, not God, speaking.[71] In the voice of Wisdom a new bearer of divine revelation is introduced. In the prophetic literature other terms were used to describe God's mode of communication and God's Presence. The prophets spoke of the Word going forth from the mouth of God to accomplish God's purpose (Isa 55:10-11); of the Spirit being set within Israel (Ezek 22:26; 37:14). In the Pentateuchal traditions God's glory and God's name dwelt in the Temple. The sages in the post-Exilic community chose the term *"Wisdom"* to describe God's self-communication in the world.

It is Job who raises the question, "Where shall Wisdom be found?" (Job 28:12). Though not located in a specific place (vv. 13b-14), somehow Wisdom is present in the world and is perceived by God (vv. 23-24). Wisdom's relationship to creation and to God is revealed more clearly in

[68] von Rad, *Wisdom in Israel,* 62.

[69] R. E. Murphy, *The Tree of Life: An exploration of Biblical Wisdom Literature.* Anchor Bible Reference Library (New York: Doubleday, 1990) 125.

[70] von Rad, *Wisdom in Israel,* 171.

[71] In using the concept of *personification,* I am following Murphy, *The Tree of Life,* 133, who argues against a term such as "hypostasis" and uses the term *personification* in a literary sense.

Proverbs 8. Here Lady Wisdom speaks publicly and directly, describing her origins at/as the beginning of God's creative activity, and her role as that of a child or artisan (Prov 8:30).[72] Sirach 24 follows Proverbs in describing Wisdom's origins in God. Her role in creation is described with greater subtlety, "'mistlike' she covers the earth (Sir 24:3), much as the spirit or wind of God came over the waters of chaos (Gen 1:2)."[73] In this poem a new element is added, in that Wisdom is given a precise location; Job's question is finally answered as Wisdom describes her dwelling in Jacob and her ministry in the holy tent:

> Then the Creator of all things gave me a commandment,
> and the one who created me assigned the place for my tent (σκηνήν).
> And he said, "Make your dwelling in Jacob,
> and in Israel receive your inheritance (v. 8).
> In the holy tabernacle (σκηνῆ ἀγίᾳ) I ministered before him
> and so I was established in Zion (v. 10).

Wisdom, who had dwelt in the heights of heaven (Sir 24:4), is now located within Israel. The words "tent" and "minister" imply a cultic context, but it is a cult that looks back to the past, bypassing a Temple-dwelling, to the older tradition of the Tent. A later verse (v. 23) clearly identifies Wisdom with Torah, "the book of the Covenant," and recalls Moses' words of Exod 24:7, when a cultic ritual sealed the Sinai covenant. The book of Baruch makes a similar identification, "She is the book of the commandments of God, and the law that endures forever" (4:1). While the dating of Baruch is problematic, the book of Sirach is probably around 180 B.C.E.[74] These passages clearly do not look to the Temple cult as the place or means of God's presence in Israel. It is in the living out of Torah that Israel is assured of the Divine Presence. The images in this poem (Sir 24:1-34) hearken back to the wilderness sojourning, only now the pillar of cloud is the throne of Wisdom (v. 4), the Tent is the place of *her* dwelling (v. 10), Wisdom provides food and drink (vv. 19-22) and the glory in the midst of the people is *her* glory (v. 1).

In identifying Wisdom and Torah, and in turning back to the pre-Temple wilderness tradition, Ben Sira offers an alternative understanding of God's presence. The Temple of Solomon was decorated with symbols of nature's fertility, with palms (1 Kgs 7:36) and pomegranates (1 Kgs 7:42), but these images pale beside the catalogue of Wisdom's abundant

---

[72] The exact meaning of the term אמון is mysterious. A brief summary of the two possible renderings as a craftsman or nursling can be found in von Rad, *Wisdom*, 152.

[73] Murphy, *Tree of Life*, 139.

[74] Murphy, *Tree of Life*, 139.

fruit (Sir 24:13-17). As Ezekiel saw waters gushing from the Temple, Ben Sira proclaims that Wisdom/Torah overflows like the Pishon, the Tigris, the Euphrates, the Jordan, the Nile, and the Gihon (24:25-27).[75] Where once God's presence in the Temple was seen as the assurance of fertility, now life is to be found in observance of the Torah/Wisdom, "Whoever finds me finds life and obtains favor from the LORD" (Prov 8:35 NRSV). The post-Exilic community had not found God's presence in a rebuilt Temple; the sages of Israel affirm the life-giving presence of God in the midst of the people, in the daily shaping of their lives according to the requirements of Torah.

Wisdom is the mode of expressing the immanence of God and in the final book of the Old Testament, Wisdom is described in ways that depict her intimate relationship with God and with humanity. Wisdom is the breath, the power, the pure emanation, the image of God (Wis 7:25-26); and Wisdom passes into holy souls (7:27) as a divine gift (8:21). Wisdom is God's gift to Israel to draw her into an intimate communion of life. In the tradition of the sages, such a communion of life is found in the Torah, rather than in the rituals of the Temple.[76]

The Temple in Apocalyptic Literature

In the biblical canon, "apocalyptic" refers to a genre whose primary concern is the end of the historical era and the imminent inauguration of a new order created by God.[77] Beyond the canon there exists another group of apocalypses concerned with revelatory journeys.[78] Both types of apocalyptic literature—eschatological and revelatory journeys—developed out of the shock of the Exile, and both offer a critique of the Temple.[79]

---

[75] The Pishon and Gihon are two of the four rivers flowing out of Eden whose location is not known and which are best understood as mythological rivers of God's cosmic abode. "The intention of the author in inserting [Gen] 2:10-14 was not to determine where paradise lay. . . but rather to point out . . . that the 'life arteries' of all the lands of the earth have their source in the river that watered paradise." See C. Westermann, *Genesis 1–11: A Commentary,* trans. John Scullion, S.J. (London: SPCK, 1984) 216.

[76] von Rad, *Wisdom,* 186–89, cautions against interpreting the various criticisms of the cult as outright rejection of cultic practices; he writes, "The wise men had, intellectually, outgrown the world of cultic action."

[77] The books of Daniel and Revelation are examples of this "end time" genre.

[78] See for example, The Apocalypse of Abraham; Testament of Abraham; Testament of Levi; Ascension of Isaiah; Apocalypse of Zephaniah; 3 Baruch; 1 Enoch 37–71; 72–82; 2 Enoch.

[79] For a discussion of the development of Apocalyptic literature see Cross, *Canaanite Myth,* 343–46; also M. Himmelfarb, "From Prophecy to Apocalypse: The

The primary motive for the tour apocalypse is to seek God's presence and revelation since God is no longer to be found in the Temple. The seer must therefore ascend to the heavenly dwelling of God to learn divine secrets.[80] In eschatological apocalypses, God's presence is in the heavens, for the wickedness of this age is incompatible with the presence of the Holy One. When this age has been brought to an end in violent conflict then God's reign can begin. In the apocalyptic visions God's dwelling is in the heavens (Dan 7:9-10; Rev 11:19), giving rise to the anguished cry "O that you would tear open the heavens and come down" (Isa 64:1 NRSV). When the final conflict is over, then there can be a new creation fit to be a dwelling place of God. In the New Testament Apocalypse the new creation itself will be God's tabernacle, and there is no need for a specific cultic location (Rev 21:1-3; 22).

The writings from Qumran preserve both types of apocalyptic mentality. Like the heroes of the apocalyptic tours, the community of Qumran understood itself to enjoy fellowship with the angels and they strove to experience mystical visions of God.[81] The community ordered its life as an eschatological people, the true Israel, fighting with the forces of Light in the final war against the children of Darkness:

And on the day on which the Kittim fall, there will be battle, and savage destruction before the God of Israel, for this will be the day determined by him since ancient times for the war of extermination against the sons of darkness. On this (day), the assembly of the Gods and the congregation of men shall confront each other for great destruction. The sons of light and the lot of darkness shall battle together for God's might, between the roar of a huge multitude and the shout of Gods and men, on the day of the calamity (1QM 1, 9b-11).[82]

The first group to settle in the wilderness of Qumran did so during the Maccabean time, considering the priesthood to have been defiled by

---

Book of the Watchers and Tours of Heaven." In *Jewish Spirituality from the Bible through the Middle Ages,* ed. Arthur Green, (London: SCM, 1985) 146–48.

[80] Himmelfarb, *From Prophecy to Apocalypse,* 161.

[81] Himmelfarb, "From Prophecy to Apocalypse," 162; B. Gärtner, *The Temple and the Community in Qumran and the New Testament.* Society for New Testament Studies Monograph Series 1 (Cambridge: Cambridge University Press, 1965) 100. G. Vermes, *The Dead Sea Scrolls in English.* 3rd. ed (Sheffield: JSOT Press, 1987) 45.

[82] The English translations come from F. Garcia Martinez, *The Dead Sea Scrolls Translated: The Qumran Texts in English* (Leiden: E. J. Brill, 1994). For the references to columns and lines I am following E. Lohse, *Die Texte Aus Qumran: Hebräisch und Deutsch* (Munich: Kösel-Verlag, 1971).

the appointment of a non-Zadokite High Priest.[83] The Temple, and its sacrificial cult, had been defiled and was therefore rejected. The Jerusalem Temple no longer constituted a fit dwelling place for God, and so this role was taken over by the community, they themselves were the "New Temple."[84] The community constituted the eschatological Temple, the true Temple; and the former function of the Temple as God's dwelling place, was now replaced by perfect obedience to Torah. "The Books of the Law are the Sukkat [סוכת] of the King, as he said, *Am 9:11* "I will raise up the fallen Sukkat [סוכת] of David" (CD VII, 15b–16). The living out of Torah replaced the blood sacrifices of the Temple and was the means of atonement for Israel:

> . . . in order to atone for the fault of the transgression and for the guilt of sin and for approval for the earth, without the flesh of burnt offerings and without the fats of sacrifice—the offering of the lips in compliance with the decree will be like the pleasant aroma of justice and the correctness of behaviour will be acceptable like a freewill offering (1QS IX:4-5).

The relationship between the community and the Temple is summed up by Gärtner:

> But when the cultus of the Jerusalem Temple could no longer be accepted, a substitute was found in the community itself: the temple, its worship, [עבדה] and its sacrifices were made to apply to the community per se, its life of obedience to the Law and its liturgy. This process may have been further facilitated by the idea, found elsewhere in late Judaism, that the works of the Law were sufficient to make atonement for sins.[85]

The proscriptions laid down for the holiness of the Temple priesthood became the proscriptions for initiates into the community, for the community, or at least part of it, lived as if it was the Temple, thus preserving the means of Israel's sanctification and redemption.[86]

[83] Brief summaries of the probable origins of the Qumran community can be found in Cross, *Canaanite Myth,* 326–342; also R. Brown, P. Perkins and A. Saldarini, "Apocrypha; Dead Sea Scrolls; Other Jewish Literature," *NJBC* (1989) 1073–74.

[84] Gärtner, *Temple and Community,* 16. Further comments on Qumran will be made in Chapter 8 under the heading "Community-as-Temple Precedents."

[85] Gärtner, *Temple and the Community,* 20–21. In an unpublished thesis, Brendan Byrne modified Gärtner's claims by showing that it was a core group and not the whole community, who were designated as the Temple. See B. Byrne, *'Building' and 'Temple' imagery in the Qumran Texts.* (M.A., Middle Eastern Studies, Melbourne, 1971) 146, 170–71.

[86] Gärtner, *Temple and the Community,* 5. Gärtner notes that living according to the ideals of the priesthood is also a characteristic of Pharisaism. Jacob Neusner claims

In discussing the Temple symbolism in Qumran, it is important to note that the Temple clearly has great significance, as does the concept of sacrifice. The community has *transferred* the meaning of these terms, according to their own ideology, but has not completely rejected the concepts.[87] Temple, Torah, Sacrifice—these basic principles of mainstream Judaism lie at the center of this community. Theologically this community still belongs within Judaism in continuity with an ethical trend found in the prophets which criticized the cult when it was divorced from covenant living.

God's Presence in the Targums

The Targums continue the movement away from an anthropomorphic understanding of God's presence dwelling in the midst of Israel. Like the earlier Deuteronomic and Priestly traditions, the Targums grapple with the paradox of speaking about an omnipresent and infinite God being located in this world with its limitations of time and space.[88] Where the Deuteronomist spoke of God's *name* dwelling in the Temple (e.g., Deut 12:5, 14:23, 16:6; 1 Kgs 3:2), and the Priestly tradition spoke of God's *glory* filling the Tabernacle and Temple (Exod 40:34; Ezek 8:4, 43:5), the Targums use a non-scriptural term and speak of God's *Shekinah.* "And the cloud covered the tent of meeting, and the Glory of *the Shekinah of* the Lord filled the Tabernacle" (*Tg. Neof.* Exod 40:34).[89]

---

that it was this aspect of Pharisaism that enabled it to survive the destruction of the Temple in 70 c.e. "In very specific ways the Pharisees claimed to live as if they were priests, as if they had to obey at home the laws that applied to the Temple. When the Temple itself was destroyed, it turned out that the Pharisees had prepared for that tremendous change in the sacred economy. They continue to live as if—as if the Temple stood, as if there was a new Temple formed of the Jewish people." See J. Neusner, "Varieties of Judaism in the Formative Age," *Jewish Spirituality from the Bible through the Middle Ages,* ed. Arthur Green, (London: SCM, 1985) 181.

[87] In her analysis of the cultic language of Qumran, Fiorenza notes that the term "spiritualization" can have an anti-cultic sense and she uses the term "transference" to describe the shift that happened when Jewish and Hellenistic cultic concepts were used to designate a non-cultic reality. See E. S. Fiorenza, "Cultic Language in Qumran and in the NT," *CBQ* 38 (1976) 161.

[88] C. G. Montefiore and H. Loewe, *A Rabbinic Anthology* (New York: Schocken, 1974) 15.

[89] M. McNamara and M. Maher, *Targum Neofiti 1: Exodus.* A detailed introduction to the Palestinian Targums can be found in M. McNamara, *Targum Neofiti 1: Genesis,* 1–46. The dating of Neofiti is problematic since it shows evidence of a number of reworkings. "Though there is evidence of "post-Mishnaic" editing of *Neof.* (e.g., it tries to reflect the Rabbinic rules regarding the Forbidden Targumim), it is not marked by any of the very late elements that feature in *Ps.-J.* It probably represents on the whole

As a cognate of the verb שׁכן (to dwell) *Shekinah* is used primarily to describe God's numinous immanence, and is commonly used in association with the term glory (יקרא—*yichra*).[90] Both terms, *Shekinah* and *Yichra* preserve the holy transcendence of God while acknowledging God's presence within Israel's midst and both are associated with fiery light:

> And the appearance of the glory *of the Shekinah* of the Lord (was) like a devouring fire, *a devouring fire* on the top of the mountain, in the eyes of the children of Israel" (*Tg. Neof.* Exod 24:17).

Although the Targums probably predate the midrashic writings of the Rabbis, the rabbinic comments about the nature of the *Shekinah* are consistent with what is found in the Targums. R. Joshua of Sikhnin explains how God's glory can be located within the Tent of Meeting (Exod 40:35) by likening the tent to a cave by the sea which fills as the tide rises, but the sea is no less full. "So the sanctuary and the tent of meeting were filled with the radiance of the Shechinah but the world was no less filled with God's Glory" (Num R., XII:4).[91] According to R. Joshua b. Karhah, God spoke to Moses from a lowly thorn bush to teach Israel about the omnipresence of God's *Shekinah,* "God spoke from the thorn bush to teach you that there is no place where the Shechinah is not, not even a thorn bush" (Exod R., XI:5).

By using terms such as *Shekinah* and *Yichra,* the Targums avoid any naive anthropomorphic ideas about God, and thus interpret the Hebrew

---

an older recension of PT than *Ps.-J.* There are no good grounds for dating anything in *Neof.* later than the 3d/4th cent. C.E." See P. Alexander, "Targum," *ABD* 6 (1992) 323.

At Qumran a Targum of Job (11Qtarg Job) and part of a Targum of Leviticus 16 (4 Qtarg Lev) were discovered. These scrolls provide evidence that at least some written Targums existed in the first century B.C.E. and possibly earlier. Work still needs to continue on the Qumran findings to see if they are related to the extant Targums and if they can provide clues to dating these Targums. See also the four criteria developed by Evans, *Word and Glory,* 114, for dating Targumic material.

[90] The term כבוד in the Hebrew text is associated with "weightiness" which gives a person importance or honor. When used of God, the term, while associated with the visible storm cloud, refers to the invisible essence of God. The cloud appears necessary to veil the radiance of God's presence. The LXX text translates כבוד with the term δόξα. As used in the LXX, δόξα takes on a distinct meaning quite different from its use in secular Greek literature. In the secular sense it usually means "opinion," while in the LXX is comes closer to the sense of כבוד, meaning the divine revelation of God's essential nature in the created world. In the Targums כבוד is always rendered יקרא. See G. von Rad and G. Kittel, "δόξα," *TDNT* 2 (1964) especially 238–46.

[91] As translated in H. Freedman and M. Simon, eds. *Midrash Rabbah.* 5 vols. (London: Soncino, 1977).

text for the listeners. By such instructive interpretation, the Targumist stands as heir to a tradition that had its beginnings with Ezra the scribe, who not only read the text but interpreted it for the people, to ensure accurate understanding (Neh 8:1-3, 8).[92] *Shekinah* and *Yichra* stand as "buffer" words, used when a direct translation would seem to bring God's utter holiness into too close contact with this world, as such, both terms are used at times as a reverent alternative to speaking of God.[93]

A further term, *Memra,* is found in the Targums, and is used in a similar way to *Shekinah* and *Yichra* as a "buffer" word. *Memra* is not simply a translation of דבר־יהוה, when this conveys the sense of the prophetic word, rather *Memra* is used to express God's self-manifestation within this world.[94] In Targum Neofiti, God creates through His *Memra, "From the beginning with wisdom the Memra of the Lord created and perfected the heavens and the earth"* (*Tg. Neof.* Gen 1:1).[95] It is the *Memra* of the Lord which gives the command, "Let there be light" (Gen 1:3).

All three words, *Shekinah, Yichra* and *Memra,* are ways of speaking of that which is of God, and which goes forth from God into the world, so that where the *Shekinah* or *Yichra* or *Memra* is present, there is God.[96] By means of these expressions, the Targumist avoids expressions such as God dwelt, or departed or ascended. Such expressions seem to be beneath the dignity of God. Where the Hebrew reads, "The Lord appeared to Abram" (Gen 17:1) and "God went up from Abraham" (17:22), Neofiti renders this "The *Memra* of the Lord was revealed to Abram" and "the Glory of the *Shekinah* of the Lord went up from Abraham."

The Targums show a close parallel with a number of Johannine terms and concepts. If clear dating can be proven, then these Scriptures from the Palestinian synagogues provide a more likely Johannine source for the *logos* concept, than Stoic philosophy or Philo of Alexandria. Following a very detailed study of this issues, Evans concludes that

[92] McNamara, *Targum and Testament,* 35.
[93] A. Unterman, "Shekinah," *Encyclopedia Judaica* 14 (1971) 1349–50. Levine argues that the primary concern of the targums is not to eliminate anthropomorphisms, but to avoid the direct use of God's name. See E. Levine, *The Aramaic Version of the Bible: Contents and Context* (Berlin: Walter de Gruyter, 1988) 57.
[94] G. F. Moore, *Judaism in the First Centuries of the Christian Era: The Age of the Tannaim.* 3 vols. (Cambridge: Harvard University Press, 1927–1930) 1:417–19.
[95] I have argued above that in the Johannine Gospel, true perfection does not happen with the creation of the world, but through the life and death of Jesus.
[96] See Moore, *Judaism in the First Centuries,* 1:371, for later rabbinic comments that contrast God's messengers, which are always in the presence of God, with human messengers which must depart and return to their sender.

the point of all this is that the Christology of the Fourth Evangelist is fundamentally indebted to the language, concepts and institutions of the Old Testament and first-century Judaism. . . . It has come as no surprise then to find the Fourth Gospel permeated by the language, exegesis and presuppositions of the synagogue.[97]

In verse 14 of the Prologue, three terms used in the Targums to speak of God's presence in this world, are combined—*Memra, Shekinah, and Yichra.* "The *Word* (Memra) was made flesh and dwelt among us (He made his *Shekinah* dwell among us) and we have beheld his *glory*."[98] In commenting on the distinction between the terms *Memra* and *Shekinah,* Manns draws on the work of Vermès in linking *Memra* with the creative and revelatory word, while *Shekinah* describes God's dwelling among humanity.[99] Whether it is God's word in creation, or the manifestation of God's glory, or God's abiding presence, all three terms express a relationship between God and humanity that is accessible to human senses. The word can be heard, the glory can be seen, albeit veiled within a cloud, and God's dwelling among us can be experienced. These terms from the Targums used in Jewish synagogue worship may have provided the Johannine author with the theological tools to express the divinity they saw, heard, and experienced in Jesus.

Conclusion

The above overview of Israel's sense of God's dwelling, shows a variety of traditions, genres, terms, cult objects, and shrines as well as a constant reinterpretation of the traditions in response to new situations. Within the plurality of religious ideas, one tradition stands out as primary, as formative of Israel's faith; this is the experience of God during the Exodus and the wilderness sojournings. All later reformulations look back to this time to support their orthodoxy. The Temple is linked to the Ark; the Prophets and Deuteronomists stress the necessity of the Sinai covenant and its ethical demands; the Priests describe a tabernacling presence on the move with Israel; the Sages speak of Wisdom dwelling within Israel in the form of the Torah; Apocalyptic literature takes Moses as the model of the seer who has ascended the heights to see God and can therefore return to reveal heavenly secrets. While the eschatological apocalyptic genre

---

[97] Evans, *Word and Glory,* 184.

[98] R. Le Déaut, *The Message of the New Testament and the Aramaic Bible (Targum).* Subsidia Biblica 5 (Rome: Biblical Institute Press, 1982) 43. Le Déaut is here using the work of A. Díez Macho.

[99] F. Manns, *L'Evangile,* 41.

emphasizes a new creation rather than a new exodus, the Qumran sect withdrew to the desert and ordered its life in preparation for the final battle, in accordance with the Wilderness battle camp traditions:

> . . . the Essene camp in the wilderness found its prototype in the Mosaic camp of Numbers. . . As God established his ancient covenant in the desert, so the Essenes entered into the new covenant on their return to the desert. As Israel in the desert was mustered into army ranks in preparation for the Holy war of conquest, so the Essenes marshalled their community in battle array and wrote liturgies of the Holy Warfare of Armageddon, living for the day of the second conquest when they would march with their Messianic leaders to Zion.[100]

In 1:14 the Prologue also alludes to the Sinai tradition by using such terms as dwelt/tabernacled, glory and gift.[101] As well as the allusions to the Sinai tradition, the context of verse 14 within the theme of the Prologue recalls the tradition of Wisdom. The story of the Word parallels that of Wisdom with God in the act of creation, seeking a place to dwell, then pitching her tent in Israel and being enshrined in Israel's Torah.[102] Though there are allusions to Sinai and Wisdom, the evangelist uses these traditions in a polemical manner, for the Gospel presents God's dwelling in the midst of humanity not by way of Israel's Torah, but in the humanity of Jesus. In continuity with Israel's own history of ongoing reflection on God's presence in her midst, the evangelist reinterprets Israel's traditions and institutions in the light of a new situation brought about in the life, death, and resurrection of Jesus.

Following the destruction of Jerusalem, the evangelist is engaged in the same task as the Jewish rabbis gathered at Jamnia. They sought to ensure the survival of Judaism and the means of redemption without the Temple cult. The rabbi's answer was Torah. In the Torah Israel had a means of atonement as effective as the Temple.[103] While rabbinic Judaism was reformulating its traditions with a focus on the Torah in place of the Temple, the Johannine community focused on the person of Jesus. Both groups

---

[100] Cross, *Canaanite Myth*, 333–34.

[101] Tabernacle and glory have been discussed above with reference to the Sinai covenant. The Law was understood to be God's gift to Israel; *". . . they told Ezra the scribe, to bring the book of the law of Moses which the Lord had given to Israel"* (Neh 8:1). The Law is linked with other gifts of bread and water given in the wilderness (Neh 9:13-15).

[102] Since Wisdom and Torah had been identified (Sir 24:23, 25; Bar 3:36-4:4) the traditions of Wisdom and Sinai are interrelated.

[103] Neusner, "Varieties of Judaism," 194–97.

turned to their common Sinai traditions and Wisdom myth to find the means of expressing their claims to cultic continuity:[104]

> Both the community and the synagogue claimed to possess the revelation of divine wisdom, and came into irreconcilable conflict over the key question of where wisdom was to be found, where God in God's knowability, visibility and audibility was to be encountered. One solution, offered by Jamnia and the local synagogue, claimed Moses' revelation in Torah as the dwelling place of wisdom. John's community offered another, Jesus.[105]

The Prologue introduces the reader to the major insights of the Fourth Gospel. The traditions and institutions of Israel were valid but incomplete gifts; in the life of Jesus something new is being offered which brings to perfection the former gifts to Israel. In Jesus the fullness of divine filiation is present and this gift of divine filiation is offered to all who are open to receive it. The Prologue makes these claims in a brief statement that is both story and testimony; the reader is now invited to enter the narrative to test the truth of these claims.

[104] The motifs of the Prologue, Creation, Exodus, and Wisdom, will continue to be reflected in the Gospel, but once the narrative begins, the Temple motif becomes more dominant, reflecting the post-70 situation of the Johannine community in its conflict with the Synagogue. Two religious communities claim to possess true revelation, and both engage in the task of interpreting the events of 70 c.e. in the light of these claims. Within this thesis I will restrict myself to the motif of the Temple. For an example of the Creation theme, see Manns, *L'Evangile,* 400–29; for Exodus, see M.-É. Boismard, *Moses or Jesus: An essay in Johannine Christology,* trans. B. T. Viviano (Minneapolis: Fortress, 1993); W. A. Meeks, *The Prophet-King: Moses Traditions and the Johannine Christology,* Supplements to Novum Testamentum 14 (Leiden: Brill, 1967); for Wisdom, see Scott, *Sophia and the Johannine Jesus.*

[105] Carter, "The Prologue," 47.

The Temple of His Body

JOHN 2:13-25

The first explicit reference to the Temple is the pericope usually termed "the Cleansing of the Temple" (John 2:13-25). The Johannine narrative combines two elements found separately in the Synoptics—Jesus' actions in the Temple (John 2:14-16; cf. Matt 21:12-13; Mark 11:15-19; Luke 19:45-48), with a *logion* about destroying and raising the Temple (John 2:19; cf. Matt 26:61; 27:40; Mark 14:58; 15:29). While the Synoptics present the Temple scene as the culmination of Jesus' ministry, closely linked to his trial and passion, the Johannine narrative places it at the beginning of Jesus' ministry in Jerusalem, at the first of three Passovers (2:1; 6:4; 11:55). The Johannine account has distinctively different elements—oxen and sheep (v. 14), a whip made of cords (v. 15), pouring out the coins (v. 15), his words to the pigeon sellers (v. 16), the presence of disciples who remember the Scripture (vv. 17, 22), and his immediate confrontation with "the Jews" (vv. 18-20),[1] which leads into the Temple *logion* placed on the lips of Jesus (v. 19) rather than on the lips of false witnesses (Mark 14:58) and scoffers (Matt 27:40; Mark 15:29).

---

[1] In this Gospel the term "the Jews" must be understood as a narrative device. The term indicates a specific group of characters in opposition to Jesus and as a narrative device these characters are to be distinguished from the historical people following Jewish religious beliefs. To highlight the narrative use of this term, I follow the convention of calling these opponents "the Jews." As well as providing characters in the text in clear conflict with Jesus, the term "the Jews" also reflects those within Judaism opposed to the early Christian community in a post-Jamnia polemic. For a detailed description of the characterization of "the Jews," see Culpepper, *Anatomy,* 125–31. The issue will be dealt with further in ch. 5.

Because of such differences in chronology and details, scholars take various positions on the historicity of the Johannine account over against the Synoptics.[2] Some ask how this action would have been understood by the audience of Jesus' time? Was it a portent of the destruction of Jerusalem in 70, or would it have been perceived as a prophetic symbol of the purification of the Temple cult, inaugurating the messianic era?[3] More recently some have questioned the historicity of the event itself.[4] Is it conceivable that Jesus could have performed such a public act, so close to the Passover, in the Temple and national treasury, under the shadow of the Antonia fortress?

Rather than focus on questions that go beyond the scope of the text, I will focus on the meaning of this scene within the Johannine presentation of who Jesus is and his mission. What does this scene mean to a post-resurrection community of believers?

The Temple in the Synoptic Tradition

Before examining the particular Johannine presentation of the Temple Act and *Logion*, it is worth commenting briefly on the manner in which these are narrated in the synoptic tradition. The Johannine focus on the Temple stands within a trajectory already established within the early Christian communities and expressed with varying emphases in the Synoptic Gospels.

A very clear and precise overview of the synoptic Temple tradition is given by Peter Walker in his recent publication on Jesus and the Holy City.[5] He finds that each evangelist has a unique point of view with regard to the Temple and its value. Mark's Gospel presents Jesus' Temple cleans-

[2] For a discussion on the merits of the Johannine or synoptic chronology, see Brown, *Gospel,* 1:116-18. According to Barrett, *Gospel,* 195, the "placing of the incident was dictated by reasons theological rather than chronological." Carson, *Gospel,* 177, favors two cleansings.

[3] Sanders argues that the scene is a prophetic portent of the coming destruction of Jerusalem. See E. P. Sanders, *Jesus and Judaism* (London: SCM, 1985) 75. Against Sanders, Evans claims that it is a purification of the Temple in the light of priestly corruption and greed. See C. Evans, "Jesus' Action in the Temple: Cleansing or Portent of Destruction," *CBQ* 51 (1989) 269–70.

[4] For a review of opinions on the historicity of the event see E. Haenchen, *John 1–2,* trans. R. W. Funk. 2 vols. Hermeneia (Philadelphia: Fortress, 1984) 1:187-90. Buchanan has suggested that the scene is a midrashic composition created by the early Church. See G. W. Buchanan, "Symbolic Money-changers in the Temple?" *NTS* 37 (1991) 289–90; see also D. Seeley, "Jesus' Temple Act," *CBQ* 55 (1993) 279–83, who argues that it is a Marcan composition.

[5] Walker, *Jesus and the Holy City,* 5–6.

ing as a critique of the Temple cult and a parabolic prophecy of its future destruction (Mark 11:15-17). In making his critique Jesus stands in continuity with a prophetic tradition.[6] In this Gospel Jesus does not speak of replacing the Temple but, according to Walker, the Gospel suggests that the Risen Jesus is the true Temple, that this is the "other" (ἄλλος) Temple Jesus will build in three days (Mark 14:58).[7]

In a recent article J. P. Heil argues that the new Temple, "not built by human hands" (Mark 14:58), is the community of disciples.[8] Heil gives attention to the Marcan quotation from Isaiah where the Temple is to be a house of prayer "for all peoples" (Isa 56:7; Mark 11:17), and the instructions to the disciples about correct prayer that follow (11:24-26). "As lord of the Temple (11:1-11), Jesus authorizes the Marcan audience to replace the Temple that failed to become God's house of prayer for all peoples."[9] The new community is to be an inclusive group of prayer, faith, and forgiveness surpassing the former handmade sanctuary.

Matthew's treatment of the Temple is more complex. Both positive and negative attitudes stand in tension with each other. The Jerusalem Temple is "of God" (Matt 26:61), unlike the Marcan Temple that is likened to an idol made with human hands (Mark 14:58). The Temple is a "Holy Place" (Matt 24:15), where God dwells (Matt 23:21). The "cleansing" in Matthew is a claim of Jesus' messianic authority and a desire for its restoration as a house of prayer, rather than a parable or portent of its destruction.[10] Unlike Mark, Matthew does not directly call the witnesses who cite Jesus' words about destroying and building the Temple "false witnesses" (Matt 26:60; cf. Mark 14:57-58). Also in Matthew, the Temple is not, as in Mark, to be replaced by another Temple (cf. ἄλλος Mark 14:58), but rebuilt (Matt 26:61). The rebuilt Temple will be in continuity with Israel's Temple.[11] Walker argues that until chapter 23:21 the Temple is treated

---

[6] Walker, *Jesus and the Holy City*, 6; also P. Dschulnigg, "Die Zerstörung des Tempels in den syn. Evangelien," *Tempelkult und Tempelzerstörung (70 n. Chr.) Festschrift für Clemens Thoma zum 60. Geburtstag,* ed. Simon Lauer and Hanspeter Ernst (Bern: Peter Lang, 1995) 168.

[7] Walker, *Jesus and the Holy City,* 9. Dschulnigg extends the meaning of the "New Temple" to include the Christian community, *Die Zerstörung,* 170.

[8] J. P. Heil, "The Narrative Strategy and Pragmatics of the Temple Theme in Mark," *CBQ* 59 (1997) 76–100.

[9] Heil, "Narrative Strategy," 100.

[10] Walker, *Jesus and the Holy City,* 28; see also D. J. Harrington, *The Gospel of Matthew.* Sacra Pagina 1 (Collegeville: The Liturgical Press, 1991) 295.

[11] Walker, *Jesus and the Holy City,* 30. Harrington, *Matthew,* 382, reconstructs a possible saying of Jesus about worship in the age of the Temple and in the new age of the Kingdom, thus presenting both continuity and discontinuity.

positively and even described as the place of God's dwelling (Matt 23:21). A change is evident at the end of chapter 23 when Jesus, the embodiment of God's presence, distances himself from the Temple, "Your house is now abandoned" (Matt 23:38). Then he departs and the divine presence, once found within the Temple, is now focused on Jesus, Emmanuel who promises to remain within the community "to the end of the age" (28:20).[12]

In the Lukan narratives there is little sense of the Temple being either rebuilt (Matthew) or replaced (Mark). There is no report in the Gospel of Jesus' words about destroying and raising the Temple. Walker believes that the Temple presentation in Luke is the most tragic of all the Gospels.[13] The cleansing in Luke, when Jesus eventually arrives in the Temple, is both a divine visitation and a divine departure (Luke 19:45-46).[14] The fact that Jesus continues to teach in the Temple (Luke 19:47), and that it is a place of gathering for the disciples in the post-Easter time (Luke 24:53), is interpreted by Walker as giving the Temple a second chance.[15] But this second chance, this possibility for a reprieve, is spurned. Like Jesus, Paul also makes a fateful journey to Jerusalem and the Temple doors are closed on him (Acts 21:30). This action seals the fate of the Temple.

Fitzmyer presents a different approach. He follows Conzelmann in interpreting Jesus' action as a "cleansing" in preparation for his own ministry of preaching within the Temple precincts.[16] Johnson refers to Jesus' action and teaching in the Temple as a "cleansing" and "occupation."[17] In agreement with Walker, I find the lack of the Temple *logion* ominous. Jesus' final words in the Temple are the warning discourse about the end of Jerusalem and its Temple. As long as the Temple is open to the word of the Gospel, either in Jesus' preaching or in the lives of the disciples, it has a function. When its doors close on Paul, the messenger of the Gospel, then the Temple seals its own fate as portrayed in the parable of the vineyard (Luke 20:9-16). The tenants who reject the servants and the son will be punished.

---

[12] Walker, *Jesus and the Holy City,* 30.

[13] Walker, *Jesus and the Holy City,* 60. This view is contrary to Dschulnigg, *Die Zerstörung,* 176, who maintains that Luke remains "sympathetique" towards the Temple.

[14] Walker, *Jesus and the Holy City,* 63.

[15] Walker, *Jesus and the Holy City,* 63.

[16] J. Fitzmyer, *The Gospel according to Luke: A New Translation with Introduction and Commentary.* 2 vols. Anchor Bible 28, 28A (New York: Doubleday, 1985) 2:1266–67.

[17] L. T. Johnson, *The Gospel of Luke.* Sacra Pagina 3 (Collegeville: The Liturgical Press, 1991) 301.

In what way will the Fourth Gospel treat this theme? Is the Temple to be replaced by another Temple as Mark obliquely suggests (Mark 14:58) or will it be raised and be in continuity with Israel's traditions as in Matthew (Matt 26:61)? Is the New Temple the Risen Jesus (Mark) or the Christian community in whom Emmanuel remains (Matthew)? Alternatively has it completely lost its significance for Jesus and for the messengers of his Gospel (Luke)?

Overview and Structure

The Temple scene follows the miracle at Cana in Galilee (2:1-11), which was the first manifestation of Jesus' glory (v. 11). At Cana, water for the Jewish purification rituals became abundant fine wine of the messianic banquet (Isa 25:6; 55:1-2). This miracle performed "on the third day" (v. 1), alludes to the gift of the Law at Sinai (Exod 19:16) when God's glory was revealed to Israel (Exod 19:16-20; 24:16-17).[18] The gift of the Law was sealed in the solemn Mosaic covenant (Exod 24:3-8), which was frequently described as a marriage between God and Israel (Hos 2:19-20; Isa 25:6-8; 62:5; Jer 2:2; 3:14). At the wedding in Cana, the six jars of water point to the inadequacy of Israel's religious institutions, an inadequacy now brought to perfection by the coming of the true bridegroom (John 3:29).[19]

The wedding at Cana provides the theological introduction for Jesus' first entry into the center of Israel's religious institutions—the Temple in Jerusalem. Just as Israel's water rituals have been perfected in the good wine provided by Jesus, the next scene shows the overturning of Israel's sacrificial cult and the passing of the Jerusalem Temple.[20] "The jars of purification and the Temple in Jerusalem give way before Jesus, who, in relation to the new, is both its giver (the wine) and the gift (his body)."[21] The Johannine chronology continues to show the influence of the Exodus

---

[18] For further details on the Sinai background to this miracle see Moloney *Belief,* 77; also Manns, *L'Evangile,* 98.

[19] Manns, *L'Evangile,* 103, writes "Jean a l'intention de montrer l'imperfection de la loi juive." Barrett, *Gospel,* 191, questions the significance of the number "six" since Jesus did not create a seventh vessel, however, Jesus himself is the true vine (15:1) bearing abundant fruit (15:5) and offering abundant life (10:10).

[20] As well as the thematic link of Israel's religious institutions being brought to perfection, Koester shows the close relationship between the two scenes on structural grounds. See C. Koester, "Hearing, Seeing, and Believing in the Gospel of John," *Bib* 70 (1989) 331.

[21] D. A. Lee, *The Symbolic Narratives of the Fourth Gospel: The Interplay of Form and Meaning,* Journal for the Study of the New Testament Supplement Series 95 (Sheffield: JSOT Press, 1994) 37.

narrative, for following the gift of the Law (Exod 20:1-17) and the covenant ceremony (Exod 24:3-8), which lie behind the words and images in the wedding at Cana, God gives instructions for the making of a sanctuary "that I may dwell in their midst" (Exod 25:8). The question of Israel's true sanctuary lies at the heart of the Temple pericope in the Fourth Gospel.

In the Synoptics the Temple cleansing is not linked with the Temple *logion*. Indeed the variety of contexts, speakers and wording of the *logion* suggests it had a separate existence in the tradition.[22] The Fourth Gospel has tied the action and the *logion* together into one literary unit in the form of a diptych with an introduction and conclusion.[23] The introduction (v. 13) stresses the Jewish context of this scene with the references to "the Passover of the Jews" and Jesus "going up" to Jerusalem for this pilgrimage feast. Both sides of the diptych contain words of Jesus spoken in the imperative—ἄρατε (v. 16b), λύσατε (v. 19b).[24] Both parts end with the disciples remembering—ἐμνήσθησαν οἱ μαθηταὶ αὐτοῦ (vv. 17, 22). The Feast of the Passover is clearly stated in the introduction (v. 13) and conclusion (v. 23), providing a liturgical frame around the action and *logion*. The proleptic reference to Jesus' death and resurrection (v. 22) anticipates the final Jewish Passover which will in turn be framed by Jesus' dying and rising.[25] The dramatic tension of both parts of the diptych surrounds the question of Jesus' identity as son and the question—where is the true house of God?[26]

---

[22] Beasley-Murray, *John*, 38.

[23] Others also note the diptych structure with some variations; see Schnackenburg, *Gospel*, 1:344; L. Nereparampil, *Destroy this Temple*, 13; Beasley-Murray, *John*, 38.

[24] Bultmann, *Gospel*, 125, claims that λύσατε is an ironic imperative of prophetic style. Conversely, Dodd, *Interpretation*, 302, argues that it is a conditional sentence representing a Hebrew idiom. The structure and polemical nature of the exchange supports Bultmann; see also M. Zerwick, *An Analysis of the Greek New Testament: Vol. 1. Gospels—Acts* (Rome: Biblical Institute Press, 1974) 291.

[25] According to the Johannine chronology, Jesus dies on the day before the Passover (19:14, 31) and his empty tomb is discovered on the day following the Passover (20:1-19).

[26] Now that the Gospel narrative has begun, the primary metaphor for describing the intimacy between *logos* and *theos* is son-father. The metaphor is not a statement about the nature of God. As Scott, *Sophia and the Johannine Jesus*, 173, points out "This relationship takes its terms not from the gender of God, but from that of the earthly Jesus." The metaphor also reflects the cultural pattern of a son being an apprentice and continuing the work of the father. Jesus as the apprentice/son doing the work of his Father is a dominant theme of Johannine Christology (5:36; 9:4; 10:25, 37; 14:10). See C. H. Dodd, "A Hidden Parable in the Fourth Gospel," *More New Testament Studies* (Manchester: Manchester University Press, 1968) 30–40.

Introduction: v. 13

[13]The **Passover** of the Jews was at hand, and Jesus went up to Jerusalem.

TEMPLE ACTION: vv. 14-17

[14]In the Temple he found those who were selling oxen and sheep and pigeons, and the money-changers at their business. [15]And making a whip of cords, he drove them all, with the sheep and oxen, out of the Temple; and he poured out the coins of the money-changers and overturned their tables. [16]And he told those who sold the pigeons, "Take these things away; you shall not make my Father's house a house of trade." [17]**His disciples remembered** that it was written, "Zeal for thy house will consume me."

TEMPLE *LOGION*: vv. 18-22

[18]The Jews then said to him, "What sign have you to show us for doing this?" [19]Jesus answered them, "Destroy this Temple, and in three days I will raise it up." [20]The Jews then said, "It has taken forty-six years to build this Temple, and will you raise it up in three days?" [21]But he spoke of the Temple of his body. [22]When therefore he was raised from the dead, **his disciples remembered** that he had said this; and they believed the Scripture and the word which Jesus had spoken.

Conclusion: vv. 23-25

[23]Now when he was in Jerusalem at the **Passover** feast, many believed in his name when they saw the signs which he did; [24]but Jesus did not trust himself to them, [25]because he knew all men and needed no one to bear witness of man; for he himself knew what was in man.[27]

The Temple Action

The introductory verse emphasizes the Jewish and cultic context. Jesus goes up (ἀνέβη) as pilgrim to the Temple,[28] where he finds animals

---

[27] The use of exclusive language in these concluding verses is required in order to provide a textual introduction to the male character Nicodemus. Vv. 23-25 clearly link these two scenes through their verbal repetitions—signs 2:23; 3:2; knowledge, 2:25; 3:2; man. 2:25; 3:1.

[28] ἀναβαίνω is almost a technical term for pilgrimage. See B. Lindars, *The Gospel of John*. New Century Bible. (London: Oliphants, 1972) 138; but note Haenchen's comment that in this Gospel Jesus is not seen to participate in the cult nor does he behave as a pilgrim, *John*, 1:182.

of sacrifice and money-changers with their tables set up in the Temple precincts. The Johannine account is unique in its mention of oxen and sheep, along with the pigeons. These larger animals were for holocausts and peace offerings (Leviticus 1, 3). As Carson notes, the provision of these sacrificial animals was a convenient service for worshippers coming from afar.[29] The money-changers were also an essential part of Temple worship for the annual Temple tax needed to be paid in Tyrian coinage which did not offend Jewish Law as the Roman coins did with their effigy of the emperor stamped on one side.[30] Pilgrims coming from other parts of the empire needed to convert their money. The tables for the money-changers were not always in the Temple precincts but were set up from the twenty-fifth of Adar (the month before Nisan).[31] This Temple tax paid for the twice-daily sacrifice of lambs which Israel was ordered to offer as *tamid,* continual, perpetual offerings. "Now this is what you shall offer upon the altar: two lambs a year old day by day continually (תמיד). One lamb you shall offer in the morning, and the other lamb you shall offer in the evening" (Exod 29:38-42). The tax therefore provided the means for Israel's twice-daily act of atonement, continually creating the covenant bond between Israel and God. This Temple tax was also linked in the rabbinic literature with the shekel offering in the wilderness[32]:

> And you shall take the atonement money from the people of Israel, and shall appoint it for the service of the tent of meeting; that it may bring the people of Israel to remembrance before the LORD, so as to make atonement for yourselves (Exod 30:16).

The money-changers and animals do not represent a corruption of Israel's religious worship, ". . . their presence made possible the cultic participation of every Israelite, and it was not only not a blemish on the cult but part of its perfection."[33] The things that represent the perfection of

---

[29] Carson, *Gospel,* 178.

[30] For further details on the Tyrian coinage and the Temple Tax see P. Richardson, "Why Turn the Tables? Jesus' Protest in the Temple Precincts," *Society of Biblical Literature Seminar Papers* 31 (1992) 512–19.

[31] *m. Shekalim* 1:3. References to the Mishnah are from H. Danby, *The Mishnah* (Oxford: Oxford University Press, 1933).

[32] J. Neusner, "Money-Changers in the Temple: The Mishnah's Explanation," *NTS* 35 (1989) 288.

[33] Neusner, "Money-Changers," 289. Talbert also recognized that the presence of animals and money-changers were essential elements for the perfection of Israel's cult. See C. H. Talbert, *Reading John: A Literary and Theological Commentary on the Fourth Gospel and the Johannine Epistles* (London: SPCK, 1992) 96.

Israel's cult are the very things emphasized in the Johannine account—
the driving out of the larger sacrificial animals and the pouring out of the
coins needed for Israel's ongoing relationship with God. Jesus' action
goes further than "cleansing" Israel's cult, "[it] represents an act of the rejection of the most important rite of the Israelite cult . . . and therefore, a
statement that there is a means of atonement other than the daily whole-
offering, which now is null."[34]

As with prophetic actions in the Old Testament, Jesus accompanies
his symbolic act with words to bring out its meaning. When he addresses
the pigeon-sellers, the language shifts from Temple, ἱερόν (vv. 14,15) to
house, reflecting the most frequent designation of the Jerusalem Temple
which the LXX usually calls the οἶκος, or οἶκος ἅγιος, τοῦ θεου,
Κυρίου, or ναός.[35] Jesus calls Israel's οἶκος τοῦ θεου, the οἶκον τοῦ πατρός μου. With these words Jesus claims a unique filial relationship with
Israel's God.

The reader, who knows the Prologue, knows of this relationship described in terms of the Word who was πρὸς τὸν θεόν, and the Son who is
εἰς τὸν κόλπον τοῦ πατρός (1:1, 18). The reader has also been informed
that Nathanael and the other disciples will see a new Bethel, a new House
of God (1:51).[36] Because of his relationship with the Father, Jesus is the
new οἶκος τοῦ θεου, for in him the glory of God is present and accessible
to human experience. The disciples saw this glory manifest at Cana (2:11).
With the coming of the true dwelling place of God, the Jerusalem Temple

[34] Neusner, "Money-Changers," 290. Note also Dodd's comments, "The expulsion
of the sacrificial animals from its courts signifies the destruction and replacement of
the system of religious observance of which the temple was the centre: a new 'temple'
for an old one," *Interpretation,* 301.

[35] The term ἱερόν like ναός, can refer to the entire Temple area as well as the inner
sanctuary, but it can also be used for pagan shrines (1 Macc 6:2; 10:84; 11:4). "A clear
distinction between ἱερόν. . .ναός. . .and τόπος . . . is not possible." See U. Borse,
"ἱερόν," *EDNT* 2 (1991) 175. See also O. Michel, "ναός," *TDNT* 4 (1967) 882. Although technically the terms are indistinguishable, in the literature of the LXX and in
the Fourth Gospel, the terms are used with precise meanings. The whole point of the
misunderstanding of "the Jews" in v. 20 lies in the ambiguity of the term ναός, which
Jesus uses with one meaning, while "the Jews" understand it in a different way. For
"the Jews" ναός and ἱερόν are interchangeable, while for the evangelist they are not.

[36] The description of angels of God ascending and descending is an allusion to the
story of Jacob's dream on the way to Haran (Gen 28:10-17). Jacob's vision of angels
ascending and descending prompts him to recognize the presence of God in that place
and to name it "Bethel." For a fuller development of this image see J. H. Neyrey, "The
Jacob Allusions in John 1:51," *CBQ* 44 (1982) 586–605; also Moloney, *The Johannine
Son of Man,* 26–41.

is relegated to the category of a public marketplace (οἶκον ἐμπορίου).[37] Rather than depicting a cleansing or portent of a future destruction, the Johannine narrative clearly shows that with the coming of the incarnate *logos,* the Temple and its cultic functions have already been abrogated.[38]

Throughout this first part of the diptych, sacrificial imagery is present in the reference to the Passover (v. 13), the larger animals (vv. 14-15) and the pouring out of coins (v. 15).[39] The words of Ps 69:9, which the disciples remember—"Zeal for Thy house will consume me" (v. 17), need to be read within such a sacrificial context. The animals named in the Fourth Gospel are those killed for sacrifices. Jesus' actions set him in conflict with "the Jews," a conflict that will lead to his death. This is what is meant by "will consume me." As Menken states:

> The fact that the zeal is "consuming", does not signify in the psalm that the zeal totally dominates the psalmist, but that it brings him close to death. This meaning of Ps. 69:10a makes it obvious that when reading the quotation in John 2:17, we should think of Jesus' death.[40]

The change of tense from aorist (κατέφαγεν LXX) to future (καταφάγεται) point the reader ahead to a future consummation.[41] "The basic inten-

---

[37] Some commentators see in this phrase a reference to Zech 14:21, "And there shall no longer be a trader in the house of the Lord of hosts on that day," see Brown, *Gospel,* 1:121; Dodd, *Interpretation,* 300. While not ruling out this possibility, I maintain that the text plays on the word "house" and contrasts the true house of God with the false house. Those who recognize Jesus' unique relationship with the Father, recognize in him the true house of God and the Temple has lost its religious significance. Haenchen, *John,* 1:184, sees in this term—οἶκον ἐμπορίου—a critique that one can buy God's favor with sacrifice, but Jesus' actions are directed at the sellers, not at the worshippers buying victims.

[38] Schnackenburg *Gospel* 1:356: "The cleansing of the temple is meant to portray the abrogation of the Jewish cult by Jesus, and its replacement by himself and his community." The community aspect will be developed later.

[39] The term ἐκχέω is frequently used with reference to blood or libations poured out in sacrificial acts (e.g., Exod 29:12; Lev 4:7, 18, 25, 30, 34; Num 28:7; Jer 7:18; 19:13; 44:17, 25). In the N.T. it is used in the Synoptics when Jesus speaks over the cup of wine at the Last Supper (Matt 26:28; Mark 14:24; Luke 22:20). See J. Behm, "ἐκχέω," *TDNT* 2 (1964) 467–69.

[40] M. Menken, *Old Testament Quotations in the Fourth Gospel: Studies in Textual Form.* Contributions to Biblical Exegesis and Theology 15 (Kampen: Kok Pharos, 1996) 41.

[41] The Hebrew text reads "Zeal for your house has consumed (אכלתני) me." Some LXX texts follow the Hebrew and use an aorist (κατεφάγεν) other variants use the future (καταφάγεται) and most of the texts of the Fourth Gospel are also in the future P66 P75 ℵ B Θ ω. This Gospel is therefore following the LXX over the Hebrew in its

tion of the Johannine Temple-cleansing becomes clear: In the first Passover, the last Passover is already contained, in his orientation."[42] The act
of remembrance recalls the wilderness experience when the atonement
money was collected to bring the sons of Israel to remembrance (זכרון
Exod 30:16). In most cases when the Fourth Gospel uses the word remember, it bears a reference to the death and resurrection of Jesus (2:22;
12:16; 15:20; 16:4, 21).[43] The remembering of the disciples at verse 17
points ahead to the death of Jesus and the gift of the Paraclete whose task
is to bring the disciples to remembrance (14:26).[44] While Israel needed
atonement sacrifices to bring them to remembrance, the community of
believers will be brought to remembrance after the death and resurrection
of Jesus, through the guidance of the Paraclete.

The Temple *Logion*

The first part of the diptych has shown Jesus overturning the core of
Israel's cultic institutions, the provision for continual sacrifices on the
Temple altar to maintain Israel's covenant relationship with God:

> The explicit explanation of the payment of the half-sheqel, therefore, is that
> it allowed all Israelites to participate in the provision of the daily whole-
> offering, which accomplished atonement for sin in [*sic*] behalf of the holy
> people as a whole.[45]

---

use of a future, and may even be deliberately changing the LXX text from a past to a
future tense in order to indicate a future consummation. See Barrett, *Gospel,* 198–99,
for a discussion on the variants in the tradition; also Schnackenburg, *Gospel,* 1:347;
Bultmann, *Gospel,* 124. For a discussion on the narrative significance of the change of
tense, see F. J. Moloney, "Reading John 2:13-22: The Purification of the Temple," *RB*
97 (1990) 443; also M. Menken, *Old Testament Quotations,* 40–41. Psalm 68 was frequently quoted in the New Testament to refer to the Passion of Jesus (cf. John 15:25,
19:29; Mark 15:36 par.; Acts 1:20; Rom 11:9-10; 15:3; 2 Cor 6:2). See also Dodd, *Interpretation,* 301.

[42] "Die Grundintention der johanneischen Tempel wird deutlich: Im ersten Passa ist
das letzte Passa in seiner Ausrichtung schon enthalten." See A. Obermann, *Die christologische Erfüllung der Schrift im Johannesevangelium.* Wissenschaftliche Untersuchungen zum Neuen Testament 83 (Tübingen: J.C.B. Mohr, 1996) 123.

[43] The only other case is in 14:26 when it is a function of the Paraclete to remind
the disciples of all that Jesus has said. Even in this case the death of Jesus is immanent
as he speaks of a time when he will no longer be present with the disciples.

[44] U. Schnelle, "Die Tempelreinigung und die Christologie des Johannesevangeliums," *NTS* 42 (1996) 362–63.

[45] J. Neusner, "The Absoluteness of Christianity and the Uniqueness of Judaism,"
Int 43 (1989) 25.

In the second part of the diptych, the focus shifts to the center of Israel's cult, the Jerusalem Temple as a place where God dwells.

"The Jews'" reply—"What sign have you to show us for doing this?"—indicates that they have at least some understanding of the meaning of Jesus' actions for they do not ask "Why have you done this?" Instead they ask for a sign that will give divine legitimacy to his deeds. Their request lies in the expectation that those who act with God's authority can perform "signs and wonders" that will testify to their authority; Moses produced such signs when he returned from Midian (Exod 4:29-31).[46] The question of "the Jews" focuses only on what Jesus has **done** and completely ignores the **words** he spoke. While they were not present as actors in the earlier scene, their presence can be assumed by the connective οὖν (v. 18), and is implied by the introductory words that the Passover of the Jews was at hand (v. 13). As characters they have been present to see the deeds and hear the words of Jesus. In overlooking his words, they fail to perceive the authority behind his action. He acts as he does because he is Son in his Father's house. "The Jews" ignore the relationship he claims, and as the dialogue unfolds they continue to reject his words, and in rejecting the words of Jesus, they reject the Word of God.

Jesus' reply is a *mashal*,[47] an enigmatic riddle which "the Jews" do not comprehend[48]—"Destroy this sanctuary (ναός) and in three days [a

---

[46] For a discussion on the significance of "signs" and their role in coming to faith, see F. J. Moloney, "From Cana to Cana (John 2:1–4:54) and the Fourth Evangelist's Concept of Correct (and Incorrect) Faith," *Salesianum* 40 (1978) 819–21, and his conclusion, 841–42. In this article Moloney presents faith based on miraculous signs as inadequate, that authentic Johannine faith is a radical belief in the word of Jesus. A recent article by Johns and Miller contradicts this approach and argues that signs have a consistently positive role for faith. See L. Johns and D. Miller, "The Signs as Witnesses in the Fourth Gospel: Reexamining the Evidence," *CBQ* 54 (1994) 525–35. In their argument they present Moses as a positive paradigm for comparison with Jesus. In discussing the Prologue, I presented Moses and the Law as the antithesis of Jesus and the gift he offers, hence I concur with Moloney and also Brown, *Gospel*, 1:530-31, who sees the demand for miraculous signs as an indicator of incorrect faith. The only authentic sign in this Gospel is the life, death, and rising of the incarnate *logos*. The σάρξ of Jesus, given to death, is the locus of divine activity which precludes the need for further wonders and miracles. For this reason the only sign that Jesus will give to his Jewish interrogators is the sign of the destruction and raising of his body (v. 19). A summary of the various faith responses and the role of signs in promoting faith can be found in R. Kysar, *John, the Maverick Gospel* (Atlanta: John Knox Press, 1976) 82–86.

[47] Schnackenberg, *Gospel*, 1:349.

[48] For further comments on the function of riddles and misunderstanding, see J. Ashton, *Understanding the Fourth Gospel* (Oxford: Clarendon Press, 1993) 189–93.

few days] I will raise it up" (v. 19).[49] At this point a distinction must be made between what the participants in the scene have heard, and what the readers of the narrative have read.[50] "The Jews" have only heard Jesus' words to the pigeon-sellers, where he called the Temple τὸν οἶκον τοῦ πατρός μου (v. 16). The reader has followed the narrator's words and has seen the Temple called τὸ ἱερόν (vv. 14, 15) as well as τὸν οἶκον τοῦ πα- τρός μου (v. 16); now, in the words of Jesus, a new term ὁ ναός (v. 19) is introduced. The middle term, "My Father's House," reminds the reader of Jesus' filial relationship with the Father (1:1, 18) and prepares the reader for the shift to the term ναός.[51] The reader already knows Jesus is the Word who has made his dwelling among us (1:14) and, because of the intimate relationship between the Word and God, where the Word dwells, God dwells. So Jesus is justified in using the term "sanctuary" (ναός) of himself.

"The Jews" understand Jesus' words to mean the actual building of the Temple complex and fail to comprehend his words about destroying and raising it again in a few days. Rather than ask for further explanation which would keep the dialogue open, "the Jews" close the discussion by turning Jesus' words against him[52]:

Jesus' words	"The Jews'" reply
καὶ ἐν τρισὶν ἡμέραις ἐγερῶ αὐτόν.	καὶ σὺ ἐν τρισὶν ἡμέραις ἐγερεῖς αὐτόν.

[49] The term "in three days" is ambiguous in this dialogue. The Hebraic idiom may simply be a means of referring to a short space of time, "a few days." On this, see J. B. Bauer, "Drei Tage," *Bib* 39 (1958) 355; also Lindars, *Gospel of John,* 143. John does not use "three day" language in his resurrection narrative, but given the tradition of "the third day" as an indicator of the resurrection, the expression may also allude to this, particularly when the following verses speak of his body and the disciples remembering his words after he was raised from the dead.

[50] This point is well developed by Léon-Dufour, "Dans la rédaction de son Évangile, saint Jean va donc jouer sur deux claviers: le temps du souvenir, celuie des auditeurs; et le temps de l'intelligence parfaite, celuie des lecteurs." See X. Léon-Dufour, "Le signe du temple selon saint Jean," *RSR* 39 (1951) 157.

[51] Stibbe comments that the change from τὸ ἱερόν (vv. 14, 15) to ὁ ναός (v. 19) represents a movement from the outer courtyard to the inner sanctuary—from the external understanding of Temple to the inner heart of what it means. See M. Stibbe, *John.* Readings: A New Bible Commentary (Sheffield: JSOT Press, 1993) 52.

[52] Moloney, "From Cana to Cana," 831. In later dialogues characters keep the conversation open by asking further questions, "How can a man be born when he is old?" (3:4); "Where do you get that living water?" (4:11).

In this exchange a common Johannine technique of misunderstanding is being used. Jesus has used the term ναός giving it a new meaning, while "the Jews" understand the term only at the literal level of a building. Not only have they failed to consider his identification with the Father in the previous action, they now fail to heed the warning given in Jesus "sign"—You destroy—I will raise. The only "sign" Jesus offers lies in the future, in the hour of his death and resurrection. Ironically "the Jews" will contribute to the making of this sign when they demand the death penalty because Jesus has made himself the Son of God (19:7). In destroying Jesus, they destroy the new sanctuary where God dwells. The narrator makes explicit the meaning of Jesus' *mashal* in the next verse where he equates the term sanctuary (ναός) with body (σῶμα) (v. 21). But even without this narrative guide, the reader has been prompted by the shift in terminology—ἱερόν, οἶκος, ναός—and the testimony of the Prologue to perceive that Jesus was not speaking of the Temple of "the Jews"—τὸ ἱερόν, but the Temple of his own person.

This second half of the diptych ends, as the first part, with the disciples remembering. In verse 17, within the actual story time, the disciples remember the words of Psalm 68 which are quoted in a manner to bring out their future, prophetic significance.[53] As I have argued, the sacrificial context and the use of the future "will consume," implicitly indicates the death of Jesus. The prolepsis is made explicit in verse 22 when the disciples' remembrance is linked to the time after Jesus was raised from the dead. At this time they are able to see the scriptural words of Psalm 68 being fulfilled in Jesus' death and resurrection.[54] In the light of Easter they believe these words of Scripture and the word of Jesus (v. 22).[55] The disciples were not mentioned as traveling companions of Jesus in his pilgrimage up to Jerusalem for the feast, nor do they have any active role in the cleansing scene or the dispute with "the Jews." Their sole pur-

---

[53] According to Moloney, *Belief,* 98, at this stage in the narrative, the disciples may simply be comparing the zeal of Jesus with that of Phineas (Num 25:11), Elijah (1 Kgs 19:10), or Mattathias (1 Macc 2:24-26). The manner in which they are said to recall the psalm foreshadows that for Jesus it is a zeal unto death.

[54] M. Hengel, "The Old Testament in the fourth Gospel," *The Gospels and the Scriptures of Israel,* ed. Craig Evans and W. Richard Stegner, Journal for the Study of the New Testament Supplement Series 104 (Sheffield: Sheffield Press, 1994) 390.

[55] Kysar interprets the reference to the Scripture as a more general belief that the Old Testament foresaw the resurrection of Jesus. See R. Kysar, *John.* Augsburg Commentary on the New Testament (Minneapolis: Augsburg, 1986) 50. Against Kysar, the repetition of the phrase, "his disciples remembered" (v. 22) links "the Scripture" back to the first use of this phrase where Psalm 68 is recalled (v. 17).

pose is to remember the Scripture and the words of Jesus and to testify to their belief. In their remembrance they function as a proleptic presence of the post-resurrection community under the guidance of the Paraclete whose task is "to bring to your remembrance all that I have said to you" (14:26).

The concluding verses (vv. 23-25), draw the time in Jerusalem to a close. Key words from the Temple scene are repeated: the Passover (vv. 13, 23) signs (vv. 18, 23) and belief (vv. 22, 23, 24). These few verses also make the point that belief based on seeing signs is inadequate. "The Jews" who confronted Jesus after the Temple cleansing had asked to see such a sign (v. 18) and in their request they turned their eyes from the Johannine sign present in the flesh of Jesus (1:14; 2:21). While many in Jerusalem came to believe in Jesus, this act of trust was not reciprocated due to their lack of radical faith that does not require signs.[56]

As well as bringing the Temple cleansing to a conclusion, these verses are also tied to the next encounter with Nicodemus (3:1-21).[57] He is one of οἱ Ἰουδαῖοι (2:13), one of the πολλοὶ (2:23) who has seen signs and through the signs recognizes Jesus as a rabbi (3:2). The repetition of the term ἄνθρωπος (2:25b, c; 3:1) links Nicodemus to the previous Temple scene. Before the dialogue with Jesus begins, Nicodemus has been allied with the many in Jerusalem who require signs in order to believe in his name (v. 23), those men to whom Jesus cannot entrust himself.[58] The Prologue spoke of those who believe in his name (1:12) as the ones who are given the power (ἐξουσία) to be come children of God. But these require a new type of birth of God (1:13). Nicodemus' "sign-faith" indicates he has not yet come to this new birth. In the following dialogue, Nicodemus is invited to complete his faith journey and be born ἄνωθεν (3:3), of water and the Spirit (3:5).

The Temple Action as Narrative Symbol

A "symbolic" reading of this scene is not of secondary importance to a traditional historical-critical exegesis. The Prologue presents a hermeneutical key that demands a "symbolic" reading of the text—"the Word became

---

[56] Moloney, "From Cana to Cana," 842, examines John 2:1–4:54 in terms of the various responses to the person of Jesus and the degree of correct Johannine faith these responses portray. "For John, true faith means a radical openness to the word of Jesus, i.e., to all that he has come to reveal. . . John himself explains that the highpoint of this revelation which must be accepted is not found in the externality of the "signs" (2:23-25) but in the event of the Cross."

[57] Vv. 23-25 are a "bridge passage," closing 2:13-25 and opening 2:23–3:21. In his structure, Beasley-Murray begins the Nicodemus discourse at 2:23, *John,* 45–47.

[58] So Brown, *Gospel,* 1:127.

flesh" (1:14). That which is of God has entered the sensory world of human history. "Jesus is the symbol of God."[59] Because the world was created through the Word and became the *locus* for the Word, material reality is open to and can mediate a transcendent reality; in John Painter's words, ". . . the world is a storehouse of symbols which can become vehicles of revelation."[60]

Within the Gospel, a number of miraculous events are designated as a σημεῖον (2:11; 4:54; 6:14; 9:16; 11:47 and 12:18). In and through these "signs" the glory of God is manifest, so the Johannine "signs" function as symbols.[61] A distinction must be made between the ordinary use of the term "sign" and the Johannine σημεῖον. "A sign is something which stands for an absent reality. Its task is to refer the observer to something other than itself."[62] A symbol is a sensory experience that makes accessible in the present a non-sensory transcendent reality.[63] Thus water opens to the reality of eternal life (4:1-42); bread gives access to the crucified and Risen One (6:1-71). A symbol contains within itself both a sensory and a transcendent reality.[64]

Paul Ricoeur uses the structure of metaphorical language, as a means of analyzing the way symbols function to communicate the transcendent.[65] In a symbol, there is both a literal meaning and a second level of meaning—what Ricoeur calls "an excess of signification." In the act of interpreting a symbol at the literal level, there arises an absurdity which destroys the possibility of this literal interpretation and demands a transformation or extension of meaning to a non-literal interpretation.[66] The literal meaning gives access to the non-literal; "it is the recognition of the literal meaning that allows us to see that a symbol still contains more meaning."[67] Such an understanding of symbol is operative in the Fourth Gospel where the σάρξ of Jesus is the means of access to the divine δόξα (1:14).

[59] S. Schneiders, "History and Symbolism," 372.

[60] J. Painter, "John 9 and the Interpretation of the Fourth Gospel," *JSNT* 28 (1986) 47. Note also the comment by X. Léon-Dufour, "Towards a Symbolic Reading of the Fourth Gospel," *NTS* 27 (1981) 441, ". . . tangible realities (i.e., light, water, bread, door, etc.) as well as the historical characters who revolve around Jesus are positively or negatively bearers of the Word of God for me today."

[61] D. A. Lee, *Symbolic Narratives,* 14; Schneiders, "History and Symbolism," 373; Léon-Dufour, "Symbolic Reading," 442.

[62] Schneiders, "History and Symbolism," 372.

[63] Schneiders, "History and Symbolism," 372.

[64] Ricoeur defines symbol in terms of "double-meaning." See P. Ricoeur, *Interpretation Theory: Discourse and the Surplus of Meaning* (Fort Worth: Texas Christian University Press, 1976) 45–46.

[65] Ricoeur, *Interpretation,* 45–69.

[66] Ricouer, *Interpretation,* 50, 55.

[67] Ricoeur, *Interpretation, 55.*

Does the Temple Cleansing constitute a Johannine "sign," or is this scene merely providing the necessary context for the Temple *logion* and the explicit symbolism of verse 21—"But he spoke of the temple of his body"?

Against the background of the Herodian Temple, a drama unfolds in two acts (vv. 13-17 and 18-22). In the first act the Temple is emptied of its sacrificial animals (v. 15), the tables are cleared of coins then turned upside down (v. 15). Israel's sacred place is empty. At the literal level, Jesus' actions are absurd.[68] From the time of the Exodus, Israel had a particular place set aside for God's presence in their midst (Exod 25:8). While there were various cult objects, (Ark, Tent, Tabernacle, Temple), the tradition of a sacred place remained constant. Interpreting Jesus' action as literally indicating that there is no longer any meeting place for God and humanity, creates an absurdity that demands a further interpretation.

Such further interpretation is indicated in Jesus' words where he calls the Temple "my Father's house" (v. 16). In the enfleshed *logos,* God and humanity meet. A building is no longer required for there is in creation a new sacred place where God dwells among us (1:14). Dramatic tension is created through the juxtaposition of the emptied Temple, the presence of Jesus already introduced to the reader as God's indwelling presence (1:1, 14, 18) and the words "my Father's house." In this scene Israel's Temple physically surrounds and stands as symbol of the new meeting place between God and humanity. The paraphernalia of Israel's cult are displaced, poured out, and overturned in anticipation of a new mode of worship. While the exact nature of the new mode of worship is still to be disclosed, in the dialogue that follows the presence of a new "Temple" is announced.

The Temple *Logion* as Symbolic Narrative

The form and function of a "Symbolic Narrative" has recently been presented by D. A. Lee and applied to six specific passages in the Fourth Gospel, 3:1-36; 4:1-42; 5:1-47; 6:1-71; 9:1-41; 11:1–12:11.[69] In this work Lee outlines five stages in a Symbolic Narrative[70]:

[68] Neusner, "Money-changers," 289, rightly states that Jesus' actions would be "incomprehensible and unintelligible."

[69] Lee, *Symbolic Narratives,* 12. Lee's five-stage structure offers a clear analysis of the Johannine technique of misunderstanding. Lee draws on the works of philosophers and literary critics to examine how symbols function to convey meaning. The question of how a symbol actually engages the reader and conveys a non-literal meaning is critical in Johannine research. Within the limitations of any interpretive model, Lee offers in precise language, a clear exposition of the hermeneutical process involved in interpreting some major Johannine symbols. For a brief discussion of Lee's work and methodology, see the review by F. J. Moloney in *Pacifica* 8 (1995) 117–19.

[70] Lee, *Symbolic Narratives,* 12–13.

Stage 1. Foundational Image or Sign
Stage 2. Misunderstanding
Stage 3. Struggle for Understanding
Stage 4. Attainment or Rejection of Symbolic Understanding
Stage 5. Confession of Faith or Statement of Rejection.

The Temple cleansing begins in this form where the foundational image is the Jerusalem Temple. Jesus' actions in emptying the Temple of the sacrificial requirements, and his words where he claims this place as his Father's house, establish the Temple as the primary image in the Johannine presentation of Jesus—the incarnate *logos* and indwelling presence of God. To perceive the Temple as symbol, it is necessary to know and believe Jesus' intimate relationship with the Father, and to perceive in the σάρξ of Jesus the δόξα of God.

The dialogue begins with "the Jews" asking for a sign. Their question moves the narrative into Lee's second stage for it already indicates a misunderstanding. "The Jews" fail to hear, in Jesus' words of his relationship with the Father, a truth that establishes his authority to act as he does. Their demand for a further "sign" testifies to their lack of perception to move beyond the σάρξ of Jesus. Jesus' enigmatic reply continues to challenge their lack of perception as he describes what is humanly absurd. The act of destroying and raising a building in a few days is impossible. Clearly Jesus is speaking in metaphorical language and inviting "the Jews" to engage with a deeper level of meaning than building-stones.

Some scholars think that in the *logion,* Jesus is speaking about the actual Jerusalem Temple.[71] They then try to reconstruct the possible meaning these words could have for Jesus and his listeners. This approach fails to take into account a pattern of Johannine discourses based on misunderstanding. In such discourses Jesus speaks of one reality, birth (3:3), water (4:10), bread (6:32), light (9:5) and this reality has a further level of meaning frequently not discerned by the listeners. The "double-meaning" of the sayings is a standard feature in Johannine misunderstanding. In the Temple *logion,* it follows that Jesus and "the Jews" must understand the Temple in two different ways. Jesus speaks of it in a metaphorical way as a symbol of his own person, whereas "the Jews" understand his words in a literal manner.[72]

---

[71] Brown, *Gospel,* 1:123, views the Temple saying as "an eschatological proclamation referring to the Jerusalem Temple." McKelvey, *The New Temple,* 78, considers it means both the actual building and the deeper meaning of Jesus' body. See Nereparampil, *Destroy this Temple,* 31–35, for a more detailed description of the various interpretations of Jesus' words.

[72] So Dodd, *Interpretation,* 301; Schnackenberg, *Gospel,* 1:349.

According to Lee's structure, the main character now enters into a process of struggling to understand the metaphorical meaning of the central image. In this case "the Jews" need to ask for a further explanation, they need to ask the right question that will keep the dialogue open. Their response, when they turn Jesus' words against him, forecloses this dialogue. Surrounded by the Temple precincts, with the Holy of Holies in the background, "the Jews" cannot move beyond the literal level of Jesus words. Standing in the midst of a desolate Temple, Jesus speaks of a further destruction of the true Temple of God (v. 19). The physical scene points to a deeper reality that "the Jews" are too blind to perceive. In their blindness, they will carry out the words Jesus speaks and destroy the true Temple. The post-70 C.E. reader, who knows this story, now has two images juxtaposed— a desolate Temple and the Crucified and Risen One.

With the foreclosure of the dialogue by "the Jews" there is no stage three represented within this narrative. The scene however, does present characters who reach stages 4 and 5 of Lee's outline. The narrative comment—"but he spoke of the temple of his body" (v. 21) indicates that there are some who achieve a symbolic understanding and in this scene they are represented by the disciples. As noted earlier, they have no direct function in the action or discussion but they stand as representative figures for a later believing community.[73] These disciples express their belief in the Scriptures and the words of Jesus. The way these characters are portrayed reveals a further level of meaning in the primary symbol, for the disciples' sole action is to remember. They stand in this scene as the nascent Christian community, in which the Spirit of Jesus, a spirit of remembrance, now dwells.

While there is no stage three within the structure of this single scene, between the time of the *auditeurs* and the time of the *lecteurs* the Gospel narrative has happened, and throughout this story the reader will see the disciples move through their own level three stage of misunderstanding. It is only when the disciples have moved through the hour of Jesus and received the gift of the Spirit that they achieve understanding and come to the stage of confessing their faith. The movement through misunderstanding to faith is not explored within the Temple cleansing but the comment which closes the scene (v. 22) does indicate that the disciples have passed through this process.

---

[73] Culpepper, *Anatomy,* 115: "Collectively and individually the disciples are models or representatives with whom readers may identify." On the Johannine techniques of characterization, see *idem* 105–6; also R. F. Collins, *These things have been written: Studies on the Fourth Gospel,* Louvain Theological and Pastoral Monographs 2 (Louvain: Peeters Press, 1990) 1–45.

Conclusion

The Temple cleansing and *logion* make explicit the hermeneutical key for understanding the Johannine use of the Temple as a narrative symbol. A possible reason why the Temple cleansing is so early in the Fourth Gospel is because this pericope provides the reader with both an explicit hermeneutical key for interpreting the Johannine Jesus as the new "Temple," and a paradigm for further scenes in the use of Johannine symbolism and misunderstandings.[74] The foundational image is the Jerusalem Temple. As this scene develops there is a transfer of meaning from a building of stones to the person of Jesus. Because of Jesus' relationship with the Father (v. 16), the reader is invited to see in the σῶμα of the Crucified and Risen One, the new sacred τόπος where God and humanity meet (vv. 21-22). The Temple scene presents in a highly refined form, the christology of the Fourth Gospel—Jesus is the dwelling-place of God, and, as this scene develops, it provides a paradigm for a narrative style that employs images and dialogue in a fusion of literary form and theological content. Through the presence of remembering disciples, a further τόπος is indicated where the Word can continue to be incarnated within a community formed and guided by the indwelling Spirit. The two motifs of πνεῦμα and τόπος will be developed in the following scenes with Nicodemus (3:1-21) and the Samaritan Woman (4:1-42).

The prolepses at verses 17, 19, 21, and 22 indicate that there is much in this scene that is still to be resolved within the ongoing narrative and perhaps beyond it in the experience of the readers. The reader does not yet know how the new "Temple" will be destroyed and raised up in three days. Nor has there been any indication of a new mode of worship that does not require physical sacrifices. The believer who has read the full narrative, may see in the disciples' remembrance the future role of the Spirit, but as yet the implied reader only knows of the Spirit who descended upon Jesus at his baptism (1:33). While there is much that is still unknown, the reader has been given one critical key to understanding the rest of this narrative—Jesus is the new dwelling-place of God. The reader has also seen in this action and dialogue the Johannine use of symbols and the ensuing misunderstanding that can happen when symbols are not recognized. Equipped with this key Johannine christological concept, and an example of Johannine misunderstanding, the reader is ready to enter further into the narrative.

---

[74] Léon-Dufour likens this scene in the Fourth Gospel to the scene in Luke's Gospel where Jesus reads from the scroll of Isaiah in the Synagogue at Nazareth (Luke 4:16-30). Both scenes function as "programmatic" statements of Jesus' identity and mission. See X. Léon-Dufour, *Lecture de l'Évangile selon Jean.* 4 vols. Parole de Dieu (Paris: Seuil, 1988, 1990, 1993, 1996) 1:249.

The Supplanter

JOHN 4:1-45

The scene beside Jacob's well provides a multiplicity of themes and images. After an initial dialogue with one woman (4:7-26), Jesus enters into a discussion with his disciples on his mission and its fruitfulness (4:27-38). The episode depicting the movement of Jesus into Samaria, and the welcome he receives there, no doubt has its historical background in the missionary activity of the early Church among the Samaritans (Acts 8:4-25).[1] Mission provides one interpretative lens through which to examine this Samaritan episode.[2] Another theme focuses on the development of faith, firstly that of the woman and then, through her words, the profession of faith by the Samaritan villagers, "It is no longer because of your words that we believe, for we have heard for ourselves, and we know that this is indeed the Saviour of the world" (4:42).[3]

The particular lens that is developed in this thesis is christological. Jesus, the incarnate *logos* is the presence of God now dwelling among us

---

[1] Brown, *Gospel,* 1:175–176, notes that there is no evidence within the New Testament that Jesus ever undertook a ministry in Samaria which raises the historical plausibility of the scene. He also points out the numerous details in the encounter that indicate accurate local knowledge. He concludes that the entire scene has some substratum of historical material that has been carefully shaped and narrated for its theological importance. Schnackenburg also discusses the historicity of this episode. See *Gospel,* 1:458–60.

[2] For a very rich development of this theme see T. Okure, *The Johannine Approach to Mission: A Contextual Study of John 4:1-42,* Wissenschaftliche Untersuchungen Neuen Testament 31 (Tübingen: Mohr [Paul Siebeck], 1988).

[3] So Schnackenburg, *Gospel,* 1:420; Moloney, *Belief,* 132–75.

(1:14). In chapter 2, within the environs of the Jerusalem Temple, Jesus was presented to "the Jews" as the new Temple (2:21). In chapter 4, under the shadow of Mount Gerizim and beside the well of Jacob, the Samaritan "sacred place," Jesus is presented to the Samaritans as the great supplanter.[4] The woman asks, "Are you greater than our father Jacob" (4:12a)? In the course of this encounter Jesus will emerge as one who far surpasses Jacob in the gift that he offers and as the bringer of a new form of worship that reaches beyond the ethnic boundaries of Jacob's descendants.

The critical issue that operates throughout the entire episode is the question of Jesus' identity.[5] The identity issue is reflected in the many titles applied to him as firstly the woman, then the villagers, struggle to identify the stranger in their midst. Jesus is called, "a Jew" (Ἰουδαῖος) (v. 9); "Sir" (κύριε) (vv. 11, 15, 19), and "a prophet" (προφήτης) (v. 19). The woman wonders if he is "the Christ" (v. 25); and the villagers call him "the Savior of the world" (v. 42). The true answer is given by Jesus in the central section, "I am" (ἐγώ εἰμι) (v. 26). Both structurally and theologically I will argue that the core of the encounter by the well is found in verses 16-26. The intimate union of Father and Son, in the person of Jesus, creates a new sacred place that does away with regional sanctuaries, and provides a new mode of worship of the Father in spirit and in truth.

Structure[6]

In spite of frequent changes of topics in the dialogues (water, husbands, worship, food), and characters who come and go (disciples, woman,

---

[4] The etymology of Jacob's name is given as "the supplanter" (Gen 27:36). The irony of the evangelist is present in this passage where Jesus supplants Israel's supplanter. See J. H. Neyrey, "Jacob Traditions and the Interpretation of John 4:10-26," *CBQ* 41 (1979) 425, for a discussion of the significance of Jacob in first-century literature. Davies shows that Jacob's well and its environs can be considered a "sacred place" by association with Jacob and Joseph, as well as the history of this location as an ancient site of worship in the ancestral narratives (Gen 33:18-20). See W. D. Davies, *The Gospel and the Land* (Sheffield: JSOT, 1974) 298–99.

[5] The identity of Jesus is one of the themes linking this chapter with the previous one. John the Baptist called Jesus the bridegroom (3:29), in ch. 4 Jesus meets a woman at a well (v. 7), a traditional meeting place for courtships (see discussion below). Other thematic links may be found in the image of water (3:5; 4:7-15), the idea of gift (3:16, 34-35; 4:10) and Spirit (3:5-8, 34; 4:23-24). The chapters are also linked in terms of the contrast between a Jewish man who comes by night (3:1-2) and a Samaritan woman who comes at midday (4:6-7) and their contrasting faith responses to Jesus.

[6] The structure shown here is based on the work of F. Manns. The modifications are not to the elements within the structure but to the naming and emphasis. See Manns, *L'Evangile,* 124–127. For a brief analysis of the stages in the formation of the text, see

villagers), the rhetorical structure shows a formal unity based on a chiasm[7]:

A 4:1-6 Jesus leaves Judea for Galilee, travels through Samaria.

    B 7-15 Jesus asks a woman for a drink. Dialogue on two 'waters'.

        C 16-18 Woman told to go and bring her husband.

            D 19-26 Place and nature of true worship.

        C' 27-30 Woman goes and brings the villagers.

    B' 31-38 Disciples ask Jesus to eat. Dialogue on two 'foods'.

A' 39-45 Jesus in the village then resumes his journey to Galilee.

As well as the structural unity, the cohesiveness of the passage is found in the primary visual image of Jesus seated at (ἐπί) the well. A further character who provides a thematic unity to the passage is Jacob, named explicitly in verses 5, 6, and 12, and whose presence is implicit throughout, in the image of the well and its miraculous flow of water associated with Jacob, in the woman's question about Jesus' identity as one who supplants Jacob, and possibly in the harvest image in verse 35.

Sections A and A': Geography

Verses 1-6 and 39-45 situate Jesus' encounter at the well within a journey from Judea to Galilee. Throughout this pericope, geography is a critical concern; indeed the question of a sacred place is at the center of the passage, "this mountain, or Jerusalem" (v. 21). Characters are described in terms of the region and religious groups they belong to, with the risk of polarization because of regional and religious animosity.[8] The woman is

---

B. Olsson, *Structure and Meaning in the Fourth Gospel: A Text-Linguistic Analysis of John 2:1-11 and 4:1-42,* Coniectanea Biblica, New Testament Series 6 (Lund: Gleerup, 1974) 116–19.

[7] J. Bligh, "Jesus in Samaria," *Heythrop Journal* 3 (1964) 329–31, and P. Ellis, *The Genius of John: A Composition-Critical Commentary on the Fourth Gospel* (Collegeville: The Liturgical Press, 1984) 66–76, also structure the passage in chiastic form. Brown, *Gospel,* 1:166–68, and Beasley-Murray, *John,* 59, propose a sequential form with two major sections determined by the two dialogues. Lee, *Symbolic Narratives,* 66, proposes a sequential structure based on three major images—living water, place, food/harvest. Manns' approach provides a balanced literary structure and, with its central focus on "true worship," gives a logical coherence to a passage which has several changes of characters and dialogue topics.

[8] The Samaritans were considered a mixed race of semi-pagans following the importation of foreign nations after the Assyrian defeat of the Northern Kingdom. Relationships between both groups were particularly strained following the destruction of the Samaritan Temple on Mount Gerizim by John Hyrcanus in 128 B.C.E. See Schnackenburg, *Gospel,* 1:425; Brown, *Gospel,* 1:170; Carson, *Gospel,* 216.

described as a γυνὴ ἐκ τῆς Σαμαρείας (v. 7) and ἡ γυνὴ ἡ Σαμαρῖτις (v. 9); Jesus is described as a Ἰουδαῖος (v. 9). The term Ἰουδαῖος is frequently translated "Jew," meaning a follower of Judaism. In the Fourth Gospel it is necessary to distinguish three different ways in which the term is used:[9]

a) *neutral sense.* At times the Gospel uses Ἰουδαῖοι with neither positive nor negative nuances to describe those people who follow the religious customs and the Laws of Moses (e.g., 2:6, 13; 3:1; 4:9; 5:1; 6:4; 7:2; 11:55; 19:42). The term Ἰουδαῖοι distinguishes them from the Gentiles.[10]

b) *positively* (4:22; 11:19, 31, 36, 45; 12:9, 11). In 4:22 Jesus states that salvation has come from οἱ Ἰουδαῖοι. This is a statement of historical fact. God's salvific activity had its origin within a group of people who were bound in covenant to God. Some of these people respond to the new offer of salvation in the person of Jesus. Ashton takes this "salvation-history" approach further in suggesting that the phrase may reflect the early Christian missionary thrust which had its origins in Judea. "Judea is conceived as the country of origin of Jesus the Messiah (John 1:41; 4:25) and *as such* the source of salvation."[11]

Jesus, his disciples and many early believers could be designated as Ἰουδαῖοι with either of the above meanings.

c) *negatively.* The Fourth Gospel most frequently uses οἱ Ἰουδαῖοι to describes those people who take a stand against Jesus and his Messianic claims (e.g., 2:20; 5:16; 7:1; 8:59; 10:31).[12] "The term οἱ Ἰουδαῖοι, characteristic of the Evangelist, gives an overall portrayal of 'the Jews,' viewed from the standpoint of Christian faith, as the representatives of unbelief . . . "[13] The Jewish leaders, the Pharisees and the High Priests are clearly Ἰουδαῖοι in this polemical sense. The term also applies to those who stand with them in opposing Jesus.[14]

---

[9] A very detailed appraisal of this term is found in J. Ashton, "The Identity and Function of the *Ioudaioi* in the Fourth Gospel," *NovT* 27 (1985) 40–75.

[10] This sense come close to Malcom Lowe's conclusion that the term has primarily a geographical sense to designate the people of Judea. See M. Lowe, "Who were the ΙΟΥΔΑΙΟΙ," *NovT* 18 (1976) 102–3.

[11] Ashton, "Identity and Function," 52.

[12] S. Pancaro, "The relationship of the Church to Israel in the Gospel of St. John," *NTS* 21 (1974–1975) 398. Note a response to Pancaro in J. Painter, "The Church and Israel in the Gospel of John: A Response," *NTS* 25 (1978–1979) 103–12. Painter argues against the Church being called the "New Israel" in the Fourth Gospel.

[13] Bultmann, *Gospel,* 86.

[14] Grelot speaks of "the Jews" as a living parable of all humanity, the world which does not know him (1:10). See P. Grelot, *Les Juifs dans L'Evangile selon Jean: En-*

These three nuances are to be understood against the background of the Johannine community's struggle with Judaism following the destruction of Jerusalem:

> The term is used in a "neutral" or "positive" sense to designate the ethnic group to whom Jn and his community still feel bound. On the other hand, Ἰουδαῖος *tends* to become identified with the religious-national community constituted by "normative" Judaism (the Synagogue) and is therefore also used in a "negative" sense which is specifically Johannine.[15]

In discussing the historical circumstances that gave rise to the choice of the term οἱ Ἰουδαῖοι over other possible designators, Ashton evokes the pain of the struggle between the Synagogue and Christian community when he describes it as a *family quarrel*, "in which the participants face one another across the room of a house in which all have shared and all call home."[16]

Within Palestine the usual self-designation uses the term Ἰσραήλ, translating the frequent Hebrew appellation "children of Israel."[17] So Jesus calls Nicodemus a teacher of Israel (3:10) and Nathanael an Israelite (1:47). In calling Jesus a Ἰουδαῖος the woman is speaking from within a Samaritan context and follows the customary way of describing a Jew as one who is outside the true (i.e., Samaritan) Israel. Both in its geographical and religious sense, there is clear polarization along ethnic and religious lines. She is from Samaria, following the religious practices of Samaritan people, while he is from Judea and she expects him to follow the customs of the Jewish people (v. 9).

Geographical interest continues in the concluding section when the journey to Galilee is completed and the text notes pointedly that the Galileans welcomed him. By the end of this passage both Samaritans and Galileans have received Jesus. The remaining chapters of the Gospel describe the growing hostility and rejection of Jesus by οἱ Ἰουδαῖοι.

Because of such strong regional and religious differences, the woman and Jesus appear to be representatives of two opposing ethnic and religious

---

quête historique et réflexion théologique, Cahiers de la Revue Biblique 34 (Paris: Gabalda, 1995) 190–91.

[15] Pancaro, *Law,* 295.

[16] Ashton, *Understanding,* 151.

[17] Lowe, "Who were the IOΥΔAIOI?" 107. See also W. Gutbrod, "Ἰσραήλ—Ἰουδαῖος," *TDNT* 3 (1965) 356–91. "ישראל is the name which the people uses for itself, whereas יהודים—Ἰουδαῖοι is the non-Jewish name for it. Thus ישראל always emphasizes the religious aspect, namely, that "we are God's chosen people," whereas Ἰουδαῖοι may acquire on the lips of non-Jews a disrespectful and even contemptuous sound. . ." (*idem,* 360).

groups, Samaritans and Jews. The dialogue between two people in verses 7-11 develops into plural forms, "*our* father Jacob who gave *us* the well" (v. 12), "*our* fathers worshipped on this mountain, *you* (pl.) say that in Jerusalem is the place to worship" (v. 20). While the woman speaks in exclusive, regional terms, Jesus uses all-inclusive terms, "*Everyone* drinking this water" (v. 13), "*whoever* drinks the water I shall give" (v. 14).[18] The final acclamation of faith is that Jesus is the Saviour of the world (v. 42). By the end of the passage, the local geography of Judea, Samaria, and Galilee, with their sectarian religious faith, is expanded to encompass the whole world.

Section B: Request followed by misunderstanding (vv. 7-15).

The two sections (4:7-15 and 4:31-38) begin with a request, "Give me a drink" (v. 7), "Rabbi eat" (v. 31), followed by a dialogue on water and food, where Jesus speaks symbolically and is understood literally.[19] When Jesus speaks of living water (v. 10) the woman takes this to mean naturally flowing water (v. 11).[20] Unlike "the Jews" of chapter 2, who literally throw Jesus' own words back at him,[21] the woman does not reject his words, but asks further questions which enable the dialogue to continue beyond her initial misunderstanding. "Where do you get that living water" (v. 11)? "Are you greater than our father Jacob. . ." (v. 12)? The exchange that follows leads the woman away from her initial hostility to Jesus' request, δός μοι πεῖν (v. 7) to receptivity to his words in framing her own request, δός μοι τοῦτο τὸ ὕδωρ (v. 15). Even though her request is still on the physical level of natural water, the religious barriers have been broken down, as this Σαμαρεῖτης and this Ἰουδαῖος converse.

The woman's questions raise a series of contrasts present in this section: living water—flowing water, eternal—limited. These dichotomies are personified in the identity of Jesus, the new Temple and House of God (2:19), contrasted with the figure of Jacob, the well giver (4:12) and one who recognized the House of God (Gen 28:17).

---

[18] Not only is Jesus' invitation inclusive in religious terms but also in gender. The use of the masculine pronoun αὐτός must be read in a generic sense especially since in this context Jesus speaks to a woman. The generic sense of αὐτός will continue to be read unless the context makes it gender specific.

[19] This is a typical Johannine technique seen in the earlier dispute with the Ἰουδαῖοι in the Temple (John 2:19-21).

[20] ὕδωρ ζῶν in oriental usage would usually mean running or spring water so the expression, used by Jesus with a different sense, has a natural ambiguity that is exploited in this encounter. See Bultmann, *Gospel*, 181; Beasley-Murray, *John*, 60.

[21] καὶ ἐν τρισὶν ἡμέραις ἐγερῶ αὐτόν (Jesus' words in 2:19); καὶ σὺ ἐν τρισὶν ἡμέραις ἐγερεῖς αὐτόν ("the Jews'" response in 2:20). See Moloney, *Belief*, 100–1.

Jacob's Well Traditions

While the Fourth Gospel makes two references to the well as that of Jacob (vv. 6, 12), Genesis has no record of such a well, although it does mention Jacob's gift of land around Shechem to his son Joseph (Gen 33:19; 48:22).[22] It is in the Targums and the rabbinic literature that well traditions linked to Jacob can be found.[23] When Jacob arrives in Haran seeking a wife, he comes to the local well. According to the Targums, Jacob's presence brings a miraculous welling up of water that lasts twenty years:

> When our father Jacob raised the stone from above the mouth of the well, the well overflowed and came up to its mouth, and was overflowing for twenty years—all the days that he dwelt in Haran (*Tg. Neof.* Gen 28:10).

A further miracle brings together this well of Haran and Jacob's dream at Bethel:

> This is the stone which he erected as a pillar and he poured oil over the upper part of it. And the third miracle: when our father Jacob raised his feet to go to Haran the earth shrank before him and he was found dwelling in Haran (*Tg. Neof.* Gen 28:10).[24]

In Targum Neofiti, Jacob's dream at Bethel is situated within legends of the miraculous well:

Gen 28:10 Miracle 3. Bethel becomes Haran
Gen 28:11-22 Jacob's dream at Bethel. "This is the house of God."
Gen 29:1-10 Jacob meets Rachel at the well of Haran
        Miracle 5. The welling up of water for twenty years

[22] Schnackenburg, Lindars, Carson and Barrett all hold that the Samaritan town was modern day Askar, which is very close to Shechem and lies on the ancient road running through Samaria from Jerusalem to Galilee. See Schnackenburg, *Gospel,* 1:433; Lindars, *John,* 178; Carson, *Gospel,* 216; Barrett, *Gospel,* 231. Others believe Sychar is a corruption of Shechem; so Brown, *Gospel,* 1:169; Davies, *Gospel and Land,* 298. For a brief history of this site and its links to the patriarch Joseph see Carson, *Gospel,* 216–17. Olsson, *Structure and Meaning,* 138–42, develops the relationship between the geographic placing of this episode and Samaritan religious traditions that claim Jacob as the ancestor of the Samaritans.

[23] In what follows I am drawing on the work of Neyrey, "Jacob Traditions" and F. Manns, *L'Evangile,* 122–40, who show the rich targumic traditions that influence this scene by Jacob's well.

[24] The phenomena of legends associated with one place attracting other sites to that place will recur in the examination of this passage. Not only is the well of Haran linked to Bethel, but Bethel is also linked to Jerusalem through the etymological origins of its name "House of God," and the most common name of the Jerusalem Temple as "The Lord's House."

The Synagogue traditions clearly associate the cultic site of Bethel with a miraculous gift of water at the well of meeting between Jacob and Rachel. The miraculous flow of water at Jacob's well was limited in its duration to twenty years; in Jesus' meeting with the woman of Samaria he promises water that will well up to eternal life (v. 14).

Rabbinic sources also associate Jacob with a travelling well that moved with him on his journey and was left at Bethel.[25] The travelling well legend is based on the story in Numbers where the children of Israel were given a well in the wilderness.[26]

> From there they continued to Beër, that is the well of which the LORD said to Moses, "Gather the people together, and I will give them water." Then Israel sang this song:
>
> *Spring up, O well! Sing to it!*
> *the well which the princes dug,*
> *which the nobles of the people delved,*
> *with the sceptre and with their staves.*
>
> And from the wilderness they went on to Mattanah (Num 21:16-18).

In the Targums the nature of the well as God's gift is emphasized by elaborating on the place name, Mattanah (Hebrew root מתן—gift). "And from the wilderness it was given to them as a gift" (*Tg. Neof.* Num 21:16). These various traditions echo behind the Johannine text—Jacob the well-giver (v. 12) producer of miraculous flowing water; the well as God's gift to Israel. In the text of the Gospel, the gift of God is Jesus;[27] he is a new wellspring able to give living water:

Εἰ ᾔδεις τὴν δωρεὰν τοῦ θεοῦ καὶ τίς ἐστιν ὁ λέγων σοι, Δός μοι πεῖν, σὺ ἂν ᾔτησας αὐτὸν καὶ ἔδωκεν ἄν σοι ὕδωρ ζῶν (v. 10).

In the above verse, there is a phrase "the gift of God" joined by καὶ to a clause beginning with the relative pronoun τίς. This type of construction is not necessarily two different concepts linked together cumulatively. The second clause could be explanatory, further clarifying the phrase "the gift of God." In English it would be expressed, "If only you knew the gift of God *who* is speaking to you."[28] This understanding that Jesus himself is

---

[25] Neyrey, "Jacob Traditions," 422, cites the late rabbinic text *Pirque R. El.* 35.

[26] In rabbinic literature this well moves with the people; see *Num R.* XIX 25.

[27] So Bultmann, *Gospel*, 181: "The gift of the Father is the Revealer Himself." (Brown, *Gospel*, 1:178) states the opposite. For Schnackenburg, *Gospel*, 1:426–31, the gift is the living water primarily associated with the Spirit or the divine life.

[28] Pridik explains that καὶ can be used in place of a relative pronoun. See K.-H. Pridik, "καὶ," *EDNT* 2 (1990–1993) 228.

the primary gift is consistent with Jesus' words to Nicodemus, "For God so loved the world that he gave his only Son, that whoever believes in him should not perish but have eternal life" (3:16). Jesus, the wellspring gift of God is also the giver of future waters of eternal life.[29]

Living Water

There are two major approaches to the interpretation of "living water." One approach sees in the image of water a reference to the wisdom and revelation that Jesus offers.[30] In the Hebrew Scriptures there are many passages where God's revelatory word is described under the symbolism of water:

Ho, everyone who thirsts, come to the waters. . .
For as the rain and snow come down from heaven
and do not return there until they have watered the earth. . .
so shall my word be that goes forth from my mouth (Isa 55:1, 10ab, 11a).[31]

While water is an image of God's word in the prophetic literature, this image is applied to wisdom in later writings, "the fountain of wisdom is a gushing stream" (Prov 18:4); "wisdom is a fountain of life" (Prov 16:22; cf. 13:14). Under the influence of the Wisdom tradition, where Wisdom became identified with Torah, the image of water was also applied to the Law:

All this is the book of the covenant of the Most High God,
the Law that Moses commanded us as an inheritance for the flock of Jacob.
It overflows like the Pishon, with wisdom,
and like the Tigris at the time of first fruits (Sir 24:23-25 NRSV).[32]

[29] The presentation of Jesus as both the gift and the giver will later be used in the "Bread of Life" discourse (ch. 6) where Jesus himself is the living bread (6:35, 48, 51a) and also the giver of bread (6:11-13; 51c). So Beasley-Murray, *John,* 60.

[30] So Bultmann, *Gospel,* 182–87; Lindars, *John,* 78–79. Brown, *Gospel,* 1:179, states there are sound reasons for seeing the living water as a symbol for both Jesus' revelation, and the Holy Spirit. "Johannine symbolism is often ambivalent, especially where two such closely related concepts as revelation and Spirit are involved. After all, the Spirit of truth is the agent who interprets Jesus' revelation or teaching to men [sic] (14:26; 16:13)." Brown, *Gospel,* 1:179–80, also raises the possibility of a secondary, baptismal motif in this discourse, linking it back to the dialogue with Nicodemus and the baptismal ministries in the intervening verse (3:22–4:2).

[31] Isa 11:9; Amos 8:11; Hab 2:14; Jer 51:16 use water as an image of the voice, knowledge or word of God.

[32] The symbolism of a well of living water as a reference to the Law and a new covenant is found also at Qumran הבאר היא התורה (CD 6:4); מבאר מים החיים (CD 19:34).

It is possible that the Gospel is using the image of water to bring out the contrast between the wisdom found in Israel's Law and the wisdom now being offered in the person of Jesus. The invitation to eat and drink of Wisdom's fare states, "Those who eat of me will hunger for more and those who drink of me will thirst for more" (Sir 24:21). In the dialogue at the well, Jesus makes the clear distinction between "this" water and the water he will give, which will fully satisfy one's thirst forever. "Everyone who drinks of this water will thirst again but whoever drinks of the water that I shall give will never thirst" (vv. 13-14a).[33]

Another approach sees a reference to the Spirit in the symbolism of water,[34] particularly since verse 14 refers to a gift in the future. The Old Testament provides examples where the outpouring of God's Spirit is imaged as a flow of water:

> For I will pour water on the thirsty land,
> and streams on the dry ground;
> I will pour my Spirit upon your descendants;
> and my blessing on your offspring (Isa 44:3; cf. 32:15; Joel 2:28; Ezek
>   36:25-27).

Also, the verb ἅλλομαι, which describes the welling up of the waters Jesus promises (v. 14), is reserved in the LXX for the gift of the Spirit when it comes mightily upon charismatic figures such as Samson, Saul, and David (Judg 14:6, 19; 15:14; 1 Sam 10:10; 17:13). The Spirit who came mightily (ἅλλομαι) upon Israel's leaders, will spring up (ἅλλομαι) in those who accept what Jesus offers (v. 14).

While living water may be a symbol of *revelation* or the action of the *Spirit,* the narrative tension in this episode concerns specifically religious differences (v. 11) particularly focussed on cultic practices (v. 20). This raises the possibility of a further interpretation of the phrase "living water." A third allusion allowed by the symbolism of water and the cultic issues raised in this scene is that of the new Temple described in Ezekiel 47. When Jerusalem had been destroyed and its Temple laid waste, Ezekiel promised a future Temple, not built by human hands, whose waters would bring life and healing wherever they flowed (Ezek 47:1-12). Behind Eze-

---

[33] Brown, *Gospel,* 1:179 : "For Jesus to refer to his own revelation as 'living water' with this background in mind is perfectly plausible, for in John Jesus is presented as Divine Wisdom and as the replacement of the Law." Barrett, *Gospel,* 233: "In Judaism the gift of God *par excellence* is the Torah." The contrast between two waters expresses the contrast between two gifts already noted in the Prologue—"the Law was given through Moses, the gift that is true came through Jesus Christ" (1:17).

[34] So Schnackenburg, *Gospel,* 1:431–32.

kiel's image of life-giving waters flowing from the Temple lies a Jewish tradition that the Temple rests upon the fissure above the great abyss which is the source of the creative waters in Gen 2:8.[35] After the flood the rock of Noah's altar sealed up the waters of the abyss. Noah's altar became the foundation stone of a new creation. Jewish traditions link the altar of Noah with the foundation stone in the Holy of Holies supporting the Ark of the Covenant.[36] According to this mythology the Temple lies upon the well-spring of the earth, the center and source of creation:

> The waters under the earth were all gathered beneath the temple, they believed, and it was necessary to ensure that sufficient was released to ensure fertility, but not so much as to overwhelm the world with a flood.[37]

Further support for Ezekiel 47 as the primary background for the symbol of water is found in the choice of the preposition used and the image it evokes. In verse 6 the evangelist uses the preposition ἐπί. Many texts translate this word as beside, and so place Jesus on the ground beside or near the well. The preposition best suited to express the idea of *beside* or *near* is παρά; the preposition ἐπί with the dative usually means *on* or *upon*. So Jesus is literally resting on the well, presumably on the rock slab that lies across the well opening.[38]

In chapter 2, within the Temple courtyard, Jesus was revealed as the new Temple. That image is now relocated from Sion to Sychar. Just as the Temple rested on the foundation stone above the waters of the great abyss, now Jesus, the new Temple, sits *upon* the rock over the waters of Jacob's well. In this way the images of Temple and well, and their life-giving waters, are juxtaposed. As Ezekiel prophesied a new Temple whose waters would overflow to bring life and healing, so Jesus, the dwelling place of God with us, is able to give waters welling up for eternal life. The subtle

[35] In commenting of the ambiguity of the term for well/cistern (πηγὴ v. 6 φρέαρ v. 11), Manns notes, "On le voit, cette ambiguité permet à Jean de présenter Jésus comme le nouveau Temple situé sur les eaux de l'abîme." See F. Manns, *Le Symbole Eau-Esprit dans le Judaisme Ancien,* Studium Biblicum Franciscanum Analecta 19 (Jerusalem: Franciscan Printing Press, 1983) 285.

[36] Manns, *L'Evangile,* 135.

[37] M. Barker, *The Gate of Heaven,* 18.

[38] W. Köhler, "ἐπί," *EDNT* 2 (1991) 21–23. W. Köhler, "παρά," *EDNT* 3 (1993) 12–13. Brown notes that Jesus was sitting "literally on the well; the well was a vertical shaft covered by a stone." He adds the comment that P[66] reads "on the ground" and that Boismard believes this may be the original text (*Gospel,* 1:169). Against Boismard, it is also possible that P[66] reads "on the ground" as a correction, due to the strangeness of the image of Jesus resting "on" the well.

interplay of image and place is characteristic of the artistry of the evangelist. Only this Gospel places the Temple *logion* within the Temple precincts (2:19). In the following chapters specific cultic images will be appropriated by Jesus to reveal his identity. In Samaria Jesus is revealing himself as the true wellspring, source of life for the world.

The analogy between Jesus—Temple—Well is helpful in clarifying the nature of this future gift that Jesus describes using the imagery of living water. Jesus is already the revealer and revelation of God. The references to the future are best aligned with the promise of eschatological salvation, ushered in by the outpouring of the Spirit.[39] As noted above, water is frequently used in the Old Testament as an image of God's Spirit, however, Olsson shows that the images of water and Spirit are primarily associated with purification and forgiveness of sin which will allow the people to draw close to the holiness of God.[40] In the scene beside Jacob's well, the emphasis is not on water for cleansing but on water for eternal life. Even when the dialogue shifts to the woman's marital status there is no suggestion of condemnation or forgiveness. Ezekiel's image of the Temple water's emphasises the future life-giving property of water. The waters will effect a recreation of the Dead Sea allowing living creatures to swarm there (cf. Gen 1:21-22):

> And wherever the river goes every living creature which swarms will live, and there will be very many fish; for this water goes there, that the waters of the sea may become fresh; so everything will live where the river goes (Ezek 47:9).

The waters will provide unfailing fruitfulness:

> And on the banks, on both sides of the river, there will grow all kinds of trees for food. Their leaves will not wither nor their fruit fail, but they will bear fresh fruit every month, because the water for them flows from the sanctuary. Their fruit will be for food, and their leaves for healing (Ezek 47:12).

The image of living water welling up for eternal life, like the image of the harvest (v. 35), speaks of an eschatological age that is now at hand with the coming of Jesus as God's gift of salvation for the world. These images will emerge in the hour of Jesus' death, when, from the Temple of his body, waters will flow (19:34) and the Spirit will be given to the nascent community at the foot of the cross (19:30).

[39] Okure, *The Johannine Approach to Mission*, 98, claims that "the gift of God can further be defined as the gift of salvation given in and through Jesus."

[40] Olsson, *Structure and Meaning*, 215.

Section C: "Go call your husband" (vv. 16-19).

The third section of this encounter raises the questions of how to interpret this dialogue:

- Literally: as a statement about the woman's marital status.
- Allegorically: as a reference to the syncretism of Samaritan worship.
- Symbolically: as an allusion to Jesus the "true bridegroom."

Those who take this section literally, explain its relevance within the entire passage as an indicator of Jesus' prophetic knowledge.[41] He knows what an ordinary person could not know. In response to his extraordinary knowledge, the woman begins to move towards a deeper understanding of Jesus' identity and she recognizes him as a prophet (v. 19).

Other exegetes take the woman's marital situation, and the reference to five husbands, as an allegorical presentation of the former history of the Samaritans.[42] During the time of the Assyrian conquest of the Northern Kingdom, five foreign nations were brought into Samaria bringing their foreign gods (2 Kgs 17:29-34). The analogy breaks down however, since the book of Kings names seven gods (2 Kgs 17:30-32)[43] which were worshipped *alongside* YHWH, while the woman had a series of husbands one after the other. There is also the consideration that, "The Evangelist does not use allegorisation, but rather symbolic representation as his main literary device."[44]

A third possibility is to see this exchange at both a literal and a symbolic level. "We have *two levels* in the text, a narrative level and a "symbolic" level; the latter appears to have shaped the text as a whole."[45] Reading the dialogue symbolically does not deny the literal sense of the words but opens the encounter to a further level of meaning. The meeting at a well between a man and a woman who will become his spouse is a typical motif

---

[41] Among those who favor this approach are B. Lindars, *Gospel*, 184; R. H. Lightfoot, *St. John's Gospel: A Commentary* (London: Oxford University Press, 1956) 123; Talbert, *Reading John*, 114; Bultmann, *Gospel*, 187; Schnackenburg, *Gospel*, 1:433; Moloney, *Belief*, 148; Brown, *Gospel*, 1:171; Barrett, *Gospel*, 235; Beasley-Murray, *John*, 61; Carson, *Gospel*, 221. Okure, *The Johannine Approach to Mission*, 111; A. Reinhartz, "The Gospel of John," *Searching the Scriptures*, ed. Elisabeth Schüssler-Fiorenza. 2 vols. (New York: Crossroad, 1994) 2:573.

[42] So Manns, *L'Evangile*, 135; Hoskyns, *The Fourth Gospel*, 243; Lindars, *The Gospel of John*, 185–87; Olsson, *Structure and Meaning*, 186.

[43] While seven gods are mentioned in Kings, Josephus records them as five (*Ant.* ix. 288).

[44] Bultmann, *Gospel*, 188 n. 3.

[45] Olsson, *Structure and Meaning*, 250.

in the ancestral narratives: Abraham's servant and Rebecca (Gen 24:10-33), Jacob and Rachel (Gen 29:1-14), Moses and Zipporah (Exod 2:15-22).[46] Robert Alter calls such meetings a "biblical type-scene" and finds five repeated characteristics of such episodes[47]:

    i. the bridegroom travels to a foreign land where
    ii. he encounters a woman or group of women at a well
    iii. one of the characters draws water
    iv. the woman returns home to tell about the encounter with the stranger
    v. there is an invitation to a meal, a betrothal followed by a wedding

In providing the good wine at Cana (2:9-10), Jesus revealed himself as the real bridegroom in this episode and later he was named as the bridegroom by John the Baptist (3:29):

> Now the new Bridegroom, who assumes the role of Yahweh, bridegroom of ancient Israel, comes to claim Samaria as an integral part of the New Israel, namely, the Christian community and specifically the Johannine community.[48]

As bridegroom he comes to the well and meets a woman who is both an individual and a representative of her people.[49] He requests water then she requests water from him. After their discussion she returns to her village to speak of her encounter and, while there is no betrothal, there is an invitation to stay (4:40) and by the conclusion of this scene there is a significant union between the Samaritan villagers and Jesus.[50]

In the prophetic literature, the infidelity of Samaria, and their worshipping of foreign *baʾalim* is depicted as adultery (Hos 2:2-5). In the dialogue there is a play on the double meaning of the word *baʾal* which also means "husband" in Aramaic. The woman is told to call her husband and Jesus commends the truth of her answer, "I have no husband." "Jesus' dec-

[46] Olsson, *Structure and Meaning,* 172, brings out the strong similarities between this well meeting and the stories in Genesis 29 and Exod 2:15. The stories all involve a man in flight meeting a woman around midday and the stranger invited to stay.

[47] R. Alter, *The Art of Biblical Narrative* (New York: Basic Books, 1981) 51–52; J. L. Staley, *The Print's First Kiss: A Rhetorical Investigation of the Implied Reader in the Fourth Gospel,* Society of Biblical Literature Dissertation Series 82 (Atlanta: Scholars Press, 1988) 100.

[48] Schneiders, *Revelatory Text,* 187.

[49] I have previously noted the use of singular and plural forms in this dialogue which would indicate the woman's individual and representative functions. See also C. Koester, "The Saviour of the World (John 4:42)," *JBL* 109 (1990) 670–71; Collins, *These things have been written,* 16–19; Schneiders, *The Revelatory Text,* 189.

[50] L. P. Jones, *The Symbol of Water in the Gospel of John,* Journal for the Study of the New Testament Supplement Series 145 (Sheffield: Sheffield Academic Press, 1997) 91–92.

laration that Samaria "has no husband" is a classic prophetic denunciation of false worship."[51] The true husband/lord of Samaria stands before her in the person of Jesus, the bridegroom. The five previous husbands plus her current one give a total of six, which symbolically indicates the inadequacy of Samaritan worship. At Cana, in a Jewish context, the six jars represented the lack of perfection of Jewish rituals, now, in a Samaritan context, the six "husbands" indicate the "less than perfect" worship of the Samaritans:

> Such implications are realistic options here. In the language of the Gospel, John the Baptist has already acknowledged that Jesus, who has the bride, is the bridegroom (3:29). Jesus, moreover, has attended a marriage feast (2:1-11) where he replaced the waters of purification with his own superb wine. Thus in matrimonial imagery Jesus has been proclaimed as winning the allegiance of new followers and as supplanting previous persons and rituals in Jewish religion.[52]

A symbolic reading of this part of the dialogue explains the shift from a discussion about the woman's marital status to a discussion about true worship.[53] Not only does the stranger have extraordinary knowledge of her life, at a deeper level the nature of his knowledge raises the central religious question, "Who is the true husband/*baʾal* of this woman"? Earlier in the dialogue she had asked "Are you greater than our father Jacob?" (v. 12); through the discussion about her *baʾal*, she begins to move in her perception of the identity of Jesus and to recognize one who is indeed greater than Jacob. The woman acknowledges Jesus as a prophet (v. 19).

Section D: The place and nature of true worship (vv. 19-26)[54]

Verses 19-26 lie at the core of the structure I have proposed. Within these verses two issues emerge:

- the identity of Jesus, and
- the place for true worship

[51] Schneiders, *The Revelatory Text*, 191.

[52] Neyrey, "Jacob Traditions," 426.

[53] Botha comes to a similar conclusion that reading the "five husbands" as a symbol of Samaritan religious practices paves the way for the shift in conversation to true and false worship. See J. E. Botha, *Jesus and the Samaritan Woman: A Speech Act Reading of John 4:1-42*, Supplements to Novum Testamentum 65 (Leiden: E. J. Brill, 1991) 150–51.

[54] The evangelist's knowledge and use of cultic sites shows great narrative skill. The discussion with "the Jews" on the true Temple took place within the Temple courtyards. The discussion with the Samaritan Woman takes place at the foot of Mount Gerizim where it is likely that the remains of the Samaritan Temple would have been visible to one standing beside Jacob's well. See R. J. Bull, "An Archaeological Footnote to 'Our Fathers Worshipped on this Mountain', Jn 4:20," *NTS* 23 (1976–1977) 461.

An understanding of Jesus himself as the new Temple conflates these two issues into one—Jesus is the living Temple of God so true worship can only happen in him.

A (v. 19) **The identity of Jesus**
The woman said to him, "Sir, I see that you are a prophet.

B (v. 20) **The place of worship**

| Our fathers | **in** this mountain worshipped |
| while you say | **in** Jerusalem is the place where it is necessary to worship." |

C (v. 21) **The future place of worship**
Jesus said to her, "Believe me woman,
the hour is coming

when neither	**in** this mountain
nor	**in** Jerusalem
	will you worship the Father.

> **D** (v. 22)   You worship what you do not know
> we worship what we know
> for salvation comes from the Jews.

C' (v. 23) **The future place of worship**
But **the hour is coming,** and now is,
when true worshippers will worship the Father
in spirit and truth
for such the Father seeks to worship him.

B' (v. 24) **The place of worship**
God is spirit,
and those worshipping him must worship
in spirit and truth."

A' (vv. 25-26) **The identity of Jesus**

| The woman said to him, | "I know that a Messiah is coming, called the Christ. When that one comes he will announce all things to us." |
| Jesus said to her, | "I am, the one speaking to you." |

The section shows a highly crafted concentric structure, where there is both a repetition of ideas and a further development. In the second part of the chiasm, the discussion of worship changes from an external, physical place of worship on sacred mountains to an internalized worship in spirit and truth. The change from external to internal requires a metaphorical reading of the preposition ἐν, and has already been prepared for by the shift in the nature of the water that Jesus offers. The gift of water he promises is not found in a physical well, but springs up from within the person—ἐν αὐτῷς (v. 14):

The outer verses focus on the woman's growing understanding of the identity of Jesus. She first perceives him to be a prophet (v. 19). As a Samaritan, her acceptance of him as a prophet can only be in terms of Deut 18:15-18, "a prophet like Moses" since the Samaritans do not accept the prophetic literature.[55] In the Samaritan tradition, Gerizim (not Ebal) was the first site of Mosaic worship when the people entered the land (Deut 27:4-7). As such Gerizim has priority over Zion, which became a site of worship only at the time of David. Samaritan traditions also shift Jacob's vision from Bethel to Gerizim, using Jacob to validate Gerizim as the "house of God" and thus as an authentic site of worship.[56]

By verse 25 the woman has shifted in her perception and now speaks of a coming Messiah, known as χριστός, who will reveal or announce all things. The woman had earlier shown an ability to shift ground and leave behind the well tradition of her people in order to request the water that Jesus could give (v. 15). In verse 25 she shows a similar readiness to leave behind strictly Samaritan traditions in response to the words of Jesus as she uses the term Messiah which lies outside her Samaritan tradition. While using a term from within Judaism, she does not say **the** Messiah, but uses the word in a generic sense without the article. Her expectations lack the rigidity of "the Jews" who know his origins and descent (7:40-42).[57] According to Josephus (*Ant.* xviii, 85–88), the Samaritans, like the Jews, had messianic hopes, but Samaritan expectations centered on a "prophet-like-Moses" figure rather than a politicized Davidic King. It is possible that the Samaritan "prophet" was later referred to as the *Taheb,* a figure found in the fourth-century *Memar Marqah,* although the late dating of the *Memar Marqah* makes it difficult to make precise claims about the *Taheb* in first-century Samaritan traditions.[58]

The *Taheb* was considered to be an eschatological figure who would uncover the Ark of the Covenant which had been hidden on Mount Gerizim when the priest Eli established at Shiloh a rival to Joshua's sanctuary on Gerizim. God caused the true Ark and its furnishings to be hidden in a

---

[55] Okure, *The Johannine Approach to Mission,* 114.

[56] Neyrey, "Jacob Traditions," 427–28.

[57] Okure, *The Johannine Approach to Mission,* 123.

[58] Brown, *Gospel,* 1:172, n. 25; also R. Lowe, "'Salvation' is not of the Jews," *JTS* 32 (1981) 342; Koester, *The Dwelling of God,* 55–59.

cave on Gerizim until true worship was restored.⁵⁹ In the woman's anarthrous use of the term "Messiah," she does not limit it to the usual Davidic, nationalistic concept of Judaism, nor to Samaritan concepts of one who will uncover the hidden sanctuary; she speaks of a Messiah in terms of a revealer, one who will announce all things. To such a messianic description Jesus can say, "I am."

In his reply Jesus shifts the focus from the **woman's** words about a Messiah, to his own words ἐγώ εἰμι, ὁ λαλῶν σοι. The woman's words do not define his identity; Jesus' "I am" is qualified by his own words, "the one speaking to you." In this way there is not an absolute identification with the woman's messianic expectations, but Okure notes that

> the woman's messianic figure is fluid enough for Jesus to identify himself "comfortably" with it, unlike the previous messianic titles given him which all proved to be inadequate.⁶⁰

Jesus' words ἐγώ εἰμι, ὁ λαλῶν σοι use the revelation formula of Deutero Isaiah 41:4; 43:10 and especially 52:6 which reads, ἐγώ εἰμι αὐτὸς ὁ λαλῶν.⁶¹ With these words Jesus claims to be more than a prophet (v. 19), greater than a Davidic Messiah (v. 25), and greater than Jacob (v. 12). He surpasses all these figures in being the incarnation in history of the God who revealed himself to Moses as I AM (Exod 3:14).

Verses 20 and 24 express an authoritative understanding about worship. The woman claims the authority of the fathers of her tradition in naming "this mountain" as the site of former worship. She also recognizes that for the Jews the single place of worship is the Temple in Jerusalem. The use of δεῖ underlines the note of necessity. Verse 24 invokes a new necessity based not on human cultic constructs, neither the fathers of the Samaritans nor Davidic claims are ultimate. Jesus introduces a new necessity based on the nature of God's activity in the world—God is Spirit. As Brown notes, "This is not an essential definition of God, but a description of God's dealings with men [sic]; it means that God is Spirit towards men [sic] because he gives the Spirit (xiv 16) which begets them anew."⁶²

⁵⁹ I. Kalimi and J. Purvis, "The Hiding of the Temple Vessels in Jewish and Samaritan Literature," *CBQ* 56 (1994) 682–83. A variant Samaritan tradition has Moses hiding the sanctuary and its vessels (683); also Koester, "The Savior of the World," 673; Olsson, *Structure and Meaning*, 190–91.

⁶⁰ Okure, *The Johannine Approach to Mission*, 124.

⁶¹ Bultmann, *Gospel*, 225–26, n. 3, does not place Jesus' ἐγώ εἰμι within his category of a sacred formula and thus he fails to see Jesus' words having a deeper revelation than the woman's understanding of Messiah. See idem, *Gospel*, 192.

⁶² Brown, *Gospel*, 1:172; also Olsson, *Structure and Meaning*, 189.

Material temples can no longer be sufficient. Since God's movement to-wards humanity is in spirit (ἐν πνεύματι), humanity's movement towards God must also be in spirit. The nature of true worship is no longer a matter of a physical place, neither in (ἐν) this mountain, nor in Jerusalem, but must be ἐν πνεύματι where the ἐν is understood metaphorically, not materially.[63]

Verses 21 and 23 establish reasons why no physical site can be an ap-propriate place for worship. Jesus speaks of an "hour" still to come, and for the first time in this dialogue he names God as Father. The word "Father" identifies God as neither the God of the Samaritans, nor the God of the Jews but God as Jesus has revealed him, and in the culminating "hour" will reveal him to perfection. Verse 21 is framed solely in the future. Verse 23 brings together both a future "hour" of worship, and a present "now" (νῦν), and in the present the Father is active in seeking true worshippers.[64]

The temporal shift from future, to present is established in the central verse 22, which is entirely in the present tense, and yet it is a verse that depends on the juxtaposition of present and future for its correct interpre-tation. Two time frames must be understood.[65] The narrative time has the meeting between a woman of Samaria and a man from Judea, with the as-sertion that the Jewish tradition of worship and its history of salvation is superior over that of the Samaritans, "we worship what we know." But, in the narrative time of the Gospel, οἱ Ἰουδαῖοι, never know correctly (cf. 6:42; 7:27; 8:14, 19, 52; 9:31). The consistent Gospel stance of οἱ Ἰουδαῖοι not knowing accurately, demands a second-level understanding of who is meant by "we" in the phrase, "we worship what we know." True worship of the Father, known in the revealing activity of Jesus, lies in the future, in the time of the believing community (v. 21). The "we" must therefore refer to the future Christian community.[66] In knowing the Father, whom Jesus has revealed, a future Christian community can assert, "We worship what we know."

The knowledge of the Father, necessary for true worship, is only pos-sible through the revelation of Jesus, as he is the only one who can make

[63] I. de la Potterie, " 'Nous adorons, nous, ce que nous connaissons, car le salut vient des Juifs'. Histoire de l'exégèse et interprétation de Jn 4:22," *Bib* 64 (1983) 94.

[64] de la Potterie, "Nous adorons," 89, speaks of an eschatological νῦν: "C'est *toute la durée du νῦν eschatologique.* Le temps messianique qui s'ouvre en ce moment peut donc se définir comme le temps de la présence *révélatrice* de Jésus, dans *l'Esprit* (v. 23: ἐν πνεύματι καὶ ἀληθείᾳ)."

[65] See de la Potterie, "Nous adorons," 99–107, for further development of the two time frames addressed in this section.

[66] Olsson, *Structure and Meaning,* 197, speaks of a co-projection of the time of Jesus and the time of the evangelist enabling Jesus to speak for the later community.

the Father known (1:18). The Son reveals the Father, because he is in the Father's heart (1:18). From the prologue the reader knows that there is a dynamic intimacy between the Word and God that is not complete identification (1:1). When the *logos* enters history the relationship is described using the analogy of a Father and Son (1:18). In verses 1 and 18 the evangelist uses prepositions of motion εἰς, and πρὸς rather than the more static ἐν or μετά. The Son is not resting passively against the Father's breast, rather there is an active giving of self to the Father, and, in turn, the Father has given all things into the hands of the Son (3:35). The dynamic self-giving of the Son to the Father is lived out in Jesus' focus on doing the work of the Father (5:19; 10:37; 14:31) and bringing it to completion (5:36; 19:30).

Because of Jesus' loving focus on the Father, he alone knows the Father and he is the only one who has already received the Spirit (1:32). Jesus is therefore the first true worshipper of the Father and so can speak in the present tense, "A time is coming **and now is** when true worshippers will worship in spirit and truth" (v. 23).[67] Jesus speaks words of promise, just as he had earlier spoken of a future gift of water (v. 14) welling up within the person. His words look to a time in the future when believers will be drawn into the Son's own intimacy with the Father. At such time believers will know the Father (14:7, 9) and so will be able to worship in Spirit and in truth:

> In that day you will know that I am in the Father, and you in me, and I in you.
> . . . whoever loves me will keep my word, and my Father will love them
> and we will come to them and abide with them (14:20, 23 [my translation]).

True worship depends on a true knowing of the Father which is only possible in and through faith in Jesus. Verse 22b has therefore a primarily christological meaning, and flowing from this comes its future application to the believing community.

The Gospel stance towards οἱ Ἰουδαῖοι, requires a similar *second level* interpretation of the phrase "Salvation is from the Jews." At one level, as Okure notes, "In its visible historical form salvation grows out of a Jewish milieu."[68] A *second level* reading opens other possibilities. In the context of this pericope, Jesus is first introduced as coming from Judea, he is then identified by the woman as a Ἰουδαῖος. In the transition verses

---

[67] The connective καὶ in the phrase ἐν πνεύματι καὶ ἀληθείᾳ may well be epexegetical as Jones, *Symbol,* 104, suggests, "True worship takes places in spirit, that is to say, in truth."

[68] Okure, *The Johannine Approach to Mission,* 117.

43-45, there is a clear statement that identifies Judea as the πάτρις of Jesus. The phrase, "salvation is from the Jews" literally depicts the physical journey of the Judean Jesus, the gift of the Father (4:10) for the salvation of the world (3:16-17). For this Samaritan Woman, and the people whom she represents, salvation—in the person of Jesus—has come "from the Jews." At the conclusion of this pericope, the Samaritans recognize this in their acclamation "we know that this is indeed the Savior of the world" (v. 42).

Section C': The Woman Goes and Brings the Samaritans (vv. 27-30)

The return of the disciples (v. 27) brings an end to the dialogue between Jesus and the woman of Samaria. At verse 16 she had been told to go and call her husband (Aramaic—*ba'al*). Through the encounter with Jesus she has named her own truth that she has no husband and has come to recognize Jesus as the revealer of all things (ἅπαντα v. 25). As the one who manifests the Father in history, Jesus claims to be the true bridegroom both of Samaria and Israel. The one who stands talking to her is I AM. In response to Jesus she leaves behind her water jar and invites the villagers to come and see a man who told her everything which she ever did (πάντα ἃ ἐποίησα).

Throughout this dialogue the woman has been able to shift her perception. Her initial, possibly hostile, reaction towards a Jew (v. 9) becomes a more respectful observation, "Sir you have nothing to draw with" (v. 11), which leads to her own request for the water he offers (v. 15), rather than the waters of Jacob's well. She begins to realize he is no ordinary man and calls him at first a prophet (v. 19), drawing on Samaritan traditions, and then a Messiah (v. 25), a term which takes her out of her own traditions. The shifts she has made in the encounter may be symbolized in the gesture of leaving the water jar behind (v. 28). She has left behind ethnic antipathy and her initial focus on Jacob's well for the gift of water that Jesus offers (v. 15); she has left behind narrow Samaritan categories of a "prophet like Moses" when she speaks about a coming Messiah who will reveal all things (v. 25). In the exchange she has become a disciple and evangelist to her community.[69]

Her words to the villagers (v. 29) must be read in conjunction with vv. 25 and 26. She has raised the issue of a future Messiah who will be a revealer and Jesus has responded for the first time in the Gospel with the revelation formula ἐγώ εἰμι. Jesus' response is hardly appropriate if the woman's concept is not in some sense valid. There must be some

---

[69] In the Synoptic Gospels male disciples leave behind their possessions as a sign of their call to discipleship (Mark 1:16-20; 2:14).

correspondence between her perception of a Messiah who will reveal all things, and Jesus' self perception which leads him to state ἐγώ εἰμι. Many times in this Gospel others will speak of him as "the Messiah" (7:26-27, 41; 10:24) and Jesus will not accept the title for it expresses narrow Davidic, nationalistic expectations. But this woman has used the term in a way that reaches beyond such expectations and so Jesus can accept the title she proposes, even as he challenges her to a deeper perception of him as the human presence in the world of I AM.

If this understanding is correct, her words to the Samaritans require further exploration. What purpose is served by the μήτι, which would appear to indicate some doubt on her part?[70] First, she is a woman and her very irregular marital background disqualifies her as a credible witness.[71] Second, I believe the μήτι is a necessary rhetorical device which allows the villagers to hear her words as an invitation and make their own journey of faith. In actual fact it matters not whether she has reached full faith or is still in a situation of imperfect faith.[72] Whatever her understanding of Jesus is, her role is to be the catalyst that will draw the villagers into their own encounter with Jesus so they can make their own response. **Her** words about him to the villagers do not matter. Full Johannine faith is a response

[70] Olsson notes that μήτι does not always expect a wholly negative answer and speaks of this phrase as a hesitant question. See *Structure and Meaning,* 130; also Lee, *Symbolic Narratives,* 85–86.

[71] I am cautious of reading into the text moral laxity on the woman's part. O'Day raises the possibility of a levirate marriage custom such as experienced by Tamar in Genesis 38. See G. R. O'Day, "John," *The Women's Bible Commentary,* ed. Carol A. Newsom and Sharon H. Ringe (Louisville: Westminster/John Knox, 1992) 296. Whatever the reason for her sequence of husbands, they are not the focus of her discussion with Jesus, but they would, in the eyes of her village, delegitimate her testimony. Maccini examines Jewish and Samaritan legal backgrounds and concludes that the woman could have been a credible witness. He does not address the fact that the Samaritan woman is not just any woman, but one whose marital arrangements, even if legal, are far from the usual which could well detract from her credibility. See R. G. Maccini, "A Reassessment of the Woman at the Well in John 4 in light of the Samaritan Context," *JSNT* 53 (1994) 43–44. For a very thorough review of the role of women in Jewish legal proceedings, see ch. 3 in *idem, Her Testimony is True: Women as Witnesses according to John,* Journal for the Study of the New Testament Supplement Series 125 (Sheffield: Sheffield Academic Press, 1996) 63–97.

[72] Scholars differ in their assessment of the faith of the woman at this stage in the encounter. Moloney, *Belief,* 158, states that she comes to "a partial, conditioned belief in Jesus." Okure, *The Johannine Approach to Mission,* 169–71, argues that she comes to complete belief. With Olsson, *Structure and Meaning,* 153, I see the exact status of the woman's faith as irrelevant. The author's primary interest is not in *her* faith but in the coming to faith of the Samaritan people.

to the self-revelation of Jesus and is only possible through a personal encounter with Jesus and listening to **his** words.[73] Later the villagers assert that their belief is not dependent on the woman's word but on their own experience (v. 42).[74]

On seeing Jesus speaking with the woman, the disciples do not voice the questions in their minds, "What do you wish? " (literally What do you seek—τί ζειτεῖς?) (v. 27). In fact their question had already been answered in the preceding dialogue in v. 23. The Father is seeking (ζειτεῖ) true worshippers. Throughout the pericope Jesus has been acting out a divine necessity, what Schnackenburg calls, "the law of the hour" (cf. the ἔδει in v. 4),[75] for it is the mission of the Son to be an instrument of salvation of the world (3:17). In and through the person of Jesus, the Father is seeking the Samaritan people and offering them the gift of salvation.

Section B': Request Followed by Misunderstanding (vv. 31-38)

As the Samaritans move out of their village and towards Jesus (v. 20), the disciples and Jesus are in conversation, and their dialogue about food (vv. 31-34) mirrors the exchange between Jesus and the Samaritan woman about drink (vv. 9-15). The disciples speak about food at a material level whereas Jesus uses the image of food to speak of a different type of sustenance. Jesus is sustained by his relationship with the Father, and the nature of his relationship is to be the "sent one" (cf. 3:17, 5:36, 38; 6:29, 57). In speaking with Nicodemus, Jesus revealed that his mission from the Father is to reach beyond Israel and encompass the world (3:16). The encounter with the Samaritan woman at Sychar is the first movement of Jesus out into the world beyond orthodox Judaism.

The disciples' request spoken as an imperative, ῥαββί, φάγε (v. 31), opens this section in the same form in which Jesus began the earlier dialogue with the woman, δός μοι πεῖν (v. 7). Then, like the woman, the dis-

---

[73] Schnackenburg, *Gospel*, 1:454.

[74] Olsson, *Structure and Meaning*, 153, correctly notes that the emphasis in the episode is not so much on the woman's faith (or possible faith) but on the coming to faith of the Samaritans and their final declaration of belief. The woman's role resembles that of John the Baptist, she hears Jesus, bears witness to him, then she fades into the background. Boers makes a similar association between the woman's missionary role and that of John the Baptist. See H. Boers, *Neither on this Mountain nor in Jerusalem*, Society of Biblical Literature Monograph Series 35 (Atlanta: Scholars Press, 1988) 183–86.

[75] Schnackenburg, *Gospel*, 1:422; Haenchen, *John*, 1:218 also speaks of "the divine will." Similarly Olsson, *Structure and Meaning*, 134; Okure, *The Johannine Approach to Mission*, 85. Barrett is more cautious and while noting the possibility that ἔδει has a theological significance, he gives more weight to the description from Josephus (*Ant.* xx. 118) that the route through Samaria was the quickest way to travel.

ciples misunderstand Jesus' words about food, and take his response literally (v. 32). Jesus' reply makes it clear that he is nourished by his relationship with the Father, in acting out who he is, the "Sent One." To be sent implies a sender, and, as long as the one sent on mission carries out his mission, a relationship exists between the sender and the one sent.[76] This relationship is what sustains Jesus. In the movement of the Samaritans towards him (v. 30), Jesus perceives that he is already accomplishing the work of the Father to be the gift of salvation for the world (3:16-17). With the visible evidence of the success of his mission, there is a shift of image from food to harvest (vv. 35-38).

In the structure I am presenting, Section B (vv. 7-15) centers on the image of living water which Jesus, the Temple of God's presence, offers. The Temple waters in Ezekiel's vision produce abundant food, and in this corresponding section B' (vv. 31-38) the primary image is that of a bountiful harvest, already ripe for reaping (v. 35).[77] The movement from living waters to harvest symbolize the effectiveness of Jesus' mission to the world. The waters of the new Temple are bringing fertility to the world.

The Harvest Image[78]

These verses, with their image of harvest rejoicing (v. 36), and the invocation "lift up your eyes" (v. 35) suggest a number of possible biblical allusions, particularly within the context of chapter 4 with its implications for Samaria, and the Johannine symbolism of Jesus the New Temple.

The words recall that time in Israel's history when the Ark returned to Israel after its years among the Philistines (1 Sam 5, 6). "The men of Bæthsamys were reaping the wheat harvest in the valley; and they lifted up their eyes and saw the ark of the LORD, and rejoiced to meet it" (1 Kgs 6:13 LXX). As the men of pre-monarchic Israel once went out joyfully to meet the ark of the Lord, so now the Samaritans move out to meet the Temple of the Lord who offers a return to a pre-monarchic time when there were no divisions along racial lines, when all were children of Israel. Jesus offers a return to a time when God's presence was not fixed in one permanent location nor worship confined to one permanent sanctuary, for

---

[76] Okure, *The Johannine approach to Mission,* 141, describes this as an "obediential relationship."

[77] The antithetical style of v. 35 supports the placement of ἤδη at the end of v. 35, rather than as the first word of v. 36. See Okure, *The Johannine Approach to Mission,* 150, and Moloney, *Belief in the Word,* 163, for references to this discussion.

[78] The image of the harvest is well developed in Olsson, *Structure and Meaning,* 242–48.

worship will be in spirit and in truth (v. 24), rather than on this mountain or in Jerusalem (v. 21).

As well as looking back to Israel's past history, the image of harvest is used to describe the future ingathering of the people at the end of time, when God will summon the nations for judgment. God's judgment may bring joy and blessings (Isa 9:3; 27:12; Joel 4:18) or condemnation and punishment (Isa 18:3-6; Jer 51:3; Joel 4:11-15). The oracle of Joel, depicting Israel's eschatological blessings, seems particularly close to the Johannine images in chapter 4:

> In that day
> the mountains shall drip sweet wine,
> the hills shall flow with milk,
> and all the stream beds of Judah shall flow with water;
> a fountain shall come forth from the house of the LORD and water the Wadi Shittim (Joel 3:18 NRSV).

One of the blessings of the eschatological harvest will be the healing of the divisions between Israel (Samaria) and Judah, and the gathering into one the scattered tribes of a divided Israel:

> Lift up your eyes and look around;
> they all gather together, they come to you (Isa 60:4).

> For you also, O Judah, a harvest is appointed.
> When I would restore the fortunes of my people,
> when I would heal Israel (Hos 6:11–7:1; see also Isa 11:11; 27:12; Jer 23:3; 29:14; Ezek 20:34; 34:13; 37:21).

A reunited Israel was part of Ezekiel's eschatological hope (Ezek 37:15-22), then God would set the sanctuary in their midst forever (Ezek 37:26). Ezekiel's vision of the new Temple and the division of the land adds a new dimension; the inheritance of Israel is extended to aliens, the strangers are to be as natives among the children of Israel. "They shall eat with you in their inheritance in the midst of the tribes of Israel" (Ezek 47:22 LXX).[79] The divisions noted in the encounter between Jesus and the Samaritan woman are completely broken down. Earlier the narrator noted that Jews had nothing in common (συγχρῶνται) with Samaritans (v. 9), a possible allusion to never eating together for fear of defilement. In the redistribution of the land, made possible because the Temple waters have recreated the earth, strangers will share the food and inheritance of the

---

[79] μεθ' ὑμῶν φάγονται ἐν κληρονομίᾳ ἐν μέσῳ τῶν φυλῶν τοῦ Ἰσραήλ.

children of Israel. Strangers are thus brought into the promise once given to Abraham and his seed. Where the promise was once made exclusively to the seed of Abraham, "Lift up your eyes and see (וראה עיניך נא שׂא). . . . for all the land that you see I will give to you and to your seed forever" (Gen 13:14-15); in the eschatological age of the new Temple, the promise is extended, giving Abraham's seed a new definition, reaching beyond religious and national boundaries. The promise is extended to all people who hold fast to God's covenant; they too will be welcome in God's house, "for my house shall be called a house of prayer for all peoples" (Isa 56:7).

The Johannine passage draws on these prophetic images of the eschatological harvest but speaks of this as a present reality, already happening in the approach of the Samaritan villagers. With the Father's sending of Jesus, and his mission in Samaria, the eschatological ingathering of fruit for eternal life is happening now. "The hour is coming **and now is**. . ." (v. 23). The theme of gathering will recur later in the Gospel as Jesus approaches his "hour" when the work for which he was sent will be brought to completion (11:52).

The image of the fields already white for the harvest may continue the allusions to Jacob that so dominated the early discussion with the Samaritan woman. In the Targums, Jacob's final blessing to Judah is given lengthy elaboration, emphasizing that the future Messiah will come from the line of Judah, and will usher in a time of fruitful abundance:

> I shall compare you Judah, to a lion's whelp. . . Kings shall not cease from among those of the house of Judah . . . until the time King Messiah shall come, to whom the kingship belongs. . . How beautiful is the King Messiah who is to arise from the house of Judah. The mountains will become red from his vines and the vats from wine: and the hills will become white from the abundance of grain and flocks of sheep (*Tg. Neof.* Gen 49:9-12).

The hills, white with abundant grain find an echo in the Johannine text, "Lift up your eyes and see how the fields are already white for harvest" (v. 35). What Jacob saw only in prophetic insight, Jesus sees in reality in the approach of the Samaritans. Jesus brings Jacob's words to their fulfillment and in doing so continues to affirm that he is greater than Jacob (v. 12).

There is a contrast between the words of the disciples and the words of Jesus "Do you not say"—"Behold I say to you" (v. 35). In ordinary time, there is an elapse of four months between the sowing of the seed and the harvest, but in the eschatological νῦν (v. 23), sowing and reaping coalesce. The collapse of normal time frames continues in verse 38 when Jesus speaks of events that have not yet taken place, of a time when the disciples will be the 'sent ones' whose task will be to reap the harvest. The use of the aorist ἀπέστειλα is a prolepsis, looking ahead to the post-Easter missioning of the disciples, and indeed, to the later experience of the Johannine community reaping the rewards of the missionary labors of others.[80]

The eschatological background to the imagery of the harvest, supports the understanding of "living waters" having their background in Ezekiel's vision of the waters of eschatological salvation, flowing from the new Temple which God will provide. The Temple waters and the abundance that they produce provide a natural continuity between the Johannine images of water, food and harvest. The gift Jesus promised in vv. 7-15 is shown to be already operative in vv. 31-38. These two sections are balanced in a creative tension around the central verses (19-26) where Jesus proclaims "the hour is coming and now is" (v. 23), for in Jesus' presence in Samaria the Father is already active and seeking true worshippers.

Section A': Geography. Samaria to Galilee (vv. 39-45)

The final verses (39-45) confirm the harvest image in the preceding section (35-38). The Samaritans at first believe because of the witness of the woman (v. 39), but finally their belief is based on their own experience of hearing Jesus, "we have heard for ourselves" (v. 42). From their personal encounter with the Word they proclaim their faith in Jesus as Savior of the world (v. 42, cf. 3:17). Jesus' journey through Samaria, prompted by the divine necessity (ἔδει v. 4) has brought the gift of salvation to the Samaritans, fulfilling the eschatological hope of Ezekiel that God would gather into one people the Northern and Southern Kingdoms:

> Behold, I will take the people of Israel from the nations among which they have gone, and will gather them from all sides, and bring them to their own land; and I will make them one nation in the land, upon the mountains of Israel; and one king shall be king over them all; and they shall be no longer two nations, and no longer divided into two kingdoms. They shall not defile themselves any more with their idols and their detestable things, or with any of their transgressions; but I will save them from all the backslidings in which they have sinned, and will cleanse them; and they shall be my people, and I will be their God. My servant David shall be king over them; and they shall all have one shepherd. They shall follow my ordinances and be careful to observe my statutes. They shall dwell in the land where your fathers dwelt that I gave to my servant Jacob; they and their children and their children's children shall dwell there for ever; and David my servant shall be their prince for ever. . . and I will bless them and multiply them,

---

[80] See Okure, *The Johannine Approach to Mission,* 159–64, for a list and discussion of the possible identity of these ἄλλοι.

and will set my sanctuary in the midst of them for evermore. My dwelling place (LXX κατασκήνωσις) shall be with them; and I will be their God, and they shall be my people (Ezek 37:21-27).

When Jesus says to the woman of Samaria, "the hour has come and now is" he announces the arrival of the eschatological age. In his own person the dwelling place of God is being established in the midst of the people (cf. 1:14). The children of Jacob who had once been given land (Ezek 37:25) have now been given a far greater gift in the true sanctuary present in their midst. True worship of the Father can now replace former apostasies.

The journey into Galilee completes the movement begun in verse 3 and establishes a stark contrast between the two groups, namely, the Ἰουδαῖοι who do not accept him and the Γαλιλαῖοι who do. Verse 44 establishes that from the Johannine perspective the Ἰουδαῖοι are Jesus' own people (τὰ ἴδια). Judea is the πατρίς of Jesus.[81] In the rejection by the Ἰουδαῖοι, the words of the prologue are depicted, "He came to his own and his own did not receive him" (1:11).

Conclusion

Jesus' journey through Samaria is an expression of his missionary task from the Father who is seeking true worshippers (4:23). Worship in spirit and in truth is the human response to the Father's gift of salvation. Such worship is no longer tied to physical cultic sites on Gerazim or in Jerusalem, for Jesus is both the gift of salvation for the world (3:16-17; 4:42), and the new Temple of God's dwelling (1:14; 2:21).

Utilizing the image of the well's living water, Jesus reveals himself to the Samaritan woman as the gift of God (4:10), as a prophet (4:17-19) and finally as the presence of the self-revealing God of Israel (Exod 3:14; Isa 52:6; John 4:26). While the woman is challenged to grow in her awareness of Jesus' identity, the readers of this Gospel already know that Jesus is the dwelling place of the *logos* (1:14) and the Temple of God's presence (2:21). The identity of Jesus as the dwelling of God among us can resolve a key issue that divided Jews and Samaritans, the issue of true worship. Within the changing images and topics, this issue of worship remains central. In contrast to the well of Jacob and its miraculous but limited flow of water, Jesus offers waters welling up for eternal life (v. 14). The symbolism

---

[81] Olsson, *Structure and Meaning*, 144. Olsson also notes that Πατρίς may mean "native land," "native town," or "father's house."

of the living water Jesus promises draws on Ezekiel's image of the waters gushing from the eschatological Temple (Ezek 47:1-12).

When the topic shifts to the woman's marital status (vv. 16-18), reading the exchange symbolically and in its context, the cultic issue still remains—who is the true husband/lord of Samaria. The centerpiece of the dialogue (vv. 19-26) offers a non-geographic, non-sectarian form of worship in the Spirit which is truth.

In the Hebrew Scriptures it was Jacob, the primary ancestor of the Samaritans, who recognized the "House of God" (Gen 28:17), in the Samaritan episode, the descendants of Jacob recognize Jesus as the messianic revealer (vv. 25, 29) and the gift of God's salvation (v. 42). In their recognition of Jesus' identity, they are invited into a new relationship with God, now revealed as the Father of Jesus (vv. 21, 23). With this knowledge true worship is possible and Temple sites where "our fathers worshipped" are inadequate. Jesus has supplanted Jacob in the gift he offers—the living waters of eschatological salvation—and as the founder of a new form of worship in Spirit and in truth.

The Tabernacling
Presence of God

JOHN 7:1–8:59

The previous two chapters analyzed two pericopes, one situated in Jerusalem and the other in Samaria. I argued that in these passages the Gospel established the interpretive key which will allow readers to understand the Johannine christology as it develops in the narrative.

Jesus Is the New Dwelling Place of God

In the human flesh of Jesus, the rich cultic traditions of Israel are brought to fulfillment as God now tabernacles in their midst (1:14). Jesus, in his very person, is the new Temple and will bring the meaning of Israel's cult to its perfection. (2:19-21). Similarly, Samaritan cultic traditions are also eclipsed by the presence of Jesus, the new wellspring, with access to the ever-flowing waters of creation's life-source. Samaria's past infidelity, her turning from YHWH to Ba'al (Hos 2:13), is overlooked as her bridegroom comes to invite her back to true worship (John 4:21-23). In chapters 5 to 10, the evangelist leads readers through a series of Jewish feasts: Sabbath (ch. 5), Passover (ch. 6), Tabernacles (chs. 7, 8, 9 to 10:21) and Dedication (10:22-42). These "feasts of the Jews" are reinterpreted in the light of the Gospel's christological claim, that Jesus is the new Temple of God's dwelling.[1] These next two chapters examine two of these feasts

---

[1] A very thorough development of the christology emerging during the Feasts of the Jews can be found in F. J. Moloney, *Signs and Shadows: Reading John 5–12* (Minneapolis: Fortress, 1996).

where the Temple and its rituals play a critical role in the Gospel narrative's revelation of Jesus' identity.

Chapters seven and eight take place within the Temple during the feast of Tabernacles, and discussions in this context focus on the identity of Jesus. The participants in the story ask the right question, "Who are you?" (8:25) but they think they know where he has come from—Galilee (7:27, 41, 52) and so fail to grasp the true identity of Jesus and his origins in the Father. The readers of the Gospel have already been given the answer to this question, "who are you?" Firstly, in the Prologue, Jesus is the tabernacling presence of the divine *logos* among us (1:14), and, in the first encounter with "the Jews," Jesus is the new Temple of God's presence (2:21).[2] During the feast of Tabernacles, the symbols of the feast (water and light) and the personages of Israel traditionally associated with Tabernacles (Moses and Abraham) highlight the identity of Jesus. This "feast of the Jews" (7:2) is thus given a christological interpretation.

Structure

An atmosphere of growing hostility pervades chapters 7 and 8 with the threat of death introducing and concluding this section. "He could not go about in Judea because the Jews sought to kill him" (7:1); and then in 8:59, "They took up stones to throw at him; he went out of the temple." The section is introduced in verses 1-13, giving the reader background information about geography (v. 1), the time of the year (v. 2), the request by his family to go to Judea (vv. 3-5), another time-frame governing Jesus' actions (vv. 6-9), and then Jesus' decision to attend the Feast (vv. 10-13).

Following the introduction, the first discussion between Jesus and his audience occurs "about the middle of the feast" (v. 14). In this initial discussion the origin of Jesus' teaching is questioned. In his argument Jesus appeals to the great teacher of Jewish Law, Moses (v. 19). As Tabernacles recalls God's care during the wilderness wanderings, Moses

---

[2] In speaking of Jesus as both Temple and Tabernacle there is no dichotomy as the two are intrinsically related as the flesh (1:14) is related to the body (2:21). The Tabernacle and the Temple serve the same symbolic function even though they recall different historical eras. Both were central in Israel's cultic awareness of God's presence. In the Gospel the images of the Tabernacle (σκηνή) and Temple (ναός) are applied to Jesus in his humanity. In the flesh/body of Jesus the divine *logos* becomes part of the human story. Throughout this study I have given emphasis to the cultic background of John 1:14. In the feast of Tabernacles, set within the physical Temple building, I will again argue that cultic imagery best illuminates the presentation of this scene.

is a key figure for the feast. Through Moses' intercession the people were sustained by gifts of manna and quail (Exodus 16), and water (Exod 17:1-7).

The discussion then moves away from Jesus' teaching authority, to the question of his identity (vv. 25-36). Each time this question is raised the audience searches for an answer in terms of Jesus' origins. The participants in the story are limited in their perception, and fail to accept Jesus' claims of a divine origin in the One who sent him and to whom he is going (vv. 28, 33).

The discussion is interrupted by another reference to time—"the last day, the great day" (v. 37). On this day, and within a feast that has had daily water libations and prayers for rain, Jesus proclaims a new source of living water. In this proclamation Jesus identifies with one of the major liturgical symbols of the feast—living water (v. 38).

At the center of the section (vv. 40-52), is a *schisma* (v. 43) based on a twofold questioning of Jesus' identity. For some he is "the prophet" (v. 40), for others, "the Christ" (v. 41). But some, who attribute his origins to Galilee reject these two titles; he is neither the Christ (vv. 41, 42), nor a prophet (v. 52). In refusing to accept that Jesus has his origins with the Father, they are blinded to his true identity.

The section continues in 8:12 with Jesus' second affirmation of his identity, using another major symbol of the feast of Tabernacles, "I am the light of the world." The two self-revelatory statements of Jesus as living water and light, bracket and bring into sharp relief the refusal of the participants to accept his claims. The discussion of Jesus' identity continues (vv. 13-30), and again the issue of identity is raised in terms of Jesus' origins and destiny.

The final section (vv. 31-58) brings the person of Abraham into the discussion and leads to Jesus' definitive non-predicated statement of identity, "I am" (ἐγώ εἰμί v. 58). Jewish tradition remembers Abraham as the first to celebrate Tabernacles. "And he [Abraham] built booths for himself and for his servants on that festival. And he first observed the feast of booths on earth" (Jub. 16:30). The discussions which began with the figure of Moses now conclude with the figure of Abraham, enabling two great Jewish forefathers associated with the feast of Tabernacles to bear witness to Jesus' claims.

Schematically, the structure can be shown thus:

Introduction: 7:1-13
"He could not go about in Judea because the Jews sought to kill him"
The Feast of Tabernacles.

Moses 7:14-24
—the issue of origins

Who Is Jesus? 7:25-36
—his origins & destiny

Jesus' first reply—LIVING WATER 7:37-39

> **Jesus' Identity—*Schisma* 7:40-52**
> reason—his origins in Galilee

Jesus' second reply—LIGHT OF THE WORLD 8:12[3]

Who Is Jesus? 8:13-30
—his origins and destiny

Abraham 8:31-58
—the issue of origins

Conclusion 8:59
"They took up stones to throw at him; he went out of the temple."

Structural considerations

Chapters 7 and 8 draw attention to a critical question in Johannine research concerning the redactional processes that led to the final format of the text. Some scholars, notably Bultmann,[4] rearrange chapters 5, 6, and 7 so that chapter 7 follows immediately after chapter 5. With this rearrangement, the geographical itinerary of Jesus seems more understandable. In 4:54 Jesus is already in Galilee so 6:1 describing a sea crossing with no mention of a journey from Jerusalem, sensibly follows. Following the sign of the loaves Jesus goes up to Jerusalem (5:1) then returns to Galilee (7:1) because of the hostile reaction to his Sabbath healing in Jerusalem.[5]

---

[3] The story of the woman taken in adultery (7:53–8:11) is not part of the narrative of Tabernacles. It can be described as a non-Johannine interpolation that is part of the gospel tradition even though there is uncertainty as to which Gospel it belongs. For further comments on this pericope and its place in the Fourth Gospel see Brown, *Gospel,* 1:335–36; Schnackenburg, *Gospel,* 1:181–82; *idem, Gospel,* 2:168–71.

[4] Bultmann, *Gospel,* 209–10.

[5] For a more detailed discussion both for and against this rearrangement, see Schnackenburg, *Gospel,* 2:5–9; Brown, *Gospel,* 1:235–36; Barrett, *Gospel,* 21–26; Haenchen, *John,* 44–51; Moloney, *Signs and Shadows,* 30, 203.

While this rearrangement may be attractive for smoothing Jesus' itin-erary, it is not supported by any textual evidence.[6] The earliest texts of the Gospel all have the chapters ordered 4, 5, 6, and 7. Apart from the textual evidence, a rearrangement of these chapters assumes that the Gospel nar-rative is governed by geographical requirements, but as Barrett rightly states, "The movement of the Gospel is dictated by theological rather than by chronological and topographical considerations."[7] When the order of the chapters is taken as given, an important chronological consideration emerges that is closely related to Johannine christology. Chapters 5 to 10 take place within particular Jewish feasts introduced by the weekly Sab-bath (ch. 5). The feasts then follow liturgically throughout the year: Pass-over (ch. 6) in the first month, Tabernacles (chs. 7–10:21) in the seventh month and Dedication (10:22-42) in the ninth month.

A number of scholars, even those who retain the current order of 5, 6, and 7, argue that 7:15-24 has been displaced and should follow on from chapter 5 and the dispute about the Sabbath healing.[8] If verses 15-24 are omitted, then 7:25 follows quite readily from 7:14 with no apparent dis-ruption. Once again, no textual evidence supports this hypothesis. Without making recourse to an ecclesiastical redactor it is possible to accept that at some stage in the composition of the Gospel, verses 15-24 were part of the Sabbath healing story, but in the final, thoroughly Johannine, editing,[9] they were purposefully moved into their current context within the feast of Tabernacles. If this supposition is correct, the question follows, what theological/christological purpose is served by having these verses in chapter 7? I will argue below, that these verses are here because of the person of Moses and his significance for the feast.

The Rituals of Tabernacles[10]

Before beginning an analysis of the passage it is necessary to discuss the meaning and rituals of this feast. The *Mishnah* (2nd century C.E.) describes

[6] Barrett, *Gospel,* 24.

[7] Barrett, *Gospel,* 24. Brown, *Gospel,* 1:236, makes a similar comment when dis-cussing rearrangements based on geography or chronology.

[8] Bultmann, *Gospel,* 238; Schnackenburg, *Gospel,* 2:130–131. Ashton, *Under-standing,* 332–33, places only vv. 19b-24 after ch. 5.

[9] See Brown's exposition of the development and composition of the Gospel, *Gospel,* 1:xxiv–xl.

[10] For a brief overview see G. MacRae, "The meaning and evolution of the Feast of Tabernacles," *CBQ 22* (1960) 251–76. A detailed analysis of the feast may be found in an unpublished master's thesis by M. Dacy, *Sukkot: Origins to 500 C.E.* Unpublished M. Phil. thesis (Dept. of Semitic Studies, University of Sydney, 1992) 1–206.

the rituals of the feast but this poses a problem as the *Mishnaic* compilation of Jewish teaching is later than the Christian era. In using the *Mishnah* as a source for understanding Jewish liturgy in the first century, scholars assume that the *Mishnah* preserves older traditions pre-dating the destruction of the Temple. As Yee states, "There is no question that some of its legislation reflected a much earlier period when the temple was still in operation."[11]

Tabernacles is the most popular and joyful of Israel's three pilgrimage festivals and it is possible that this feast was the original pilgrimage festival. It is unclear whether its origins lie in an agricultural celebration borrowed from the Canaanites, or whether it was always linked to Israel's covenant faith.[12] Its antiquity is attested to by the various names given to the feast: "Tabernacles" (סכה) (Lev 23:34; Deut 16:13, 16; Ezra 3:4; Zech 14:16, 18-19); "the feast of ingathering" (Exod 23:16; 34:22); "the feast of the Lord" (Lev 23:39; Judg 21:19) and simply "the Feast" (1 Kgs 8:2, 65; 2 Chr 7:8; Neh 8:14; Isa 30:29; Ezek 45:23, 25).

The feast began on the fifteenth day of Tishri shortly after the day of Atonement (the 10th day of Tishri) and lasted for seven days, with the addition of a special eighth day of observance. During these days, the pilgrim slept and ate within a specially constructed booth originally made of myrtle, willow, and palm branches (Neh 8:13-18). These booths recalled Israel's sojourn in the wilderness at the time of the Exodus and God's care for them in providing the cloud of glory, the manna, and water during this time.[13] The booths were probably derived from an agricultural practice of building temporary shelters during autumn to protect the olive and grape harvest.

Commenting on the description of the booths in Lev 23:43, Ulfgard insists that there was a gradual theologizing of the feast.[14] The booths were seen as gifts from a caring God as "I made the people of Israel live in booths" (Lev 23:43). The primary meaning of the word סכה is "protection." Whatever the historical origins, the feast came to be a memorial of God's protective care and presence during the wilderness time.

In post-Exilic times, the feast developed an eschatological motif, looking ahead to the end time when all the nations would gather to worship in

[11] G. A. Yee, *Jewish Feasts and the Gospel of John* (Wilmington, Del.: Michael Glazier, 1989) 74.

[12] J. C. Rylaarsdam, "Booths, Feast of," *IDB* 1 (1962) 457.

[13] F. Manns, *Jewish Prayer in the time of Jesus,* Studium Biblicum Franciscanum Analecta 22 (Jerusalem: Franciscan Printing Press, 1994) 214; G. Bienaimé, *Moïse et le don de l'eau dans la tradition juive ancienne: Targum et Midrash,* Analecta Biblica 98 (Rome: Biblical Institute Press, 1984) 210.

[14] H. Ulfgard, *Feast and Future: Revelation 7:9-17 and the Feast of Tabernacles* (Stockholm: Almqvist & Wiksell, 1989) 121.

Jerusalem (Zech 14:16-19; Isa 2:2-4; 56:6-8). In later times Zechariah 14 was one of the *haphtarah* (selection from the Prophets) passages read on the first day of the festival.[15] The Zechariah text indicates a further aspect of this feast in its connection with prayers for the autumn rains. The libation ceremony also drew on traditions of Moses as a well-giver, where the well is a symbol for the gift of Torah. In recalling Moses, and the gift of water in the wilderness, the people looked forward to a new Moses-like figure. "The Targums on Gen 49:10 play on the digging of the scribes to promise a future Messiah who digs from the well of the Torah, a final 'giving of water' from the Torah, the well of God."[16]

Each morning of the festival a water-libation ceremony was conducted. A procession of priests filed down to the Pool of Siloam to draw a flagon of water which was carried with great solemnity back to the Temple. When the procession passed through the Water Gate, the *shofar* was blown (*m. Sukk.* 4:9). By the end of the first century C.E., the Water Gate was identified as the south gate of the eschatological Temple in Ezekiel's vision (ch. 47).[17] Through this gate the waters flowed from the Divine Presence out into the desert lands bringing life and healing. During the procession the pilgrims sang the *Hallel* (Pss 113–118) and carried a bouquet of myrtle, willow, and palm branches (the *lulab*) in the right hand, and a citron representing the harvest produce, in the left.[18] The *lulab* was waved aloft at particular verses in the psalms (*m. Sukk.* 4:5). On reaching the altar, the priest carrying the golden water-flagon circled the altar then ascended the ramp of the altar to perform the libation of water and wine. On the altar were two silver bowls, one for water and one for wine. These bowls were pierced, allowing the libations to flow onto the altar then down into the deep reservoirs below the Temple. On the seventh day, the priests circled the altar seven times.

A second aspect of this feast occurred each night in the Court of the Women:

Four huge Menorahs fitted out with wicks made from the worn-out garments of the priests, illumined the entire temple area. Under them the celebrants danced a torch dance to the accompaniment of flute playing, and the Levites chanted the Psalms of Ascent (120–134), one each on the fifteen steps that led down from the court of Israelites to the Court of the Women.[19]

---

[15] G. A. Yee, *Jewish Feasts,* 73. H. H. Donin, ed. *Sukkot,* Popular Judaica Library (Jerusalem: Keter Books, 1974) 81.

[16] Moloney, *Signs and Shadows,* 68.

[17] G. Bienaimé, *Moïse et le don de l'eau,* 202.

[18] Yee, *Jewish Feasts,* 74.

[19] Rylaarsdam, "Booths," 456.

According to the *Mishnah*, "there was not a courtyard in Jerusalem that did not reflect the light of the *Beth hasheʾubah* [i.e., House of the Water Drawing]" (*m. Sukk.* 5:3).[20]

The third ritual of this feast was carried out each morning by the priests. Before sunrise they processed to the East Gate of the Temple area looking towards Mount Olives. At the moment of sunrise, they turned round to the west with their backs to the rising sun and facing the Temple they said:

> "Our fathers who were in this place *turned with their backs toward the Temple of the LORD and their faces toward the east, and they worshipped the sun toward the east* (Ez. 8:16). 'But as to us, our eyes are to the Lord'" (m. Sukk. 5:4).

In chapters 7 and 8 the three rituals of this feast involving water, light, and an affirmation of faith in God are given a new interpretation in the person of Jesus.

Introduction (vv. 1-13)

On a feast celebrating the ingathering of the olive and grape harvests and also anticipating the eschatological ingathering of the nations, the introduction (vv. 1-13) ironically indicates a number of divisions which will be developed in the discussions that take place during this feast:

- between Jesus and "the Jews" (v. 1)
- between Jesus and his family (vv. 2-9)
- amongst the people (v. 12)

During this feast, called "the festival of ingathering" (Exod 23:16; 34:22), there is the first of several mentions of a *schisma* (7:43; 9:16; 10:19). Whereas the Tabernacle, and later the Temple, were focal points of unity, Jesus, the new Tabernacle/Temple is a focus of conflict and division.

The first mention of "the Jews'" seeking to kill Jesus occurred within the Sabbath healing (5:18). This threat is voiced repeatedly within the celebration of Tabernacles (7:1, 19, 20, 25; 8:22, 37, 40). In chapter 2 Jesus had said to "the Jews," "*Destroy this temple, and in three days I will raise it up*" (2:19). His prophetic words are recalled with deep irony as "the Jews" now set about the destruction of the new Tabernacle/Temple.

The introductory verses and the conflict with his family indicate Jesus' motivation for attending the feast. He is not going to give a demonstration of his mighty works (v. 3), nor is he seeking personal recognition by the

---

[20] See the discussion by Dacy on the translation of the term *Beth hasheʾubah*, (*Sukkot*, 108–11).

world (v. 4). Jesus is following a different time-frame, determined for him by the will of the Father. "Jesus knows that he is not yet summoned by his Father to the journey to Jerusalem, which will mean for himself the decision to accept death."[21] As he says, *this feast* is not yet *his* time (vv. 6, 8).[22] His words suggest there will be another feast which will be the right time for his *going up* to Jerusalem. It is possible that the term ἀναβαίνω is used with the double sense of the pilgrim's "going up" to the festival, and an indication of Jesus' future ascent to the Father (20:17).[23] The family of Jesus understands only the ordinary sense of the word "to go up" to the festival, but Jesus understands the deeper sense with its reference to the Father.

Moses—The Issue of Jesus' Origins (vv. 14-24)

Jesus' public teaching occurred "*about the middle of the feast*" (v. 14). This would be the fourth day. If later synagogue worship retains worship traditions from the Temple period, it may be possible to explain the discussion about Moses and the Sabbath that occur in the middle of this feast. Since the festival takes place over seven days, there would usually be a Sabbath within the feast. On this intermediate Sabbath Guilding calculates that in one of the three-year lectionary cycles, the reading is from Deut 10:1-5 which describes the directives to Moses to carve out the Ten Commandments.[24] This may explain the rather strange statement, "Moses gave you circumcision" (v. 22), when this ritual is attributed to Abraham (Gen 17:9-14). Through Moses the ritual was drawn into Israel's Law. Even if the "middle of the feast" did not coincide with the intermediate Sabbath, Moses is a key figure in the biblical narrative of the Tabernacle.[25]

A later custom recorded in the Middle Ages but based on earlier traditions, was inspired by Abraham's hospitality. In Targum Neofiti we read,

[21] Schnackenburg, *Gospel*, 2:140.

[22] There are differences in the manuscript traditions allowing for reading both "not" and "not yet" in v. 8. It is possible that "yet" was a scribal addition to harmonize vv. 8 and 10, which would otherwise appear contradictory. See Schnackenburg, *Gospel*, 2:141; Barrett, *Gospel*, 312–13.

[23] Hoskyns, *The Fourth Gospel*, 313; Brown, *Gospel*, 1:308.

[24] A. Guilding, *The Fourth Gospel and Jewish Worship* (Oxford: Clarendon Press, 1960) 96. Statements about the first-century cycle of lectionary readings cannot be made with absolute certainty as no actual lectionary exists and scholars need to reconstruct the lectionary cycle using literary methods and making deductions from the later Mishnaic writings. A. Guilding's work presents her reconstruction of this lectionary cycle and the early chapters discuss the methodology she uses in her reconstruction.

[25] Barrett, *Gospel*, 317, raises the possibility that this day is the intermediate Sabbath but note the caution of Moloney, *Signs and Shadows*, 75 n. 35.

"And Abraham planted an orchard in Beersheba and within it gave food to the passers by" (*Tg. Neof.* Gen 21:33). Each night a special guest would be invited into the *Sukkoth,* one of the following biblical figures: Abraham, Isaac, Jacob, Moses, Aaron, Joseph, and David.[26] In this list Moses is the fourth guest, the middle guest, of Tabernacles. The lateness of this tradition makes a definite conclusion impossible, but it is reasonable to assume that the liturgy of Tabernacles provides a context for the focus on Moses, circumcision, and Sabbath. This liturgical context would be familiar to first-century readers.

The discussion in this section begins with the question of the origins of Jesus' learning (v. 15). In this discussion there are two groups of participants. There are "the Jews," apparently the ones present at the Sabbath healing who have already decided to kill Jesus (5:18; 7:1, 11, 13, 15). Also present is another group called the crowd (ὄχλος), who are divided in their opinion but not yet threatening death (7:12, 20). Since Jesus was not part of a scribal school, his teaching is a cause of wonder. Within the scribal schools authority was based on two credentials; first, the teaching had to be grounded in the Scriptures, and second, it must be possible to trace the line of argument back to a great teacher of the Law. "In Judaism a teacher acquires his knowledge at the school of some other rabbi; he belongs to an unbroken line of tradition which goes back to Moses."[27] Jesus traces his teaching authority back to the Father, the one who sent him (vv. 16-18). Jesus also appeals to the Scriptures (vv. 19-23) and uses as an example an earlier episode known to "the Jews" concerning his healing on the Sabbath (5:1-9).

The Mosaic Law allows Sabbath regulations to be set aside for circumcision, "And all things required for circumcision do they perform on the Sabbath" (*m. Sukk.* 18:3). Using a rabbinic form of argumentation, from a lesser to a greater,[28] Jesus claims he is therefore able to set aside the Sabbath law to heal a whole person. Circumcision draws a person into the fullness of covenanted life that takes precedence over Sabbath restrictions; Jesus' healing gives a person fullness of human life (ὅλον ἄνθρωπον 7:23) and so his actions also have precedence over the Sabbath.[29] The discussion about the Sabbath and the appeal to the Father attempt to answer the initial query about the origin of his teaching.

---

[26] Donin, *Sukkot,* 43.

[27] S. Pancaro, *The Law in the Fourth Gospel,* 82.

[28] Manns, *L'Evangile,* 314. Manns develops a more detailed description of rabbinic exegesis in *idem,* 307–19.

[29] Moloney, *Signs and Shadows,* 79.

Who Is Jesus? (vv. 25-36)

These verses attend to the crucial question raised within the feast celebrating God's gifts to Israel in their wilderness experience. As they rejoice in the gifts of God's presence in the cloud and Tabernacle, God's sustenance and care in the gifts of water and manna, God's covenant with them in the Torah, they are challenged to recognize in Jesus a new gift of a loving God (cf. 3:16; 4:10). The issue of Jesus' identity is discussed in terms of where he has come from and where he is going. Limited by their "this-worldly" perceptions, the people of Jerusalem think they know Jesus' origins.

In reply to their clear statement, "We know where this man comes from," (v. 27), Jesus replies with a rhetorical question that undermines the truth of their statement, "You know me, and you know where I come from?" (v. 28). In fact, the people of Jerusalem should know where Jesus comes from for he told them clearly after the Sabbath healing, "The Father has sent me" (5:36); "I have come in my Father's name" (5:43). In rejecting the words of Jesus, they reject not only him but also the one who sent him. In the context of Tabernacles and its daily ritual and affirmation of faith in Israel's one true God, the Jerusalemites are blind to the identity of Jesus and so repeat the act of their fathers who rejected God and turned to the sun (*m. Sukk.* 5:4).

Jesus' Reply—Living Water (vv. 37-39)

The preceding verses posed a series of questions concerning Jesus identity:

Is not this the man whom they sought to kill? (v. 25)
Can it be that the authorities really know that this is the Christ? (v. 26)
When the Christ comes, will he do more signs than this man has done? (v. 31)
Where does this man intend to go that we shall not find him? (v. 35)

In verses 37-39 Jesus gives his first reply to these questions by referring to one of the major rituals of the feast, the Water Libation, and the accompanying prayers for rain (Zech 14:16-19):

Jesus stood up and proclaimed, "If any one thirst, let him come to me and drink. He who believes in me, as the Scripture has said, 'Out of his heart shall flow rivers of living water'" (vv. 37b-38).[30]

(εἰστήκει ὁ Ἰησοῦς καὶ ἔκραξεν λέγων, Ἐάν τις διψᾷ ἐρχέσθω πρός με καὶ πινέτω. 38 ὁ πιστεύων εἰς ἐμέ, καθὼς εἶπεν ἡ γραφή, ποταμοὶ ἐκ τῆς κοιλίας αὐτοῦ ῥεύσουσιν ὕδατος ζῶντος.)

[30] Schnackenburg, *Gospel,* 2:153, lists the Eastern and Western Church Fathers who followed this translation with the believer as the referent of "his" (v. 38).

Now this he said about the Spirit, which those who believed in him were to receive; for as yet the Spirit had not been given, because Jesus was not yet glorified (v. 39).

Verse 37 and 38 present three main difficulties for exegetes:

- What is the correct punctuation?
- Whose "heart" is referred to in verse 38, the believer's or Jesus'?
- What is the Scripture that is cited by Jesus?

Since these verses pose great difficulty and yet are critical for my hypothesis, I will set out in some detail the arguments supporting the above punctuation and translation. This in fact, is the more traditional approach and has the support of the oldest manuscript tradition P[66]. The above translation which has the believer as the referent of the "his" in verse 38, has the support of a number of commentators such as Barrett, Haenchen, Lightfoot, Leon-Dufour, Kysar, Lindars, Marsh, Morris, Pfitzner, and Schwank. Menken follows this punctuation but retains Jesus as the referent in verse 38.[31]

The oldest text of the Fourth Gospel is that of papyrus 66, dated around 200 C.E., and it has a full-stop after "drink." This papyrus has been followed in the critical editions of the New Testament Greek, Nestle-Aland (1963), United Bible Society (1993), British and Foreign Bible Society (1958). P[75] (175–225 C.E.) also supports this punctuation. The participial phrase ὁ πιστεύων, "who ever believes," at the start of a new sentence is very common in the Fourth Gospel; according to Brown, this pattern is found forty-one times, whereas the participle is never attached to the preceding sentence.[32]

The statement in 7:37-38 is very similar to the earlier dialogue with the Samaritan woman, where Jesus promised that the believer would never thirst, and indeed within the believer there would arise a "spring of water" (4:13-14). Cortés refutes the objections of some scholars that the believer is never promised to be a *source* of living water *for others* by pointing out that 7:37 maintains *Jesus* as the water source and verse 38 does not necessarily mean that the believer is to be a source for others.[33] This argument of Cortés is not supported by the text. While 4:14 spoke of a spring of water *within* the believer, (ἐν αὐτῷ), 7:38 speaks of water flowing *out of* the believer (ἐκ τῆς κοιλίας αὐτοῦ). Earlier I argued that a key text behind the Johannine image of living water in the encounter with the Samaritan Woman was Ezekiel 47. In 7:38 the depiction of the eschatological

---

[31] Menken, *Old Testament Quotations,* 189–94.

[32] J. B. Cortés, "Yet another look at Jn 7,37-38," *CBQ 29* (1967) 78, refers to Brown to support this grammatical argument. See Brown, *Gospel,* 1:321.

[33] Cortés, "Yet another look," 79.

Temple from Ezekiel continues to influence the interpretation of Jesus' words.[34] In Ezekiel's vision the actual source of the water is not seen; the waters are simply flowing from beneath the threshold of the sanctuary (Ezek 47:1). The waters have their source in the divine presence and the Temple is the point of intersection between heaven and earth and thus the locus of the divine presence on earth.

According to Hodges, "The Lord Jesus remains its true and ultimate source, while the believer might be more fittingly described as a 'channel' for the waters he actually receives by coming to God's Son."[35] In presenting a case for the water flowing from the side of the believer, there is no suggestion that the believer is an independent source. The believer possesses living water only because he/she has already come πρός με (v. 37; cf. 4:14). "Jesus gibt lebenspendendes Wasser, so daß jeder, der an diesem Wasser (im Glauben) teilhat, selber zu einer Quelle lebendigen Wassers werden kann (7,38).[36] The later image of the vine and branches will similarly insist that only the one who remains in Jesus can be fruitful: "apart from me you can do nothing" (15:5).

Verse 38, with the αὐτοῦ referring to the believer, has a shift in case from the nominative case "He who believes. . ." to the genitive "from within him," but while this is not grammatically perfect, it is quite "common," "Semitic," and used elsewhere in this Gospel (6:39; 8:45; 15:2; 17:2). For example, "But **I**, because I am telling the truth, you do not believe in **me**" (8:45).[37]

Some commentators, Ashton, Brown, Burge, Bultmann, Beasley-Murray, Boismard, Dodd, Hoskyns, Moloney, Schnackenburg, argue for an alternative *christological* interpretation and punctuation because it allows poetic parallelism,

"If any one thirst, let him come to me;
and let drink he who believes in me."

Menken, Cortés, and Hodges point to the imperfection of the parallelism, and Dodd asserts that such parallelism is not common in John.[38]

---

[34] There are many views on what passage of Scripture is referred to in 7:38. I will discuss this issue below and present arguments in support of Ezekiel 47.

[35] Z. Hodges, "Rivers of Living Water—John 7:37-39," *Bibliotheca Sacra* 136 (1979) 242. See also the similar comment by Léon-Dufour, *Lecture,* 2:237, that the believer is necessarily related to Jesus.

[36] Obermann, *Die christologische Erfüllung,* 357.

[37] Cortés, "Yet another look," 79.

[38] Menken, *Old Testament Quotations,* 190–91; Cortés, "Yet another look," 79–80; Hodges, "Rivers," 240; Dodd, *Interpretation,* 342.

Cortés shows that the Fourth Gospel has numerous instances where there is an invitation to believe followed by an offer of a reward, which is the pattern of the expression I have argued for. Thus—"He who believes in me will never thirst" (6:35).[39] The invitation to come and drink is offered to the one who thirsts, and is a metaphor expressing an invitation to believe.[40] The believer is then promised a reward, living waters shall flow from within him (7:38). With this pattern of invitation and promise, the alternative punctuation—"and let drink, he who believes in me"—does not make sense as it offers an invitation to drink to the one already believing, who has metaphorically already drunk and has been promised that he will never thirst (6:35).

Following Fee and Lindars,[41] it is important to read verse 38 in the light of verse 39; "Now this he said." The translation I argue for has Jesus as the speaker of verse 38 in its entirety.[42] Jesus quotes the Scriptures "Out of his heart shall flow rivers of living water," and it would be most unlikely that Jesus would cite a passage using a third-person pronoun while referring to himself. If the scriptural quotation is a later addition by Bultmann's ecclesiastical redactor, then, as Fee argues, the redactor would be making such addition to add weight to Jesus' words and so would surely cite Scripture "with enough accuracy as to be identifiable."[43] But as already noted, the scriptural passage is one of the questions that puzzles exegetes.

The discussion above, on the punctuation and on the identity of the referent in the biblical text, Jesus or the believer, is important for the interpretation of the scriptural citation and for identifying the text Jesus refers to. It is also important to note that Jesus' words are proclaimed on "the last day" of the feast. The time indicator forms an essential part of the context of his words and is critical for their interpretation.

On the last day, the great day (v. 37)

The expression Ἐν δὲ τῇ ἐσχάτῃ ἡμέρᾳ τῇ μεγάλῃ τῆς ἑορτῆς is open to various interpretations. The celebration of Tabernacles lasted for seven days, (Deut 16:13) with the addition of an eighth day of solemn assembly similar to the Sabbath (Lev 23:34-36). If the expression is a reference to a specific day of the festival, does it mean the seventh, *Hoshanna Rabbah,* or the eighth, *Shemini Atzeret*? Both are possible. The image of

[39] Also 3:18, 36; 6:47; 11:25; 14:12; 12:44.
[40] Hodges, "Rivers," 240-241; Cortés, "Yet another look," 81.
[41] G. D. Fee, "Once More—John 7[37-39]," *ExpT* 89 (1978) 116–17; Lindars, *Gospel,* 301.
[42] Agreeing with Menken, *Old Testament Quotations,* 187.
[43] Fee, "Once More," 117.

water in verses 37 and 38 suggest the seventh day when the participants process with the water libation seven times around the altar.[44] According to the *Mishnah,* the water and light ceremonies did not continue into the eighth day (*m. Sukk.* 4:1).

Alternatively, the eighth day, a special Sabbatical day (Lev 23:36), may have provided the vacuum in which Jesus' offer of water and light would have been more keenly appreciated. The eighth day of the feast had particular significance as it ". . . was the last festival day in the Jewish calendar and is called 'the last good day' (*m. Sukk.* 4:8)."[45]

A third possibility proposed by Hodges is that the expression is distinctly Johannine and has its full meaning beyond the actual feast in the "hour" of Jesus.[46] The text of verses 37 and 38 supports this interpretation and its eschatological thrust, without becoming totally divorced from its meaning within the feast. Within the Gospel "the last day" has been mentioned in the "Bread of Life" discourse (6:39, 40, 44, 54) and will occur again in 11:24 and 12:48. All these occurrences speak of the resurrection of the believer. The next time the reader hears of a "great" day is the Passover-Sabbath day after the crucifixion (19:31).[47] During this Sabbath, "while it was still dark" and so according to Jewish reckoning, not yet over, Mary Magdalen discovers the empty tomb (20:1).

The "great" day in the Johannine Gospel is the day of Jesus' resurrection, with a promise that the believer will share this resurrection experience. Because of these textual links to the resurrection of the believer and Jesus, the "last day, the great day" has a particular Johannine eschatological perspective which continues in the next two verses. Verse 38 looks to a future time when rivers of living water "shall flow." Verse 39 makes the future reference quite explicit in mentioning the Spirit who has "not yet" been given, because Jesus has "not yet" been glorified.

The eschatological emphasis within verses 37-39 is not foreign to the celebration of the feast. Indeed the text states explicitly, "on the last day of the feast." Even as the verses look to "the hour" for the fulfillment of their meaning, the feast itself offers an eschatological perspective which must interplay with "the hour." Zechariah 14, one of the *haphtarah* readings for the feast, describes the last days when the Lord will come to Jerusalem, and the surviving nations will come to celebrate Tabernacles.

---

[44] Brown, *Gospel,* 1:327.

[45] L. Morris, *The Gospel According To John* (Rev. Ed.), New International Commentary on the New Testament (Grand Rapids, Mich.: Eerdmans, 1995) 373, n. 79.

[46] Hodges, "Rivers," 247.

[47] Hodges, "Rivers," 247.

The Water gate, through which the libation ceremony passed, was identified as "the south gate" of the eschatological Temple in Ezekiel. While the *Mishnah* makes no overt reference to Ezekiel or Zechariah, the elaborate water ceremony within the Temple surely recalled, for those who had once participated in them, these texts, and their eschatological hopes.[48] The rituals of Tabernacles provide the liturgical context for the proleptic interruption of the Johannine "last day."

The arguments so far have reached beyond the narrative time to the time of the Johannine community to find a meaning for the phrase, "on the last day, the great day" (v. 37). Within the actual feast, the narrative time that best expresses the Johannine meaning of Jesus' words on "the last day of the feast," is the eighth day. In the stark absence of water rituals and light, Jesus announces that the water has not dried up and the light has not been extinguished. He is a source of water for the thirsty (v. 37) and light for those in darkness (8:12). In asserting the eighth day as most appropriate, I point to a key Johannine theme that has been developing throughout the narrative—the paradox of presence in absence. For a Christian community living at the end of the first century when the Temple has been destroyed and they no longer have access to synagogue worship, how can God be present to them? In the absence of a physical Temple, Jesus provides a new Temple where God may be encountered and worshipped (2:21; 4:21). In the absence of water rituals, and Temple candelabras, Jesus provides water and light. The significance of the eighth day is also reflected in the post-Easter stories. The eighth day, which is also the first day of the Jewish week, is the day when Jesus breathes the gift of the Spirit onto the community of disciples (20:19-22), fulfilling the words of 7:39. On the next "eighth" day Jesus comes to Thomas who, in the absence of Jesus, cannot believe. On this day Jesus announces a blessing to all who come to faith without seeing his presence. Within this Gospel the eighth day juxtaposes presence and absence and invites all to experience the eschatological blessings of the eighth day.

What is the Scripture passage cited by Jesus?

Commentators who accept a christological reading of verses 37 and 38 suggest Isa 12:3; Zech 13:1; Ezek 47:1; Exod 17:5-6; Num 20:7-16 and Ps 78:15-16. Those favoring the alternative interpretation I have adopted

---

[48] A very thorough discussion on the rich historical and eschatological symbolism of Tabernacles can be found in Bienaimé, *Moïse et le don de l'eau*, 200–229. In summary, see especially 229, "Dès une date ancienne, à la signification primitive de la fête des Tentes liée au rythme des saisons s'étaient ajoutées la commémoration du don de l'eau au désert et l'attente des eaux eschatologiques jaillissant du Temple."

suggest Zech 14:8; Prov 4:23; 5:15; Sir 24:30-33 and others.[49] To this list can also be added Isa 58:11 and Prov 18:4. The obvious lack of agreement in identifying the text leads to great differences in interpretation. Since there is no exact parallel to Jesus' words in either the MT or LXX versions of the Hebrew Scriptures, it is possible that a targumic text lies behind Jesus' words, or that he was not quoting exactly but simply alluding to a text (or texts) from the scriptural tradition.

The Greek expression ποταμοὶ **ἐκ τῆς κοιλίας αὐτοῦ** ῥεύσουσιν ὕδατος ζῶντος (v. 38) arises from a distinctly Aramaic idiom, which indicates that, if Jesus is quoting a text exactly, it will be from the Targums.[50] Grelot suggests that the expression is not a single verse of Scripture but a combination of two texts following rabbinic exegetical principles.[51] A text, usually taken from the Torah, is combined by means of verbal repetition with a second text, often from the prophets.[52] In this case Grelot points to Num 21:20 and Zech 14:8—"From his side shall flow rivers." This text from Numbers recalls the incident in the desert, when Moses struck the rock producing a flow of waters. To this is added the phrase "Living waters" from Zechariah, which elaborates further on this flow. To support his view, Grelot refers to sections of a third-century rabbinic commentary the *Tosefta* (*t. Sukk.* 3:3-18).[53]

In the *Tosefta* the ritual of the water libation is firstly linked with the waters from the Temple (Ezek 47)[54] and then Zechariah 14. Quite a long passage (*t. Sukk.* 3:3-8) explains the meaning of the name "Water Gate." The witness of a first-century rabbi who had known the Temple prior to its destruction in 70 C.E. identifies the Water Gate through which the libation ceremony passed, with the south gate of Ezekiel's Temple vision[55]:

---

[49] Cortés, "Yet another look," 85.

[50] P. Grelot, "Jean, VII, 38: Eau du rocher ou source du Temple?," *RB* 70 (1963) 43; Bienaimé, *Moïse et le don de l'eau*, 283. Menken, *Old Testament Quotations*, 199, accepts the Aramaism but disputes that this necessitates a targumic citation.

[51] Grelot, "Jean, VII, 38," 47–48.

[52] See Manns, *L'Evangile*, 314, for a more thorough discussion of this technique called *gezerah shawah*.

[53] This rabbinic text is also discussed by B. Grigsby, "'If Any Man Thirsts. . .': Observations on the Rabbinic Background of John 7,37-39," *Bib* 67 (1986) 105–8.

[54] The cautionary comments made about the *Mishnah* and its reliability for knowing the rituals in the first century apply even more so to the *Tosefta* which is a commentary on the Mishnah ca. 200–300 C.E. For further analysis of the relationship between the Mishnah and Tosefta, see J. Neusner, *The Classics of Judaism: A textbook and reader* (Louisville: Westminster John Knox, 1995) 19, 53.

[55] Grelot, "Jean, VII 38," 46; Bienaimé, *Moïse et le don de l'eau*, 202.

Whence is the name "Water Gate"? It is so called because through it they take the flask of water used for the libation at the Feast. R. Eliezer b. Jacob says of it: "The waters are dripping," intimating that water oozing out and rising, as if from this flask, will in future days come forth from under the threshold of the Temple; and so it says, When the man went forth eastward with the line in his hand, he measured a thousand cubits, and caused me to pass through the waters. . ." (*t. Sukk.* 3:3).[56]

Grelot also argues that the passage from Ezekiel is singular *(un fleuve)* where the Johannine passage speaks of "rivers." But although Ezekiel speaks of one river (6, 7, 12), in verse 9 the first reference in the Hebrew is in the dual form נחלים, which could be reflected in the plural ποταμοὶ of John 7:38.[57]

Grelot's solution is only sustainable if one accepts the christological interpretation and punctuation. Jesus is then the rock providing from his side a flow of living water. I have argued above that the manuscript tradition and the syntax of the verse, as well as Johannine theology and expression, point towards the *believer* as the one from whom the living waters will flow.

The clearest text indicated by the *Tosefta* is Ezekiel 47, the vision of the eschatological Temple, which in Jewish tradition was associated with Zephaniah 14:8. The waters of Ezekiel's Temple are "living" in the sense that they are moving, and also in the sense that they give life (Ezek 47:9). The image of life-giving waters flowing from the side of the eschatological Temple provides a most appropriate scriptural text for Jesus to allude to, given a daily liturgical procession through Ezekiel's "south gate" (Ezek 47:2), even if there is not exact verbal parallelism.[58] The eschatological Temple vision is also consistent with Johannine symbolism (1:14; 2:19) and suits the physical context within the Temple, and the time reference to "the last day." It must also be noted that the waters in the Zecharian text flow from Jerusalem (14:8), the city, while Ezekiel's text by naming the Temple as the water source (Ezek 47:1) has more in common with the Gospel symbolism. In the Johannine text, Temple imagery is applied to

[56] Quotation from A. W. Greenup, *Sukkah, Mishna and Tosefta: With introduction, translation and short notes,* Translations of Early Documents. Series 3. Rabbinic Texts (New York: Macmillan Co., 1925).

[57] Hodges, "Rivers," 245, n. 22. See also D. Bodi, "Der altorientalische Hintergrund des Themas der "Ströme lebendigen Wassers" in Joh 7, 38," *Johannes-Studien,* ed. Martin Rose, (Zurich: TVZ, 1991) 152.

[58] S. H. Hooke, "'The Spirit was not yet," *NTS* 9 (1962–1963) 377, comments that after the Temple *logion* in ch. 2, there is a similar reference to an unspecified word of Scripture, testifying to future post-resurrection events. It is also possible, as I noted above, that the text quoted in the Gospel came from a targumic tradition rather than from the MT or the LXX.

Jesus (2:21) so that when he says, "come to me and drink," he is able to offer water because he is the new Temple and source of living waters.

In his analysis of the significance of the rituals of Sukkot for the Second Temple period, Rubenstein argues that the meaning of the libation ceremony must be found in the ancient myths about the Temple and its "foundation stone" resting directly above, and therefore giving access to, the primordial flood-waters of the deep *(tehom)*. "The libation descended through channels beneath the altar, stimulated the waters, and set in motion a process which led to the refertilization of nature."[59] The very focus of this festival is the Temple and its abundant life-giving waters which the cult actualizes through its rituals. In this context, the Temple therefore provides a more likely image of a source of water than the Rock. But can this Temple imagery be applied to the believer?

The first-time reader of verses 37-39, who has only what has been read so far as an interpretive guide, would certainly be puzzled by this citation. The alert reader has already been led to understand Jesus as the tabernacle (1:14) and Temple (2:21), and as one who supplants Jacob in the gift of living water (4:7-15). Given the dynamic interplay of these images, the reader would expect the stream of living water to come from the side of *Jesus,* but that is not what the text says. The third-person pronoun αὐτοῦ, (v. 38) rather than the first, sounds a jarring note that is not immediately comprehensible. Verse 39 confirms that the text cannot be deciphered accurately in the present time, as there is a "not yet" time and a future gift to which the text refers, "For the Spirit had not yet been given" (v. 39). In narrative time, the words, "Out of **his** heart shall flow rivers of living water" (v. 38), can only be a promise, not fully clear, of something still to happen. The proleptic nature of the verses transfers to the believer cultic imagery that rightly applies only to Jesus during the narrative time of his ministry. In his flesh (1:14) and body (2:21) he is the divine presence dwelling with us and the source of living water. There will come a future time when, through the gift of the Spirit to the believer, such cultic images will also apply to the believer. The future, post-resurrection time, forcefully interrupts the narrative bringing the eschatological "last day" into the present moment in Jesus' words.

The Spirit who was not yet[60]

There is a strong scriptural tradition linking water and the Spirit, stretching back to creation and forward to the endtime (Gen 1:3; Ezek

---

[59] J. Rubenstein, "Sukkot, Eschatology and Zechariah 14," *RB* 103 (1996) 83.

[60] On the manuscript traditions for the addition of "given" see Hoskyns, *The Fourth Gospel,* 324.

36:25-26; Isa 44:3; Joel 3:1).[61] The liturgy of Tabernacles also makes this association of water and Spirit, for according to rabbinic traditions, the place where the candelabra were set up was called the "House of Drawing" because "from there they draw the Holy Spirit."[62] "In arid Palestine, such an effluence was the perfect metaphor for the abundance of the divine Spirit in the Messianic age."[63] In Isaiah 44, Spirit and water are eschatological gifts promising life to the exiles:

> For I will pour water on the thirsty land, and streams on the dry ground. I will pour my Spirit upon your descendants, and my blessing on your offspring (Isa 44:3).

This text may have been one of the *haphtarah* used during the feast of Tabernacles.[64] In the Johannine narrative, the Spirit is already given to Jesus (1:32) but is not yet a living power in the life of the believers. The Spirit will only be released upon the community in the hour of Jesus' glorification (19:30; 20:22).

Jesus' Identity—*Schisma* (vv. 40-52)

The response to Jesus' proclamation and invitation is schism. Within the narrative, the hearers of Jesus' proclamation at the feast, and not the readers who have been guided by the Johannine narrative, have probably heard in his words echoes of the Mosaic miracle, producing water from the side of the rock (Num 20:9-11; cf. Exod 17:6); for the participants at the feast are celebrating the wilderness wanderings and remembering all the Mosaic gifts.[65] For these listeners, Jesus is the expected prophet-like-Moses repeating his wonders,[66] "This is really the prophet" (v. 40). Others, given the messianic hopes expressed in Zechariah 9–14 and the liturgy of Tabernacles, perceive that these longings have now been fulfilled, "This is the Christ" (v. 41). While others in the audience, who fix on Galilee as the place of Jesus' origins, deny these assertions, pointing to the Scriptures to support their blindness. ". . . the Christ is descended from David, and comes from Bethlehem" (v. 42); ". . . no prophet is to rise

[61] Brown, *Gospel*, 1:324.

[62] Dacy, *Sukkoth*, 150; *y. Sukk.* 55a.

[63] G. H. Burge, *The Anointed Community: The Holy Spirit in the Johannine Tradition* (Grand Rapids, Mich.: Eerdmans, 1987) 92.

[64] Guilding, *The Fourth Gospel and Jewish Worship*, 105.

[65] There are two descriptions of Moses striking the rock and producing a flow of water. Bienaimé, *Moïse et le don de l'eau*, 285, argues that the incident that best aligns with John 7:37 is found in Exod 17:6. See also Grelot, "Jean, VII, 38," 48.

[66] M.-É. Boismard, *Moses or Jesus*, 6-10; Brown, *Gospel*, 1:329.

from Galilee" (v. 52). A feast anticipating the eschatological gathering of the nations has brought about division among the people of Israel (v. 43). Those who cannot accept Jesus, even in the limited designation of "prophet" or "Christ," will most certainly reject his further claim to be "I Am" (8:58).

While some do make a positive response, understanding Jesus as "the prophet" or "the Messiah," their response is far from a true understanding of Jesus' identity. Jesus goes beyond the limited categories of Jewish expectations. The gift of bread he offers is true bread surpassing the Mosaic gift of manna (6:32); the gift of living water he brings quenches thirst forever (4:13; 6:35). Jesus is the very presence of the divine *logos,* now dwelling among us (1:14).

Jesus' Reply—I am the light (8:12)[67]

Faced with the confusion and denial of his listeners, Jesus makes a second self-disclosure, again in terms of the symbols of Tabernacles. "On the last day . . . the great day" (7:37), when the *menorahs* have been extinguished, Jesus offers a new guiding light, not just for Israel but for the entire world, "I am the light of the world; whoever follows me will never walk in darkness, but will have the light of life" (8:12 NRSV).[68] In the wilderness the people of Israel had been accompanied by a pillar of cloud by day, and a pillar of fire by night.[69] The fire/cloud settled upon the tabernacle and the people were guided to journey or rest by its movements:

> On the day that the tabernacle was set up, the cloud covered the tabernacle, the tent of the testimony; and at evening it was over the tabernacle like the appearance of fire until morning. And whenever the cloud was taken up from over the tent, after that the people of Israel set out; and in the place where the cloud settled down, there the people of Israel encamped (Num 9:15, 17).

The cloud, called consistently in Targum Ps. Jonathan "the cloud of glory," is clearly associated with the Tabernacle during the wilderness time. Later, when the Temple was built and the Tabernacle placed within

[67] Ball presents this "I am" saying of Jesus against a background of the Servant of YHWH in Isa 42:6; 49:6; 51:4. See D. Ball, *"I Am" in John's Gospel: Literary Function, Background and Theological Implications,* Journal for the Study of the New Testament Supplement Series 124 (Sheffield: Sheffield Academic Press, 1996) 215–224.

[68] As Tabernacles was celebrated at the full moon during the autumnal equinox, the "world" was lit by the sun during the day and by the radiance of the moon by night. See H. Ulfgard, *Feast and Future,* 115.

[69] The pillar of cloud/fire was one of three Mosaic gifts associated with Tabernacles, which looked to a second redeemer to fulfill their promise. These gifts were the manna, the well, and the cloud. See Bienaimé, *Moïse et le don de l'eau,* 210–11.

it, the glory cloud of God filled the Temple (1 Kgs 8:4-11). Jesus offers a light surpassing the wilderness cloud, for Jesus is the *logos* who has already been described as a light and life for all people and a light that the darkness could not extinguish (cf. 1:4-5). The tabernacling presence of God that formerly nourished, refreshed, and guided Israel, is once more dwelling in Israel's midst offering bread (ch. 6), water and light (chs. 7 and 8).

Who Is Jesus—His Origins and Destiny (vv. 13-30)

Jesus' second self-disclosure does not resolve the schism. There is still the possibility of arrest (v. 20) and belief (v. 30). Following the appeal of Nicodemus to give Jesus a proper hearing (7:51), verses 13 to 30 take on a forensic tone as the Pharisees require a witness to support Jesus' testimony (v. 13).[70] The discussion of Jesus' origins in chapter 8 recall words and themes from a similar discussion in chapter 7:

Chapter 7	Chapter 8
we know where this man comes from (27)	you do not know whence I come (14)
him you do not know (28)	you know neither me nor my **Father** (19)
no-one laid a hand on him,	no-one arrested him,
because his hour	because his hour
had not yet come (30)	had not yet come (20)
I go to him who sent me (33)	I go away (21)
you will seek me and you will not find me (34)	you will seek me and die in your sin (21)
what does he mean ? (36)	they did not understand (27)

The primary addition to these verses is the naming of the Father as the one who sent Jesus and who bears witness to Jesus (vv. 18, 27). The union of Jesus and the Father who sent him is forcefully expressed in the triple use of the absolute ἐγώ εἰμι (vv. 18, 24, 28). Unlike verse 12, these three verses have no predicate to "I am." Many scholars trace the Johannine unpredicated use of "I am" to the self-revelatory formula of Deutero-Isaiah

---

[70] Barrett, *Gospel,* 316, makes the comment that the interrogations during Tabernacles replace the synoptic "Jewish Trial" narratives. Moloney, *Signs and Shadows,* 94, does not consider these verses a true trial, rather an attempt by the Pharisees to understand Jesus in terms of their legal traditions. See also J. Neyrey, "The Trials (Forensic) and Tribulations (Honor Challenges) of Jesus: John 7 in Social Science Perspective," *BTB* 26 (1996).

(41:4; 43:10, 25; 45:18; 46:4; 51:12; 52:6)[71]. The phrase ἐγώ εἰμι is regularly used in the LXX to translate the Hebrew phrase אֲנִי־הוּא.[72]

In Isaiah, the first references to the phrase אֲנִי־הוּא occur in trial scenes where over and against the gods of the world, God's singular sovereignty is asserted. "I am YHWH, the first and the last; I am (אֲנִי־הוּא)" (Isa 41:4).[73] In these trial scenes YHWH summons Israel to bear witness, to **know**, **believe** and understand:

> "You are my witnesses", says the LORD, "and my servant whom I have chosen, so that you may **know** and **believe** me and understand that I am (אֲנִי־הוּא) (Isa 43:10).

In the context of a legal hearing the Pharisees reverse roles and demand that Jesus produce witnesses (v. 13). Jesus' first witness is none other than Israel's ἐγώ εἰμι. "I am (ἐγώ εἰμι), the one witnessing to myself, and the Father who sent me bears witness to me" (v. 18). The phrase is repeated two more times in words that recall God's words to Israel:

> "You will die in your sins unless you **believe** that I Am" (v. 24).
> "When you have lifted up the Son of Man then you will **know** that I Am" (v. 28).

The possibility of the expression having its background in Deutero-Isaiah is strengthened by the uniquely Johannine word ὑψόω ("lift up") which has the double sense of being lifted up in the crucifixion, and in exaltation (3:14; 8:28; 12:32, 34).[74] The Servant of Deutero-Isaiah, whom God calls to witness will also be lifted up (Isa 52:13).

The rituals of Tabernacles may also explain the strong concentration of the phrase ἐγώ εἰμι within this particular chapter, where it occurs five times (8:12, 18, 24, 28, 58). A variant of the Hebrew אֲנִי־הוּא was used in the Festival of Tabernacles as an oblique way of referring to YHWH and thus avoiding saying the sacred name. During a procession with willow branches the supplicant would pray "ʿani wᵉhu (literally I and He) come to our aid."[75] Having celebrated the feast and heard the daily recitation of

[71] Dodd, *Interpretation*, 94–96; Schnackenburg, *Gospel*, 2:79–89; Brown, *Gospel*, 1:533–38.

[72] P. Harner, *The "I Am" of the Fourth Gospel: A Study in Johannine Usage and Thought*, Facet Books (Philadelphia: Fortress, 1970) 6.

[73] Harner, *I Am*, 9.

[74] G. Lüdemann, "ὑψόω," *EDNT* 3 (1993) 410. G. Bertram, "ὑψόω," *TDNT* 7 (1971) 602–20.

[75] Harner, *I Am*, 18–21; Manns, *Jewish Prayer*, 214. Dacy, *Sukkot*, 116. H. Ulfgard, *Feast and Future*, 111, n. 466.

אֲנִי־הוּא Jesus' use of the phrase "I Am" as a term of self-designation would have been both striking and offensive to his opponents.

Abraham (vv. 31-58)

Corresponding to the focus on Moses in 7:14-24, which opened the discussions at Tabernacles, 8:31-58 close the discussions by referring to another of Israel's forefathers associated with the feast. This section is dominated by references to the figure of Abraham (vv. 33, 37, 39 x3, 40, 52, 53, 56, 57, 58):

"The Jews'" Words	Jesus' Words
we are descendants of Abraham 33	I know you are descendants of Abraham 37
Abraham is our Father 39	if you were children of Abraham 39
	you would do what Abraham did 39
	this is not what Abraham did 40
Abraham died 52	
Abraham who died 53	
	Abraham rejoiced to see my day 56
You have seen Abraham? 57	
	Before Abraham was, I am 58

The first part of the discussion raises the issue of the origins of "the Jews," who claim Abraham as their father, "We are seed of Abraham" (v. 33). Jesus supports this assertion. In a physical sense, they are of Abraham's seed. Verse 39 changes the language from seed (σπέρμα) to children (τέκνα). Although physically descended from Abraham, "the Jews" are not true children for they do not *do* what Abraham did. In chapter 5 Jesus had claimed to be a true son of the Father because he did only what he saw the Father doing; *"for whatever he does, that the son does likewise"* (5:19). Doing as the father does is the true measure of sonship. In rejecting Jesus who spoke the truth, and in seeking to kill him (v. 40), "the Jews" show that they are sons of the Devil who is "a murderer" and "has nothing to do with the truth" (v. 44). The deeds of "the Jews" testify to their true lineage for they *do* what their father does, namely, murder and destroy truth.

The concluding verses of chapter 8 contain some of the harshest words in the Christian Scriptures about "the Jews," and it is essential that the term be understood in its narrative context. The conflict in the Johannine narrative is best understood as a struggle between adolescent siblings trying to establish their own self-identity in the aftermath of the destruction of Jerusalem. Therefore I reiterate that the term the *Ioudaioi* in the Johannine Gospel must be read as a narrative device rather than as a description of members of Second Temple Judaism. According to Bultmann the *Ioudaioi* portrays the Jews "from the standpoint of Christian faith as the representatives of unbelief" and "the unbelieving world in general."[76] They are, in John Ashton's words, an "archetypal symbol of the sinfulness of all humanity."[77] "The Jews" in the gospel narrative are a caricature of the unbelieving world that rejects Jesus, and in their rejection show they are not true *sperma Abram*.

What is it that Abraham *did,* that "the Jews" are not doing? "Abraham rejoiced that he was to see my day" (v. 56). The action of rejoicing in the day of Jesus is what "the Jews" fail to do. Frequently Abraham is described as a man of faithful obedience; he is mainly remembered for that in the Jewish tradition (Gen 12:4; 22:1-14; 26:5), and also in the early Christian writings (Rom 4:3, 13, 16; Gal 3:6; Heb 11:8, 17; Jas 2:23). But in this feast, it is not Abraham's faith or obedience that is commended by Jesus, but his joy (8:56). The book of Jubilees and the celebration of Tabernacles provide a likely context for this unusual emphasis.[78]

The book of Jubilees, written in Hebrew and probably completed around 160 B.C.E.,[79] names Abraham as the first to celebrate Tabernacles, "And he first observed the feast of booths on the earth" (Jub. 16:21). Abraham's joy in this feast is striking. The text of Jubilees mentions joy many times:

> He built an altar there to the LORD who delivered him and who made him rejoice in the land of his sojourn. And he celebrated a feast of rejoicing in this month (16:20).

> He observed this feast seven days, rejoicing with all his heart . . . (16:25).

> And he blessed and rejoiced and called the name of this festival 'the festival of the LORD' a joy acceptable to God Most High (16:27).

The cause of Abraham's joy and blessing lies in the future that he is permitted to see.[80] ". . . for he knew and perceived that from him there would be a righteous planting for eternal generations and a holy seed from him. . .(Jub. 16:26). Abraham's perception enables Jesus to say "Your Father Abraham rejoiced that he was to see my day; he saw it and was glad" (John 8:56).

In failing to rejoice in Jesus, as Abraham did, "the Jews" reveal that they are not true children of Abraham. In this confrontation where "the

---

[76] Bultmann, *The Gospel of John,* 86.

[77] J. Ashton, "The identity and function of the Ἰουδαῖοι," 68.

[78] In celebrating the feast of Tabernacles, the Israelites are specifically commanded to celebrate it with joy (Lev 23:40; Deut 16:14).

[79] J. Charlesworth, ed. *The Old Testament Pseudepigrapha.* 2 vols. (London: Darton, Longman & Todd, 1985) 2:43; Hayward, *The Jewish Temple,* 85.

[80] Moloney, *Signs and Shadows,* 112: "Early Jewish tradition held that Abraham had been privileged with a disclosure of the secrets of the ages to come, especially the messianic age . . ." See this reference for further Jewish sources on Abraham's foreknowledge.

Jews" call upon Abraham to add legitimacy to their argument (v. 33), Jesus shows that their claim is not true. The post-70 Christian readers of this dispute may at this point be thinking that the narrative is going to reveal that **they** are the true children of Abraham because they have responded positively to Jesus. But there is more!

Abraham as a Witness to Jesus' Origins

It is not just a question of the identity of the son/daughter; also at stake is the question of the identity of the father. "The Jews" insist that their father is Abraham (v. 33, 39) and even God (v. 41), a claim Jesus challenges by pointing to what they *do* to him (v. 40), and showing that in fact they cannot have their origins in either Abraham or God. By contrast, Jesus does the will of his Father. He speaks what he has seen and heard with his Father (v. 38, 40). Jesus is a true son and his Father is none other than the one "the Jews" claim as their God (v. 54). There is a contrast established between "our/your father Abraham" (vv. 53, 56) and "my Father"/"God" (vv. 49, 54). The sonship Jesus claims goes far beyond the sonship of belonging to the "seed" of Abraham; his is a divine sonship. The Christian reader may well recall that the Prologue promised that they too would become children of God (1:12) sharing in Jesus' divine filiation. The promised Christian filiation far transcends "the Jews'" claim to be children of Abraham.

"The Jews'" question, "Are you greater than our father Abraham?" (v. 53), recalls an almost identical question posed by the Samaritan woman, "Are you greater than our father Jacob?" (4:12). The site of Sychar was linked in the Scriptures to Jacob, and, for the Samaritans, was the sacred place close to the remains of their Temple. For "the Jews," their holy place was the Temple Mount chosen by David, a site which was also associated with Abraham and the sacrifice of Isaac:

> Take your son, your only son Isaac, whom you love, and go to the land of Mori'ah, and offer him there as a burnt offering upon one of the mountains of which I shall tell you (Gen 22:2).

> Then Solomon began to build the house of the LORD in Jerusalem on Mount Mori'ah, where the LORD had appeared to David his father, at the place that David had appointed, on the threshing floor of Ornan the Jeb'usite (2 Chr 3:1).

At two sacred places, associated with the founding patriarchs, Jesus' identity is challenged, "Are you greater than Jacob/Abraham?" Jesus concludes both discussions with the affirmation, "I am" (4:26; 8:58).

Throughout the encounters at Tabernacles a critical issue has been the identity of Jesus. His opponents accuse him of leading the people astray

(7:47), and of being possessed by a demon (8:48). Even those inclined to accept him do so within the limitations of their own expectations, he is the prophet (7:40), the Christ (7:41). There is a failure to see the answer to the question asked, "Are you greater than our father Abraham?" (8:53). Jesus is indeed greater than Israel's patriarchs. He is the incarnate *logos,* "the only Son who is in the bosom of the Father" (1:18). As son and not slave, he continues forever, ὁ υἱὸς μένει εἰς τὸν αἰῶνα (v. 35), within a relationship that transcends all time, as was stated in the Prologue, Ἐν ἀρχῇ ἦν ὁ λόγος (1:1). His concluding "I am" affirms his identity with Israel's God whom he calls Father (8:54), and who is the God of Israel's patriarchs, Abraham and Jacob.[81] "I am the God of Abraham your father" (Gen 26:24; cf. Exod 3:6).

In the discussion of the phrase ἐγώ εἰμι in verses 8:18, 24 and 28, I followed the work of a number of scholars who look to Deutero-Isaiah as the most likely background for the Johannine expression. The context of the final ἐγώ εἰμι in verse 54 may also be best elucidated through Isaiah, particularly the targumic version:

MT Isa 43:10-12	**Tg Isa 43:10-12**[82]
10. You are my witnesses, says the LORD	You are witnesses before me, says the Lord
and my servant whom I have chosen	and my servant the **Messiah** with whom I am well pleased,
that you may **know** and **believe** me	that you might **know** and **believe** before me
and understand that I am He.	and understand that I am He.
	I am he that was from the beginning, even the ages of the ages are mine and there is no God beside me.
11. I, I am the LORD	I, I am the Lord,
and beside me there is no savior.	and beside me there is no savior.
12. I declared and saved and proclaimed	I declared **to Abraham your father what was about to come,** I saved you from Egypt, just as I swore to him between the pieces, I proclaimed to you the teaching of my Law from Sinai, when you were present
when there was no strange god among us.	and there was no stranger among you.

[81] Freed discusses some contemporary Jewish literature, where only the *name* of the Messiah and not the Messiah himself was thought to pre-exist. The Gospel goes further in asserting the pre-existence of a personal *logos*. See E. D. Freed, "Who or what was before Abraham?," *JSNT* 17 (1983) 52–59.

[82] B. Chilton, *The Isaiah Targum,* ed, Martin McNamara. The Aramaic Bible 11 (Edinburgh: T. & T. Clark, 1987).

Abraham has been inserted into the text of the Targum in connection with the deliverance from Egypt. Abraham is added to Isaiah in other places expressing a similar theme of Abraham as savior. In some cases he replaces the original reference to Cyrus who was considered a savior figure (41:2; 48:15-16).[83] The reference above to 43:10-12 is particularly striking as the Gospel picks up the theme of "knowing" and "believing" (8:24, 28). The Gospel (v. 56) and Targum (v. 12) follow the Jewish tradition found already in Jubilees (16:26) that future events were revealed to Abraham:

> Targum—I declared to Abraham your father what was about to come
> Jubilees—He knew and perceived that from him there would be a righteous
> planting for eternal generations
> Gospel—Abraham rejoiced to see my day.

> Both Targum and gospel speak of the pre-existence of the "I Am."
> Targum—"I am he that was from the beginning" (Is. Tg. v. 10).
> Gospel—"Before Abraham was I am" (8:58).

The similarities between the Gospel and Targum suggest that both draw upon a common source of traditional material concerning Abraham available to a first-century author.

The fivefold repetition of the phrase ἐγώ εἰμι (8:12, 18, 24, 28, 58) in the Temple, within the feast affirming worship of Israel's one God, gives the phrase the character of a theophany. "I am the light of the world" (8:12), recalls the theophany in the glory cloud above the tabernacle and later within Solomon's Temple (Num 9:15,17; 1 Kgs 8:4-11). Verses 8:18, 24, 28, and 58 recall the self-revelation of YHWH in Deutero-Isaiah when Israel is called to acknowledge YHWH as the one true God.

On the Temple mount, the place that recalled the obedience of Abraham and his sacrifice, and during a feast which remembered Abraham's perception and joy, Jesus confronts the seed of Abraham with their disobedience and true paternity disclosed in their seeking to kill the "only son" of the Father. The Father of Jesus is the one "the Jews" claim as their God (8:41, 54) and whom, every morning during the feast of Tabernacles they profess to worship. The challenge to believe that Jesus is "I am" speaks precisely to this ritual profession of faith carried out each morning during the feast. Will the Israel of Jesus' day repeat the sins of their fathers or accept a new manifestation of God's tabernacling presence? Will they move beyond their identification with "our father Abraham" (vv. 33, 39) to perceive in Jesus the one Abraham "rejoiced to see" (v. 56), and their true Father (v. 41) whom Jesus' reveals (1:18; 8:58)?

---

[83] Harner, *I Am,* 39–41.

Conclusion (v. 59)

The reaction of "the Jews" to Jesus' "I am," testifies that they have understood his words even though they reject them as blasphemy. "By their reaction 'the Jews' show that they regard such a point of view as reserved for God."[84] Jesus' response is to leave the Temple. The departure of the one who is "the light of the world" is ominous. Once before the glory cloud of God's presence departed the Temple and it heralded the forthcoming destruction of the Temple (Ezek 10:18-19; 11:22-23). The departure of one who has consistently during this feast affirmed his relationship with the Father (7:16, 28, 29; 8:18, 19, 29, 38, 42, 54, 55) and so revealed himself as the tabernacling presence of Israel's God (8:12, 58) acts as a judgment on Israel's cult. As their ancestors once "turned their backs to the Temple" (Ezek 8:16), now "the Jews" turn from the true Temple of God. Jesus, the enfleshed glory "as of the only son" is driven from his Father's House. Neither the witness of Moses (7:14-24), nor of Abraham (8:31-58) has changed the original intention of "the Jews" to kill him (7:1).

The feast of Tabernacles has continued to apply Temple and cultic symbolism to Jesus. He has revealed himself as a source of water (7:37), as light (8:12) and as the very presence of Israel's God ἐγώ εἰμι (8:58). There has also been an intimation that Temple symbolism will in the future, with the gift of the Spirit, apply to the believers (7:38). No explanation is given at this stage as to how this shift of meaning will occur. This promise must simply stand, along with other promises of a Temple that will be raised up (2:20) and of a place where the Father will be worshipped in Spirit and truth (4:23). The narrative presses forward to see how these promises will be fulfilled.

---

[84] D. M. Ball, *I Am*, 88.

The Consecrated One

"It was winter" (10:22). With these words the evangelist sets the tone for this final "feast of the Jews." The sequence was introduced by the Sabbath festival, that weekly affirmation of the creative sovereignty of God (ch. 5). There followed the springtime festival of Passover (ch. 6) and the autumn feast of Tabernacles (7:1–10:21). In a Gospel that is sensitive to the symbolism of light and darkness, the movement through the seasonal year suggests the coming to closure of Jesus' ministry, a closure that will result in the departure of "the light of the world." This section of the Gospel began in the Temple precincts (5:2) and concludes with Jesus' complete withdrawal from the Temple (10:40), never to return.[1]

Dedication was not one of the three pilgrim festivals. Its significance in this Gospel lies in the christology that has been developing from the Prologue—Jesus is the dwelling place of God's glory (1:14) and the Temple (2:21). Jesus' ministry among "the Jews" draws to its climactic end as Jesus is presented to them as the one consecrated and sent by the Father (ὁ πατὴρ ἡγίασεν καὶ ἀπέστειλεν) (v. 36). Within a festival celebrating the consecration of the Temple after it had been desecrated by idolatry, Jesus' self-revelatory words are a final challenge and appeal to "the Jews." Jesus can speak of himself as the Consecrated One because of his intimate relationship with the Father. He is the Son who is in the heart

---

[1] Stibbe, *John,* 117, notes an *inclusio* in the architectural description of the colonnades of Solomon and the colonnades (στοά) near the Bethesda pool (5:2) where this section on "the feasts of the Jews" began. The section begins and ends within the Temple precincts.

of the Father (1:18). Where "the Jews" sought the presence of God in the Temple, Jesus comes to them as the enfleshed dwelling place of the Father (1:14). But "the Jews" reject his claims, and the consecrated glory of God finds no home within Israel's House of God (בת י יהוה).

Structure

Throughout this section of the Gospel there has been an emphasis on showing a relationship between Jesus' identity and the primary symbols and rituals of Israel's festivals. Other motifs also were present such as Jesus' authority to heal on the Sabbath and the relentless confrontation with the Jewish leaders during Sabbath and Tabernacles. During the feast of Dedication the issue of identity and how the identity of Jesus is revealed in the symbols of this feast continue to be central. The focus on identity guides my choice of structure and argument. As in the overall context of chapters 5 to 10, this is the primary issue. Carson comments on this passage, "The governing themes of this chapter, indeed of this Gospel, are christological, leading up to the moving conclusion (20:30-31)."[2]

The feast can be divided into two major blocks within an introduction (vv. 22-23) and conclusion (vv. 40-42).[3] The first section begins with a question, asked with a degree of hostility, which leads to the statement, "If you are the Christ, tell us plainly" (v. 24). Jesus' reply points to the witness of his works, then to his own "messianic" definition in terms of shepherd and life-giver, and finally to his subordination to the Father.[4] He concludes his reply with a statement affirming his union with the Father, "I and the Father are one" (v. 30). "The Jews" respond by taking up stones against him (v. 31).

[2] Carson, *Gospel,* 390. So also Brown, *Gospel,* 1:404–5; Schnackenburg, *Gospel,* 2:304.

[3] Von Wahlde proposes an alternative structure which shows the relationship between this confrontation and those in 6:31-59; 8:13-19. See U. Von Wahlde, "Literary Structure and Theological Argument in Three Discourses with the Jews in the Fourth Gospel," *JBL* 103 (1984) 575–84. His outline has a strong community orientation. The structure I propose gives greater emphasis to the issue of Jesus' identity for reason given above.

[4] The repetition of the pastoral metaphor from 10:1-21, is not an indication of displacement, as proposed by Bultmann, *Gospel,* 358–60. It is the metaphor Jesus uses to redefine his messianic program. For arguments tying 10:1-21 to the story of the man born blind (9:1-41) see U. Busse, "Open Questions on John 10," *The Shepherd Discourse of John 10 and its Context,* ed. Johannes Beutler and Robert Fortna, Society for New Testament Studies Monograph Series 67 (Cambridge: Cambridge University Press, 1991) 1–17; also Brown, *Gospel,* 1:390. I will demonstrate that the text as we have it from 10:22-42 is a unity and reflects a careful ordering to express the christology of the evangelist.

The second section begins with Jesus' question and leads into the accusation by "the Jews," "you, being a man, make yourself God" (v. 33). Jesus' defense begins again by appealing to a witness, this time the testimony of the Scriptures, "Is it not written in your law, 'I said, you are gods'?" (v. 34). Again he reveals his own identity as the Consecrated One and his role as the Sent-One of the Father. His conclusion to this section (vv. 32-37), rephrases the earlier conclusion in verse 30, "the Father is in me and I am in the Father" (v. 38). "The Jews" again respond by rejecting his words and trying to arrest him. The passage concludes with Jesus' escape (v. 39b) and departure across the Jordan. As in previous passages, this pericope shows a structural and christological coherence testifying to the artistry of the evangelist.

The final verses 40-42 not only bring the narration of this feast to its end, but also function as a conclusion to Jesus' entire ministry among "the Jews." Jesus' first appearance in the Gospel was "in Bethany" beyond the Jordan where John was baptizing (1:28-29). He now returns to that place. The first verse after the Prologue names Jerusalem (1:19), and in chapters 1 through 10 Jesus has been engaged in a ministry to Israel, even those no longer considered true Israelites by the Jews, but who never the less, claim Jacob as their Father (ch. 4). He has come to his own and his own have not received him (1:11). From chapter 11 onwards the narrative moves into a story of death leading to glory (11:4). Jesus' own "hour" will be prefigured in the story of Lazarus whose illness "is not unto death; it is for the glory of God" (11:4).

Introduction: vv. 22-23 Time, place, season, and location

Interrogation: v. 24. If you are the Christ . . .

    First reply—witness of works v. 25
        —Jesus is shepherd & life-giver vv. 26-28
        —the Father v. 29
    Conclusion: I and the Father are one. v. 30
Response: They took up stones. v. 31

Accusation: vv. 32, 33. You make yourself God.

    Second reply—witness of Scripture vv. 34, 35
        —Jesus the consecrated and sent one v. 36
        —the Father vv. 37, 38 abc
    Conclusion: The Father is in me, I am in the Father. v. 38d
Response: They tried to arrest him. v. 39

Conclusion: vv. 40-42. He went away across the Jordan.

The Feast of Dedication[5]

Dedication is called in Hebrew חנוכה *(Hanukkah)* and Josephus refers to it as the feast of Lights *(Ant.* xii, 325). It celebrates the rededication of the Temple in 164 B.C.E. by Judas Maccabeus. In 175 B.C.E. the Seleucid ruler Antiochus IV became ruler of Palestine. In order to consolidate his power he instigated a ruthless program of hellenization, with some support by segments of the Jewish aristocracy and priesthood. He deposed the legitimate High Priest and installed the High Priest's brother Joshua, who hellenized his name to Jason (2 Macc 4:7-10). In support of Antiochus, Jason established a gymnasium in Jerusalem in which some Jews hid their covenantal sign of circumcision in order to compete naked in the athletic events (1 Macc 1:11-15). In effect, these Jews repudiated their heritage and revoked their identity as a covenant people. As Yee says, "it was apostasy in the worse sense."[6]

Antiochus stripped the wealth of the Temple treasury (1 Macc 1:20-28) and established himself as divine. He gave himself the title "Epiphanes" or "God Manifest" and decreed the worship of the Greek god Zeus as the national religion. On the 25th of Kislev (November–December) 167 B.C.E., a pagan altar was erected over the altar of burnt offerings in the Temple and sacrifices were offered to Zeus (1 Macc 1:59). A Jewish revolt was led by Mattathias and his sons, who, using guerilla tactics from the hills of Modein, defeated the Greek forces in 164 B.C.E. and established an independent Jewish kingdom later ruled by the Hasmoneans.

Judas immediately set about the task of purifying the Temple from all signs of pagan defilement (1 Macc 4:36-51; 2 Macc 10:1-6). On the 25th Kislev 164, the Temple was rededicated and the first celebration of *Hanukkah* took place. There is no description of the rituals of Dedication in the *Mishnah.* According to the description in the book of Maccabees, the festival lasted for eight days and was patterned on the feast of Tabernacles, since, as earlier in Israel's history, the rebels had been wandering homeless in the mountains (2 Macc 10:6). The lighting of the *Hanukkah* lamps plays an important part in the ritual both in the Temple and in private homes. The lamps are associated with the fire that was miraculously preserved when the Temple was first destroyed (2 Macc 1:18-36).

Dedication celebrates a Jewish victory over foreign oppression and a victory over those sections within Judaism that conspired to destroy covenant faith. The apostasy of those Jews who sacrificed before the "desolat-

---

[5] Yee, *Jewish Feasts,* 83–92; J. C. Rylaarsdam, "Dedication, Feast of," *IDB* 1 (1962) 812–13.

[6] Yee, *Jewish Feasts,* 85.

ing sacrilege" (1 Macc 1:54) threatened the very identity of the Jewish nation as a people belonging to God alone. In the light of this experience,
when many succumbed to pagan influence and denied their faith, Dedication is both a celebration of victory and a reminder of failure. It is a summons to faith and an affirmation "Never Again!"[7] The memory of Judas'
victory gave to this feast a strong "messianic" outlook.[8] Judas was hailed
as "the savior of Israel" (1 Macc 9:21) and when he died he was mourned
with the refrain sung by David at the death of Israel's first king, Saul "How
is the mighty fallen" (1 Macc 9:21), "Your glory, O Israel, lies slain upon
your high places. How the mighty have fallen" (2 Sam 1:19).

Against the nationalistic messianic hopes evoked by the memories of
this feast, the major issue remains clearly focused on the identity of Jesus.
Remembering the exploits of Judas Mattathias, "the Jews" ask at first, "Is
he the Christ?" When Jesus answers openly in terms of his union with the
Father (v. 30), he is then accused of being a second Antiochus Epiphanes,
"you make yourself divine" (v. 33).[9]

Jesus—The Messianic Shepherd King

In reply to "the Jews'" request, "if you are the Christ tell us
plainly" (v. 24), Jesus indicates his works (v. 25). There was an expectation that when the Messiah appeared his authenticity would be
demonstrated by signs and wonders. Such an expectation lies behind the
earlier statement "When the Christ appears, will he do more signs than
this man has done?" (7:31).[10] Jesus does not respond in terms of "sign"
expectations, he speaks of his works (τὰ ἔργα). Signs and wonders direct attention to the wonder-worker. Jesus comes to complete the work
(τὸ ἔργον) of the Father (4:34), and this work is manifest in the many

[7] Yee, *Jewish Feasts,* 88.

[8] Nodet compares the differing interpretations of the Maccabean revolt given in
Maccabees 1 and 2. He argues that 1 Maccabees presents the feast as the missing
fourth pilgrimage festival celebrating the successful venture through the wilderness,
but it was subsumed within the celebration of Tabernacles. In the first century it was
celebrated like Tabernacles, but, with its strong messianic theme, the feast declined
after the failure of the Bar Kokhba revolt. See E. Nodet, "La Dédicace, les Maccabées
et le Messie," *RB* 93 (1986) 373–75.

[9] The lack of the definite articles suggests the use of ἄνθρωπος and θεόν as adjec-
tives: "you being human make yourself divine" (v. 33).

[10] Ashton, *Understanding,* 273–78, discusses the place of miraculous signs associated with eschatological figures such as the "prophet-like-Moses" and Elijah. There is no
clear evidence that such signs and wonders were to accompany the Messiah, but from the
comments in 7:31 it seems that this may have been a popular expectation with some.

works Jesus accomplishes.[11] Jesus' works witness that he is the sent one of the Father (5:36) and point beyond his own person to the one who sent him (5:19).

At a festival commemorating a military victory and looking to a future Messiah, Jesus' speaks again of the only messianic model he will ascribe to, that of the Shepherd King who will ultimately lay down his life for his sheep (10:11).[12] "Jesus will not fit the model of the expected Davidic shepherd-Messiah. He may be the Messiah, but he will exercise his messiahship by giving himself freely to death."[13] The shepherd image as a symbol of care and leadership was first applied to God (Gen 48:15; 49:24; Pss 23:1; 80:1). True leaders and kings of Israel were then called shepherds (2 Sam 5:2; 7:7) and the false leaders depicted as false shepherds (Jer 23:1,2; 50:6; Ezek 34:2, 5, 7-10). With the failure of these shepherds the promise was given that God would raise up true shepherds (Jer 23:4) and that God would be the shepherd of Israel (Ezek 34:12, 15). The promised Davidic king would be a shepherd (Ezek 34:23, 24), and even Cyrus, the one responsible for the rebuilding of Jerusalem and its Temple, was called shepherd (Isa 44:28).[14]

The Shepherd-King of Israel is now present in Jesus, and those who belong to him hear and follow his voice (10:3, 4, 27). But "the Jews" have never heard the Father's voice (5:37) since their father is the devil (8:44); nor do they listen and hear the Son.

The discussion has now moved from an initial query about Jesus' messianic status to a redefining of the Messiah as the long awaited Shepherd-King. Since Israel's primary Shepherd-King is God, Jesus can only claim to be the Shepherd-King because of his union with the Father. The power of God's hand displayed throughout Israel's history (cf. Exod 13:14; 15:6; Ps 118:15; Isa 48:13), is now in the hand of Jesus (vv. 28, 29).[15] Jesus' final words of identification with the Father affirm his true identity, "I and the Father are one" (v. 30). Jesus goes far beyond the expectations of the ini-

---

[11] Moloney, *Signs and Shadows,* 22.

[12] Schnackenburg, *Gospel,* 2:305, suggests that the readings for the Feast of Dedication utilized pastoral images; similarly Guilding, *The Fourth Gospel,* 129–32. On the kingship theme hinted at in the gospel and its links with the shepherd image, see A. Reinhartz, *The Word in the World: The Cosmological Tale in the Fourth Gospel,* Society of Biblical Literature Monograph Series 45 (Atlanta: Scholars Press, 1992) 110–12.

[13] Moloney, *Signs and Shadows,* 136.

[14] Koester, *Symbolism,* 16–17, explores the dynamic of the shepherd image as it recurs throughout the Gospel and the way in which it evokes various associations, both scripturally and culturally.

[15] Schwank [*Evangelium nach Johannes* (Ottilien: EOS, 1996) 293], develops the image of God's hand as a symbol of power.

tial inquiry of "the Jews." "His identity is found not in any traditional messianic title but in a unique, unparalleled relationship with God."[16]

Jesus' union with the Father is demonstrated in *the works* he performs in order to bring to completion *the work* of the Father. Pollard calls this a "moral sonship."[17] Jesus is also Son in a unique sense, in that he participates in the divine being of God, καὶ Θεὸς ἦν ὁ λόγος (1:1c).[18] In spite of the intimate union of Father and Son, the Gospel never collapses the distinction between them.[19] The distinction is there when Jesus speaks of the Father as "greater" and as the one who gave the sheep to the Son (10:29). The distinction in union is best expressed in terms such as mutuality or reciprocity. Again Pollard expresses this very carefully:

> Everywhere in John from the first verse of the prologue the unity of the Father and Son is never the undifferentiated unity of identity. It is a unity which permits distinctions. Always the relation between the Father and the Son is the paradoxical relation of distinction-in-unity.[20]

"The Jews" do not believe what they have been told (v. 25), nor the works they have seen (v. 26). They hear his words as blasphemy and take up stones against him as they had done once before in the feast of Tabernacles (8:59).

Jesus—The Consecrated and Sent One

The second section, while still a reply to the initial query "If you are the Christ tell us plainly" (v. 24), continues to develop the theme of Jesus' identity. "The Jews" state clearly their opposition to Jesus, "you being human, make yourself divine" (v. 33), which to them is blasphemy. This is the charge "the Jews" bring to Pilate demanding the death penalty, "We

[16] R. Kysar, "John 10:22-30," *Int* 43 (1989) 68.
[17] T. E. Pollard, "The Father-Son and God-Believer Relationships according to St. John: A brief study of John's use of Prepositions," *L'Évangile de Jean: Sources, rédaction, théologie,* ed. M. de Jonge, Bibliotheca Ephemeridum Theologicae Lovaniensis 44 (Gembloux: Duculot, 1977) 363.
[18] Through a careful exegesis of the Prologue and the anarthrous naming of God eight times in these first 18 verses (1a, b, 2, 6, 12, 13, 18a,b) Fennema establishes that deity is ascribed to the *logos,* so that the *logos* shares in the divinity of God. "He [the *logos*] is the only Son (μονογενής), who shares the deity (θεός) which has traditionally been ascribed only to God/the Father (ὁ θέος / πατήρ)." See D. A. Fennema, "John 1:18: 'God the Only Son'," *NTS* 31 (1985) 131.
[19] Painter maintains the unity and distinction by speaking of ontological equality and functional subordination. See J. Painter, "Tradition, history and interpretation in John 10," *The Shepherd Discourse,* 69.
[20] Pollard, "Father-Son," 367.

have a law, and by that law he ought to die, because he has **made himself** son of God" (19:7). To defend himself Jesus appeals to the witness of the Scriptures and quotes from LXX Ps 81:6, "I said, you are gods" (v. 34).[21] As Reim indicates, the context for this saying in the psalm sounds a warning to "the Jews." It is a psalm where God indicts the other gods for their judgments and refusal to listen. "Weil die Richter aber nicht hören, werden sie trotz der ehemaligen Bezeichnung als Götter und Kinder der Höchsten wie Menschen und Tyrannen sterben."[22] "The Jews," through their lack of hearing the voice of the shepherd, and their poor judgment in wanting to commit deicide, stand condemned.[23] Here, Jesus is using an argument following a rabbinic principle of arguing from the lesser to the greater *(a minori ad maius)*.[24] If the ones who receive the *logos* of God can be called "gods" how much more should the one who *is himself* God's *logos* be able to call himself "Son of God":

> If the word of God came to men, that they might be called gods, how can the very Word of God, who is with God, be otherwise than God? If by the word of God men become gods, if by fellowship they become gods, can He by whom they have fellowship not be God? (Augustine, *Homilies on the Gospel of John*, Tract. 48:9).[25]

---

[21] Ashton, *Understanding*, 147–50, discusses the possible identity of the ones addressed in this psalm: unjust judges, Israel, angels. He concludes that the "gods" are to be understood as divine beings who are members of God's heavenly court. Schuchard holds that the addressees are Israel's judges. He then reads this passage as a contrast between Jesus and Moses. See B. G. Schuchard, *Scripture Within Scripture: The Interrelationship of Form and Function in the Explicit Old Testament Citations in the Gospel of John*, Society of Biblical Literature Dissertation Series 133 (Atlanta: Scholars Press, 1992) 62–64. For a similar contrast between Jesus and Moses derived from this passage, see Boismard, *Moses or Jesus*, 105–6. In trying to identify the "gods" of the psalm, Ashton and Schuchard shift the focus away from Jesus' primary identity as 'the Word of God'. I maintain that the contrast is made between those who are merely recipients of the word, who can be called "gods" and the one who is the Word himself.

[22] G. Reim, *Studien Zum Alttestamentlichen Hintergrund des Johannesevangeliums* (Cambridge: Cambridge University Press, 1974) 23.

[23] As Stibbe notes, "the Jews," as portrayed in the narrative, have been trying to commit deicide throughout chs. 5 to 10 (*John*, 118). But note the earlier comments on the importance of reading "the Jews" as a narrative artifice and not as a generalized term depicting all followers of Judaism.

[24] Yee, *Jewish Feasts*, 91; Moloney, *Signs and Shadows*, 149; Manns, *L'Evangile*, 313–14.

[25] P. Schaff, ed. *Augustin [e sic]: Homilies on the Gospel of John, Homilies on the First Epistle of John, Soliloquies*, Nicene and Post-Nicene Fathers 7 (Peabody, Mass.: Hendrickson, 1995) .

In this study I have shown the narrative technique of using Israel's cult to point to Jesus' identity. This same technique is used in verse 36. Jesus, speaking during the feast commemorating the reconsecration of the altar and temple, describes himself as the Consecrated and Sent One, ὃν ὁ πατὴρ ἡγίασεν καὶ ἀπέστειλεν εἰς τὸν κόσμον. In the restoration program following the victory of the Maccabees, the same verb ἁγιάζω is used to describe the consecration of the Temple courts, καὶ τὰς αὐλὰς ἡγίασαν (1 Macc 4:48, similarly 3 Macc 2:9, 16). The very word central to the celebration of this feast of Dedication is now applied to Jesus. The Mosaic Tabernacle and the Solomonic Temple had also been consecrated by God (Ps 45:4; 2 Chron 7:20; 30:8) and filled with God's glory (Exod 40:34-35; 2 Chron 7:3). Jesus, the tabernacling presence of God in the world, is the new locus of God's glory (1:14). As in the Tabernacle and the Temple, God's glory dwells in him, consecrating him as a new House of God.

The one whom Jesus calls "Father," "the Jews" recognize as God, as shown by their readiness to stone him for blasphemy. Jesus is therefore implicitly calling himself a son of God. His sonship has a far deeper sense than the general sonship applied to all Jews and to Jewish kings in particular. Jesus claims a unique oneness with the Father (v. 30) that gives his sonship a particular sense. As Obermann states:

> Dieses Eins-Sein Jesu mit dem Vater ist mehr als ein im ethischen oder moralischen Sinn verstandenes Gleichgesinnt-Sinn . . . Die hier angesprochene Einheit ist wesentlich eine Einheit im Ursprung (so 1,1-3 mit 1,12; 7,29) und im Wesen (z.b. 8,8.19).[26]

Jesus supports his claims of sonship by once again appealing to his works (v. 37; cf. v. 25). Because Jesus is son of the Father, he does the work of his Father. The works of the son are evidence of his paternity. This principle has run throughout the feasts of "the Jews." In the Sabbath controversy of chapter 5, Jesus had said, the son can do "only what he sees the Father doing" (5:19). Jesus' opponents during Tabernacles deny the truth of his identity and wish to kill him and so reveal that their father is the devil (8:44). The works Jesus has done in giving fuller life and forgiveness on the Sabbath (ch. 5), in giving bread to the multitude at Passover (ch. 6), and in giving light to a man born in darkness during Tabernacles (ch. 9), should be sufficient for his opponents to recognize in

---

[26] Obermann, *Die christologische Erfüllung,* 171. See also the discussion by P. Meyer, "'The Father': The Presentation of God in the Fourth Gospel," *Exploring the Gospel of John: In Honour of D. Moody Smith,* ed. R. A Culpepper and C. C. Black, (Louisville: Westminster John Knox, 1996) 255–73.

him the God of their festivals. They should by now know and understand that "the Father is in me and I am in the Father" (v. 36).

Within the Feast of Tabernacles there was a movement beyond the narrative time to a future gift of the Spirit, when the disciples, like Jesus, could be providers of living water (7:37-39). In the Feast of Dedication, there is no such prolepsis, but it is important to note that the words used of Jesus, as the Consecrated and Sent One (10:36), will later be applied to the disciples. In Jesus' prayer to the Father, he uses the same verbs ἁγιάζω and ἀποστέλλω, of his disciples as he prays that they may be consecrated in truth (17:17, 19) and sent into the world (17:18). They are to be given the glory given to the Son, and they are to be drawn into a unity with Father and Son (17:22-23). There will come a time when Jesus is no longer present in the world, but the disciples, who remain in the world (cf. 17:11, 15), will continue to be a consecrated presence of the Son in the world (17:17). How this is to happen remains to be unfolded, but this present chapter introduces themes, applied here to Jesus, which will recur later and be applied to the disciples.

"The Jews" respond to Jesus' words by trying to arrest him, as they had done previously at the feast of Tabernacles (7:32, 44; 8:20). Jesus then moves out of the Temple, away from Jerusalem and to the east across the Jordan (10:40). This movement of one who is the consecrated dwelling-place of God's glory is ominous. During the feast of Tabernacles Jesus is within the Temple (7:14). Following his initial confrontation with "the Jews" he moves outside (8:59). At the feast of Dedication Jesus walks in the colonnades around the perimeter of the Temple Courts (10:23). With the final refusal of "the Jews" to believe either his words or his works, Jesus permanently leaves the Temple Mount. He goes east, probably crossing Mount Olives and then across the Jordan. Jesus' movement from within the Temple, to the colonnades, then east across the Jordan traces the path of God's glory when it left the Solomonic Temple prior to its destruction by the Babylonians. Ezekiel described a similar progressive movement:

> Then the glory of the LORD went forth from the threshold of the house, and stood over the cherubim. And the cherubim lifted up their wings and mounted up from the earth in my sight as they went forth, with the wheels beside them; and they stood at the door of the east gate of the house of the LORD; and the glory of the God of Israel was over them (Ezek 10:18-19).

> And the glory of the LORD went up from the midst of the city, and stood upon the mountain which is on the east side of the city (Ezek 11:23).

God's glory was then seen by Ezekiel among the exiles in Babylon following the destruction of Jerusalem (Ezek 1:1-28). In the Gospel, God's glory will next be manifested in the hour of Jesus' death and resurrection, prefigured in the next section of the Gospel in the raising of Lazarus.

Conclusion

During the cycle of Israel's feasts, throughout chapters 5 to 10, Jesus has come up to his Father's House in obedience to the requirements of Torah. He has celebrated Israel's festivals and revealed himself as the one fulfilling Israel's festal traditions. He has offered life and judgment on Sabbath, bread during Passover, light and water at Tabernacles, and his own consecrated presence, which is the presence of Israel's God, during Dedication. The narrative has shown that during this time with 'his own' "the Jews" have refused his offer. In their blindness they refuse to see the glory of God now revealed in their midst in the person of Jesus as witnessed by his words and works. Within the feast of Dedication, Jesus twice affirms that in his very person Israel encounters the presence of the Father (10:30, 38). The God of Israel's festivals has become incarnate in their midst, no longer in symbols or rituals but in the *sarx* of Jesus. The year's cycle of feasts comes to its dramatic climax in this revelation "I and the Father are one" (v. 30 cf. 38), and "the Jews" give their definitive response, "they tried to arrest him" (v. 39). The words of the Prologue are now fulfilled, "he came to his own and his own did not receive him" (1:11). At a festival reaffirming their faith in Israel's God and repudiating idolatry, "the Jews" have rejected Jesus and in so doing have rejected the Father. The glory of the God of Israel, revealed in Jesus, permanently leaves the Temple. The cultic institutions of Israel are left emptied of the reality they once symbolized and celebrated.

My Father's House

JOHN 14:1-31

Chapter 14 falls within Jesus' final meal and discourse. The setting was established earlier in chapter 13: "Jesus, knowing the hour had come to depart out of this world to the Father, having loved his own, who were in the world, he loved them to the end" (εἰς τέλος) (13:1). In the previous chapters I have shown that the actual settings described in the narrative interact with the christology being presented, as the cultic setting and its symbols are reinterpreted in terms of Jesus' identity. This same narrative technique continues in chapter 14. In the context of a final meal among his friends (15:15) Jesus will speak of a new depth of intimacy only possible through his departure.

Chapters 14, 15, and 16 of the Fourth Gospel use a number of images (παροιμία) (16:25) such as the vine and the branches (15:1-11) and the woman in childbirth (16:21). The references to "my Father's house" and its "many rooms" belong to this same constellation of παροιμία and cannot simply be understood as Jesus' return to heaven and his preparation of a heavenly place for his disciples. Interpretations along these lines fail to give full weight to the figurative language of the verse and its context in a highly symbolic Gospel narrative. In what follows I will develop a reading of this verse that allows the Gospel itself to provide the primary hermeneutical clues to its interpretation. In the words of James McCaffrey, "The evangelist is his own best commentator."[1]

Chapter 14 develops around three statements of Jesus (vv. 1-3; 18-21; 27-28), with a brief conclusion (vv. 29-31), which also functions as a

---

[1] McCaffrey, *The House With Many Rooms,* 27.

157

bridge to the continuation of the narrative. The first and third statements form a frame around the entire passage; there is the repetition of the phrase "Let not your hearts be troubled" (v. 1 and v. 27), and in both statements there is the teaching of Jesus' departure and his return to the disciples, "I go to prepare a place for you" (v. 2) "I will come again" (v. 3); "I go away, and I will come to you" (v. 28). Following the first two statements there is a response by the disciples leading into a dialogue with Thomas and Philip (vv. 5-14) then with Judas (vv. 22-24). Each of these dialogues concludes with the promise of the Paraclete (vv. 15-17; 25-26).

The structure can be shown as follows[2]:

Statement 1. vv. 1-4
"Let not your hearts be troubled. . ." (v. 1)

> Response: Dialogue Thomas and Philip (vv. 5-14)
> Promise of the Paraclete (vv. 15-17)

Statement 2. vv. 18-21
> "I will not leave you orphans" (v. 18)

> Response: Dialogue with Judas (vv. 22-24)
> Promise of the Paraclete (vv. 25-26)

Statement 3. vv. 27-28
"Let not your hearts be troubled. . ." (v. 27)

Two Paradoxes Raised

The three statements create two paradoxes. First, they speak of Jesus' going away to the Father:

- I go to prepare a place for you (v. 2)
- the world will see me no more (v. 19)
- I go away (v. 28)

At the same time they promise a return to and presence with the disciples:

- I will come again (v. 3)
- I will not leave you orphans (ὀρφανούς) (v. 18)
- I will come to you (v. 28)

---

[2] As stated in my methodology, I am taking the text in its final form and trying to perceive in its current arrangement the thinking that gave it this literary coherence. The Last Discourse shows obvious signs of editorial development. For a discussion on the tensions and disjunctions in the text see Brown, *Gospel,* 2:581–604. A diachronic analysis of the Discourse attempting to explain the problems in the text we now have can be found in Segovia, *Farewell,* 319–28. See also Schnackenburg, *Gospel,* 3:7–15; 89–93.

But there is no sense that these two locations—presence with the Father, and with the disciples—are mutually exclusive. The Father does not send Jesus again, or gift the world a second time with the Son (3:16-17). The function of being the sent one and gift of the Father passes to the Paraclete (vv. 15, 25). In a way that is not yet clear, Jesus will be able to be present with the Father and with the disciples.

The second paradox arises from the first. Even as the discourse promises a future presence, there is no denying that there will also be an experience of absence, "The approaching physical absence of Jesus is the substratum of the farewell discourse."[3] The function and tone of the discourse is to prepare the disciples for this absence and offer consolation. The second paradox is, therefore: How can there be presence in absence?

The key to penetrating the first paradox, of Jesus' presence simultaneously with the Father and with the disciples, lies in the Johannine concept of mutual indwelling, expressed in the verb μένω and its cognates. The key to the paradox of presence-in-absence lies in the role of the Paraclete. The two concepts are inter-related but will be dealt with separately.

The Divine Indwelling

Forms of the verb μένω with the sense of "dwelling" occur primarily in chapters 14 and 15 (14:10, 17, 23, 25; 15:4 [x3], 5, 6, 7 [x2], 9, 10). The mutual abiding of Jesus and the Father (14:10; 15:10), and Jesus and his disciples (15:4, 5, 6, 7, 9, 10), enables the evangelist to hold together the apparently contradictory statements of presence with the Father and also with the disciples. The departure of Jesus will be no ordinary departure; in a way still to be clarified in the ongoing narrative, Jesus' going to the Father will also be a coming to the disciples.

The theology of mutual indwelling developed in chapters 14 and 15 is introduced in both chapters with a παροιμία, firstly the house of the Father and its many rooms (μοναί 14:2), and then the vine and branches (15:1, 5). In chapter 14 the Father, Jesus and the Paraclete are the ones abiding, with Jesus (v. 10) and the believer (vv. 17, 23, 25) the locus of their presence. In chapter 15 it is the believers who are called to abide (vv. 4, 5, 6, 7, 9, 10) and the locus of their abiding is Jesus. The first image "my Father's house and its many rooms" introduces the theme of the abiding of the *divine presence* and I will argue that this image draws upon and transforms Israel's Temple traditions.

[3] R. H. Gundry, "'In my Father's House are many Monai' (John 14:2)," *ZNW* 58 (1967) 68–69.

The second image "the vine and branches" describes the community of believers abiding in Jesus as branches in a vine.

Again the Gospel draws upon and transforms the traditional designation of the community of Israel as the Lord's vineyard (Jer 12:10; 32:15; Isa 5:1-7). The two images are related to each other in that they both become the vehicle for developing the Johannine theology of indwelling, first from the perspective of the divine presence (ch. 14), and then from the perspective of the believing community (ch. 15). The metaphor of the vine and branches is more easily perceived as a symbol since it makes no sense to speak of dwelling or abiding "in" a vine. The metaphorical use of the term "my Father's house" is not so readily perceived as it is possible to dwell or abide in a house. Even when the term "house" is understood as an image it is usually taken to mean the heavenly abode of God. Such an understanding does not give sufficient attention to the specifically Johannine context of this image and the fact that the image of my Father's house has previously occurred within this Gospel.

My Father's House

In chapter 14, the phrase ἐν τῇ οἰκίᾳ τοῦ πατρός μου needs to be interpreted in the light of a similar expression τὸν οἶκον τοῦ πατρός μου (2:16), which referred to the Jerusalem Temple. Even in this earlier scene, there was an obvious process of reinterpretating the meaning of Temple. The scene in chapter 2 began in the physical Temple building (ἱερῷ) but concluded with the enigmatic phrase "he spoke of the temple (ναοῦ) of his body" (2:21). In this Fourth Gospel the Temple means more than a physical building. In the early part of the Gospel, beginning with the announcement of the *logos* tabernacling with us (1:14) and reiterated in 2:21, the function of providing a locus for the divine presence shifted from the Jerusalem Temple to the living flesh of Jesus.[4]

The choice of terms οἶκος (2:16) and οἰκία (14:2) immediately resonates with the dominant term for the Jerusalem Temple in the Hebrew text—the House of the Lord (בית יהוה).[5] The very naming of this place as "House" indicates its function as a dwelling for the Divine Presence, appropriately furnished in all its accessories:

All of them are shaped as furniture of a dwelling-place and testify that the house is really arranged as a habitation: the lamps for light, the tables for

---

[4] See the earlier discussion in ch. 4 "The Temple of His body."

[5] The terminology בית יהוה occurs 231 times while the expression היכל occurs 60 times.

bread, the small altar for incense (an item which was not lacking in any luxurious residence in antiquity), the altars bearing the epithet of God's tables (Ez 41,22; 44,16; Mal 1,7), the sacrifices being called God's bread (Lv 21,21-22; Num 28,2), the typical image of the gods as eating the fat of the sacrifices and drinking the libations of wine (Deut 32,38) and the like.[6]

Because of Jesus' identity as the incarnate *logos* and his unique relationship with God, the Temple, which Israel calls "the Lord's House," Jesus can call "my Father's house," a term that is never used of the Temple in the Hebrew text. In speaking of the Temple in such familiar terms, Jesus proclaims that an entirely new and unique situation has arrived.

The term "my Father's house" is open to further levels of meaning. In the Scriptures this phrase usually means the group of people who make up the household, such as the family and servants, even the future descendants.[7] It is rarely used in the sense of a building. In speaking of the Temple with this phrase, in chapter 2, the evangelist began to move away from Temple-as-building to something more personal and relational. In chapter 2 the image of Temple shifted to a single person, Jesus (2:21). In chapter 14 this movement continues and extends beyond one person to a group of people in a household or familial relationship.[8]

Chapter 14 develops this personal and relational understanding even further with the shift from the word οἶκος to οἰκία.[9] In the Gospel the term οἶκος is used only with the sense of a building, the Temple building (2:16, 17) and also the house at Bethany (11:20). The term οἰκία is used with a more fluid range of meanings in that it can mean both a physical building (11:31; 12:3), and also the household (4:53; 8:35).[10] Whereas in

---

[6] M. Haran, "The Divine Presence in the Israelite Cult and the Cultic Institutions," *Bib* 50 (1969) 255.

[7] For example, "So Joseph said to his brothers and to his father's house, 'I will go and tell Pharaoh and say to him, My brothers and my father's house have come to me'" (Gen 46:31); similarly, Gen 24:38; 28:21; Josh 2:13; Judg 6:15; 9:18; 16:31; 1 Sam 22:15; 2 Sam 14:9; (1 Chr 28:4). Often the expression "father's house" is translated as "family" in the RSV.

[8] Dettwiler is a recent commentator who develops the imagery of this verse in some detail. He presents the root-metaphor of 14:2 as "house" but while elaborating on the imagery of the "house" and its cultural meaning, he does not extend it further to the sense of a "household." He sees the "dwellings" as a metaphor for religious salvation. See A. Dettwiler, *Die Gegenwart des Erhöhten: Eine exegetische Studie zu den johanneischen Abschiedsreden (Joh 13:31–16:33) unter besonderer Berücksichtigung ihres Relecture-Charakters* (Göttingen: Vandenhoeck & Ruprecht, 1995) 155–56.

[9] O. Michel, "οἶκος, οἰκία," *TDNT* 5 (1964–1976) 119–34.

[10] Agreeing with Gundry, "My Father's House," 71.

2:16 the initial reference was to the οἶκος in the sense of a building, here in chapter 14, through the change of the word to οἰκία there is a continuation of the movement begun in 2:21 to understand the phrase, "my Father's house," not as a building but as a quality of personal relationships.[11] In Gundry's words, "The father's house is no longer heaven, but God's household or family."[12]

Many dwellings—μοναὶ πολλαί

While μοναί can mean the physical chambers within a house, and so could at one level be understood as many rooms within a physical Temple building, the shift from building to personal relationships suggested by the phrase "in my Father's house" requires a similar shift in understanding what the evangelist means by "dwellings" (μοναί). The chapter itself and chapter 15 provide the best interpretive clue to the particular Johannine meaning of this phrase. Chapters 14 and 15 use derivatives of μένω and μονή to describe a variety of interpersonal relationships between the Father, Jesus, Paraclete, and believers. The relationships are usually described with the translation "abiding," or "dwelling." These various relationships are appropriately introduced by the phrase "many dwellings" (μοναὶ πολλαί).

As stated earlier, chapter 14 focuses on a series of divine dwellings:

- the Father who dwells (μένων) in Jesus (v. 10)
- the Paraclete who dwells (μένει) with believers, and in the future will dwell in them (v. 17)
- the Father and Jesus who will make their dwelling (μονὴν) with the believer (v. 23)
- Jesus dwells with the disciples (v. 25)[13]

McCaffrey's analysis of the metaphor "my Father's house" does not give sufficient attention to the subject of the verb μένω and the action thereby suggested. He, along with many commentators, would see the

---

[11] McCaffrey, *The House With Many Rooms,* 31.

[12] Gundry, "My Father's House," 70.

[13] The imagery of μοναὶ πολλαί continues into ch. 15 where the verb μένω is again used to describe the believers dwelling in Jesus. The shift to the community of believers is reflected by a shift in the metaphor from "house" to "vine" since the vine was a common image for the community of Israel. On the use of this image see A. Jaubert, "L'Image de la Vigne (Jean 15)," *Oikonomia. Heilsgeschichte als Thema der Theologie. Oscar Cullmann zum 65. Geburtstag gewidmet,* ed. F. Christ (Hamburg-Bergstedt: H. Reich Verlag, 1967) 93–96.

metaphor as a reference to God's heavenly dwelling, where the believers
will abide at some future time:

> The Father's house with the many rooms of the first member (Jn 14, 2a)
> designates the heavenly temple as the inner spiritual "space" where Jesus
> abides permanently in union with his Father, and where there are also pos-
> sibilities (enough and more than enough) for all believers to abide there
> spiritually in union with Jesus.[14]

Against this "heavenly" dwelling place, it must be noted that the subject
of the verb μένω, throughout chapter 14, is not the *believer* but *God*. The
action therefore is not the *believers* coming to dwell in God's heavenly
abode, but the *Father,* the *Paraclete* and *Jesus* coming to dwell with the
believers. It is a "descending" movement from the divine realm to the
human, not an "ascending" movement from the human to the divine. In
the words of Andreas Dettwiler, it is a "grosse Bewegung von der Tran-
szendenz zur Immanenz Gottes."[15] Given that the emphasis in chapter 14
is on the divine dwelling with the believers, it is not altogether surprising
to find this theology introduced with an image that draws on Israel's symbol of the divine presence in its midst—the Temple, Israel's house of the
Lord, now renamed by Jesus as the house of my Father.[16]

From the above analysis the phrase "in my Father's house there are
many dwellings" is best understood, within the context of this Gospel, to
mean a series of interpersonal relationships made possible because of the
indwelling of the Father, Jesus and the Paraclete with the believer. The divine indwelling in the midst of a believing community makes it appropriate to speak of the community as a living Temple. The community is the
House (household) of God.[17] Aune goes so far as to claim that this image
is so all pervasive that it is the self-perception of the believing community. "It is probable that in John 14:2 (and also 8:35) the term οἰκίᾳ (τοῦ
πατρός) reflects the self-designation of the Johannine community."[18]

---

[14] McCaffrey, *The House With Many Rooms,* 220. Similarly Schnackenburg,
Gospel, 3:60–61; Brown, *Gospel,* 2:625; Lindars, *Gospel,* 470; Pfitzner, *John,* 238;
Segovia, *Farewell,* 82.

[15] Dettwiler, *Die Gegenwart des Erhöhten,* 202.

[16] In his analysis of 14:2, Gundry does not address the metaphorical use of "my
Father's house" against its earlier reference to the Temple (2:16).

[17] To ensue that the term "House" has the more personal sense of family rather than
building I will use the word "household" which is the more frequent meaning of οἰκίᾳ
in the Fourth Gospel.

[18] D. E. Aune, *The Cultic Setting of Realized Eschatology in Early Christianity,*
Supplements to Novum Testamentum 28 (Leiden: E. J. Brill, 1972) 130. Other passages

The familial language of the discourse supports this "household" interpretation. The discourse begins with Jesus gathering his own (τοὺς ἰδίους) and in 13:33 they are called children (τεκνία). These words recall the words of the Prologue (1:11) and the affirmation that those of his own who do receive the *logos* are given the power to become τέκνα θεοῦ. With the departure of Judas in 13:30, those gathered with Jesus are the ones receptive to his word and so in 13:33 they can be called τεκνία. The language of family relationships continues in 14:18 with the word "orphans" to describe a state of Jesus' absence, followed later by the allegory of the woman in childbirth (16:21).

To prepare a place for you

In the M.T. the terminology of a *prepared place* is used almost exclusively of the Ark. The one exception is found in Exodus where from the context the phrase refers to the land (Exod 23:20). All other M.T. references are to the Ark. *"David built houses for himself in the city of David, and he prepared a place for the ark of God and pitched a tent for it"* (1 Chr 15:1 also 15:3, 12; 2 Chr 1:4). The LXX extends these references to include a place prepared for the building of the Temple. "And Solomon began to build the house of the LORD in Jerusalem in the mount of Amoriah where the LORD appeared to his father David, in the place which David had prepared in the threshing floor of Orna the Jebusite" (2 Chr 3:1).

The entire process of constructing the Temple is called a preparation, "Now all the work had been prepared from the day when the foundation was laid, until Solomon finished the house of the LORD" (2 Chr 8:16).[19] Ark and Temple can both be seen as a *prepared place* since the Temple prepared by David and Solomon is a copy of the Tent prepared by God, "You have given a command to build a Temple on your holy mountain, and an altar in the city of your habitation, a copy of the holy tent that you prepared from the beginning" (Wis 9:8).

The task of forming a people is also called a preparation, "And you have prepared (ἡτοίμασας) for yourself your people Israel, to be a people forever" (2 Sam 7:24). Temple preparation and people preparation are very clearly linked in the description of the Temple purification during the religious reforms at the time of Hezekiah. Following a long description of the sanctification of the Temple and its sacrifices (2 Chr 29:3-35),

---

that reflect the use of οἶκος as an image of the community are 1 Pet 2:5; 4:17; 1 Tim 3:15; Heb 3:2-6.

[19] Further references to temple-building as preparation can be found in 1 Kgs 5:18; 6:9; 1 Chr 22:2, 5, 14; 28:2; 29:2, 3, 16; 2 Chr 2:9; 31:11.

the chronicler adds, "And Hezekiah and all the people rejoiced, because God had prepared the people" (2 Chr 29:36). The first reference above to building/preparing a people is in the context of the promise of a future Temple to be built by David's son (2 Sam 7). In this context the word 'house' is also used with two meanings, referring to both a Temple building and a family dynasty. The later reference in Chronicles is linked to restoring and sanctifying the Temple. Temple-building and people-building enable the divine presence to dwell with Israel. Just as the terminology of "in my Father's house" juxtaposes the imagery of Temple and people in the household, the concept of "preparation" also links Temple-building to people-building.

The word τόπος also has theological significance both in the Hebrew Scriptures and within this Gospel. In an earlier encounter with the Samaritan woman, I discussed the use of τόπος and the place of true worship (4:20). In chapter 11 Jesus' opponents are concerned that, if they allow Jesus to continue, the Romans will destroy their *holy place* (11:48). The irony is that, through their plotting, they themselves destroy the true holy place in this narrative, so fulfilling the words of Jesus in chapter 2, "Destroy this temple" (2:19). In their desire to protect their Temple, they become the destroyers of the true Temple.

In the ancestral narratives there are two scenes associated with the future site of the Temple where the word "place" features prominently and suggests more than a neutral locality. The first story is that of the sacrifice of Isaac (Gen 22:3-14). The Mount of Moriah, the Temple Mount according to Chronicles (2 Chr 3:1), is the place where Abraham is told to sacrifice his beloved son (v. 2) his only son (v. 12). The word "place" (מקום) occurs four times in this short episode (vv. 3, 4, 9, 14). In examining the exchange with "the Jews" during Tabernacles I pointed out a God/Abraham typology. The Gospel also exploits a Jesus/Isaac typology. In the Fourth Gospel, like Isaac, Jesus bears the wood of his own sacrifice and in the description of Golgotha the evangelist repeats the word *topos* giving it greater emphasis. "So they took Jesus and he went out, bearing his own cross, to the place called the place of a Skull" (19:17).[20] The second scene from the ancestral narratives which emphasizes the word *topos* is Jacob's dream at Bethel (Gen 28:11-19). "Surely the LORD is in this place. . . this is none other than the house of God" (vv. 16-17). He called

---

[20] A further unique Johannine insight into Isaac typology is the reference to the binding of Jesus by soldiers in Gethsemane (18:12); the Synoptics simply say they seized him (Mark 14:46; Matt 26:50; Luke 22:54). Further discussion on the Isaac typology will emerge in the following chapter.

the name of that place Beth-el" (v. 19). In these narratives, the term "place" has a cultic significance that receives its full meaning in the Jerusalem Temple.

The Temple is frequently simply called "the Holy place" (e.g., Exod 26:33; Leviticus 16; 1 Kgs 8:6, 8, 10); the place where God will set his name (e.g., Exod 20:24; Deut 12:5, 11, 21); and God's dwelling place (e.g., Ps 74:7; 76:2; 132:7; Ezek 37:27). In the discussion on the background of the phrase "to prepare," reference was made to the passages from Micah and Isaiah where the eschatological Temple was the place for the gathering of the nations. Such an understanding lies behind the prayer of Nehemiah:

> Gather together our scattered people, set free those who are slaves among the Gentiles, look on those who are rejected and despised, and let the Gentiles know that you are our God. Punish those who oppress and are insolent with pride. Plant your people in your holy place, as Moses promised (2 Macc 1:27-29; see also 2 Macc 2:17-18).

From this survey of the Scriptural background to the words "prepare" and "place" it is possible to see in the phrase "to prepare a place for you" a clear allusion to the Jewish Temple traditions, particularly the later traditions of the Temple as the eschatological gathering place which God will prepare for his people. There is also evidence from the Targums testifying to a strong Palestinian tradition where the phrase "to prepare a place" is associated firstly with the Exodus wanderings and then, by extension, to the Temple sanctuary, the place where God's name and God's *Shekinah* would dwell[21]:

> "My presence will go with you, and I will give you rest" (Exod 33:14), becomes:

> "The glory of my Shekinah will accompany amongst you and will prepare a resting-place for you" (*Tg. Neof.* Exod 33:14).

Similarly,

> "And the ark of the covenant of the LORD went before them three days' journey, to seek out a resting place for them" (Num 10:33), becomes:

> "And the ark of the covenant journeyed before them a three days' journeying distance to prepare for them a place, a place of encampment" (*Tg. Neof.* Num 10:33).[22]

---

[21] M. McNamara, "'To prepare a resting-place for you'. A Targumic expression and John 14:2f.," *Milltown Studies* 3 (1979) 106–7.

[22] In John 2:19 Jesus spoke of raising the Temple "in three days." The phrase may have its basis in this passage referring to the ark, rather than in the more traditional "on the third day" terminology that is not used in the Johannine Easter narratives.

Difficulty in dating the Targums prevents firm conclusions but, according to McNamara, the use of this paraphrase across three Targums and the Syriac Pershitta, shows "that the expression 'to prepare a resting place for you' was an established interpretation in the New Testament period."[23]

Taken together, the two key phrases of 14:2—"in my father's house there are many dwellings," and "I go to prepare a place for you," show a uniquely Johannine concern with the Temple, reinterpreted in a radically new way as the household of God. When the disciples fail to understand Jesus' words, his explanation leads into the promise of the Paraclete and an indication that "my Father's house(hold)" will be established through the indwelling of the Father, Jesus and Paraclete with the believer (14:17, 23, 25). A prepared people becomes a fitting "holy place" for the dwelling of God, as surely as the prepared building was in the time of Solomon. In some way, the action of Jesus "going" to the Father, is simultaneously the action when he "prepares/builds" the "place" (Temple) for the disciples. Dettwiler expresses this precisely: "Es werden zwei Aktivitäten Jesu, jeweils mitsamt ihrer Finalität, genannt."[24] The Father's house will no longer be a construction of stones, but will be a *household* of many interpersonal relationships (μοναί) where the divine presence can dwell within believers.

Temple-as-Community Precedents

The shift of Temple imagery from a building to a community is not without some precedents both within Judaism and pre-Johannine Christianity. Firmly rooted in Israel's theology is the concept of Israel as a holy people, a kingdom of priests. "You shall be for me a priestly kingdom and a holy nation" (Exod 19:6; also Deut 28:9; Isa 62:12; 63:18; Wis 10:15; 3 Macc 2:6). The holiness of the people is linked to the presence of God's sanctuary in their midst. "Have them make me a sanctuary so that I may dwell among them" (Exod 28:8). Ezekiel's vision of a restored Israel has as its geographical and religious center the sanctuary where God will dwell (Ezek 37:26-27). These texts still speak of a sanctuary as something distinct from the people. But other texts do not make such a sharp distinction and begin to make possible the Temple-as-community image found in later Jewish and Christian writing.

In discussing the background to the word ἑτοιμάσαι, I noted two texts that applied the language of Temple-preparation to the people (2 Sam 7:24 and 2 Chr 29:36). Even more significant is the passage in Sirach:

---

[23] McNamara, "To prepare a resting-place," 106–7.
[24] Dettwiler, *Die Gegenwart des Erhöhten*, 148.

And so was Jeshua the son of Jozadak;
in their days they built the house and raised a temple (people) holy to the
Lord,
prepared for everlasting glory (Sir 49:12). [25]

Some manuscripts have the word people, (λαός) while others have
Temple (ναός).[26] In late second Temple Judaism it was possible to speak
of the *lifting up* of both a holy Temple and a holy people. A community
perceiving themselves as a new Temple, prepared by the *lifting up* of Jesus
in death, could well look back to this text and its many associations with
Johannine terms: Jesus (Ἰησοῦς), house (οἶκον), lift up (ἀνύψωσαν), prepare (ἡτοιμασμένον), glory (δόξαν).

Qumran

The writings that have emerged from the excavations at Qumran also
testify to a late Jewish concept of the community-as-Temple. In three of
the Qumran scrolls there are clear references that point to the community
understanding itself as a living Temple; the Community Rule 1QS 8:4-10;
9:3-6; 5:5-7; the Damascus Scroll CD 3:18-4:10, and the Habakkuk Commentary 1QpHab 12:3. These documents describe the community as a
holy house for Israel (1QS 8:5); the holy of holies for Aaron (1QS 8:6); a
most holy dwelling for Aaron (1QS 8:9).[27] The Temple-as-community
imagery found in these scrolls is more functional than the imagery found
in the Fourth Gospel. The Johannine text develops the imagery of Temple-
as-people around the concept of divine indwelling expressed in the various forms of μένω in chapters 14 and 15. The Qumran literature does not
have this concept. Their notion of community-as-Temple is tied up with
the concept of sacrifice and atonement. They, as a community, perform
the functions of the Temple, "in order to offer a pleasant aroma" (1QS
8:9); "they shall make atonement for all" (1QS 5:6). When this community made its break with the Jerusalem Temple and its priesthood, they
faced the question about atonement—Where is atonement to be made?

[25] οὕτως Ἰησοῦς υἱὸς Ἰωσεδεκ, οἳ ἐν ἡμέραις αὐτῶν ᾠκοδόμησαν οἶκον καὶ
ἀνύψωσαν **λαὸν** (**ναὸν**) ἅγιον κυρίῳ ἡτοιμασμένον εἰς δόξαν αἰῶνος.

[26] ναόν A L' alii Zi; λαον B-S V 336 Syh Sa Aeth. See J. Siegler, ed. *Sapientia Iesu
Filii Sirach.* Vol. X11, 2, Septuaginta Vetus Testamentum Graecum (Göttingen: Vandenhoeck & Ruprecht, 1980) 356.

[27] A more detailed discussion on these scrolls and their Temple allusions can be
found in D. Juel, *Messiah and Temple,* Society of Biblical Literature Dissertation Series 31 (Missoula, Mont.: Scholars Press, 1977) 159–68.

One response of the community was to rekindle hopes for a renewed or new sanctuary where legitimate sacrifices could be offered. But another response seems to have been to reinterpret cultic imagery and to "spiritualise" sacrifice, substituting proper obedience to the Law for bloody sacrifices. Part of this second response seems to have been the development of the notion that the community was the temple, the place where proper atonement could be made.[28]

A further significant difference between the Qumran community-as-Temple imagery and that found within the Christian Scriptures is that this image does not apply to the entire community but to a select group within the community called the "council of union."[29] "This restriction of the 'community-Temple' ideology to a definite focal group within the larger membership emerges as a characteristic feature of Qumran."[30]

Pauline Literature

In turning to the pre-Johannine Christian literature that uses Temple-as-community imagery there are a number of significant passages in the Pauline literature:

Do you not know that you are God's temple and that God's Spirit dwells in you? If anyone destroys God's temple, God will destroy that person. For God's temple is holy, and you are that temple (1 Cor 3:16-17).

Or do you not know that your body is a temple of the Holy Spirit within you, which you have from God, and that you are not your own? (1 Cor 6:19).

What agreement has the temple of God with idols? For we are the temple of the living God; as God said, "I will live in them and walk among them, and I will be their God, and they shall be my people" (2 Cor 6:16).

In him the whole structure is joined together and grows into a holy temple in the LORD; in whom you also are built together in the Spirit into a dwelling place for God (Eph 2:21).

Each of these passage calls the community a Temple and does so not because of its function, but because God (2 Cor 6:16) or the Holy Spirit (1 Cor 3:16; 6:19; Eph 2:21), dwells in its midst. Compared to the Qumran ideas, this is quite a different and enriched notion of Temple. These texts have moved away from what the community does, how it functions as Temple, to what God has done by dwelling within them and so building

---

[28] Juel, *Messiah and Temple*, 166.

[29] Byrne, "'Building' and 'Temple' imagery," 146.

[30] Byrne, "'Building' and 'Temple' imagery," 171.

them into a Temple. This Pauline concept is closer to the Johannine understanding than Qumran, as it defines Temple in terms of a relationship of indwelling rather than in terms of how the community functions.

Three of these four Pauline passages relate Temple to the indwelling of the Spirit. Here we may be touching on the initial impetus within the Christian community to see itself as the new eschatological Temple, for both Spirit and Temple were perceived as gifts in the last days. It would be a simple step for a community experiencing pneumatic gifts to interpret this as the dawn of the *eschaton* and to relook at and reinterpret Israel's Temple hopes. During the time of the Pauline writings the Jerusalem Temple still existed. Paul's image of the community-as-Temple is not in opposition to the existing Temple but is used to promote the living of holy lives. Paul's primary image of community and its relation to Christ is the body.[31]

The Johannine community existed in a different milieu. The Temple had been destroyed and there was conflict between some Jews and the Jewish-Christian believers. The Jewish community, led by the Pharisees, began a process of self definition and reinterpretation of their traditions. Like the sectarians at Qumran they turned to the Torah as a means of making atonement. Torah would enable them to continue living as a kingdom of priests and a holy nation even without the Temple. I have argued that the Johannine community reinterpreted Israel's Temple traditions firstly in terms of Jesus and ultimately in terms of the community. For the Johannine community *they* can be the house(hold) of God because of the indwelling of the Father, Jesus and the Spirit-Paraclete.

The above survey of Jewish and Christian literature shows that there was, in the post Exilic and first-century writings, a milieu that would provide a background for a Christian community to see itself as the new Temple, especially so after the destructive events of 70. It is not necessary to look for direct links between the Pauline churches, the Qumran sect and the Johannine communities. It is enough to show that the idea of temple-as-community predates the Johannine writing and has a basis in first century Jewish and Christian thinking. While the image may not be unique to the Fourth Gospel, the manner in which the image is used shows a highly original and theologically sensitive understanding of Jesus and the community he left behind. The uniqueness and creativity of the Fourth Gospel is shown in its use of the Temple as the major christological and ecclesial theme. The community-as-Temple is not an image about how the community is to live or what its function is, but the image describes the very essence of the community, what it is because of the divine indwelling.

---

[31] Rom 12:5; 1 Cor 12:12-13, 27; Eph 3:6; 4:12; 5:30; Col 1:18, 24; 2:19.

Having shown what the new Temple is, namely, the community or house(hold) of God, it is now necessary to examine when this community comes into existence. Temple building is a divine task and since the time of the exile, it was linked to the "last days" and the eschatological outpouring of the Spirit (Isa 44:3; Joel 2:28; Ezek 11:19; 36:26-27; 39:29; Zech 12:10). An issue for all Johannine studies is to determine where and to what extent this Gospel reflects a realized eschatology and where and to what extent it reflects the more traditional end-time eschatology? Related to the question of when the community as the new Temple comes into being, is the question: When does Jesus return to his disciples?

The Eschatological Temple

The builder

The clearest statement about the builder of a future Temple is found in Zechariah within a series of eschatological visions. "Thus says the LORD of Hosts: here is a man whose name is Branch:[32] for he shall branch out in his place, and he shall build the temple of the LORD" (Zech 6:12). The Targums translate Branch (צמח) as Messiah (משיחא), thus identifying the person "Branch" with the Davidic Messiah,[33] no doubt drawing on the Isaian reference to the shoot (נצר) from the stump of Jesse (Isa 11:1). The Targum of Isaiah identifies the Temple-builder as the Servant who is renamed as the Messiah, "Behold my Servant, *the Messiah*" (*Tg. Isa* 52:13)[34]. The targumic treatment of Isaiah 53 is most surprising in that it goes well beyond a paraphrase to give an entirely new interpretation of the Servant/Messiah's task. Juel suggests that the targumist has departed from the M.T. by reading the participle מחלל as "profaned" instead of "pierced" or "wounded" which leads to the insertion, speaking of the Servant/Messiah "*and he will build the sanctuary* which was profaned for our sins, handed over for our iniquities" (*Tg. Isa* 53:5).[35] Juel's first conclusion is

> that at some point in the development of the targumic tradition, it became customary to refer the prophecy in Zech 6:12-13 to the Messiah, and that at some point the phrase was added to Isa 53:5, reflecting the belief that the Messiah would rebuild the fallen temple.[36]

---

[32] לֵאמֹר הִנֵּה־אִישׁ צֶמַח שְׁמוֹ

[33] R. P. Gordon and K. J. Cathcart, *The Targum of the Minor Prophets,* ed. Martin McNamara. The Aramaic Bible 14 (Edinburgh: T. & T. Clark, 1989) 198.

[34] Chilton, *The Isaiah Targum,* 103.

[35] Juel, *Messiah and Temple,* 183, also McCaffrey, *The house with many rooms,* 97.

[36] Juel, *Messiah and Temple,* 189.

Juel then attempts to date the targumic tradition of the Messiah as the
builder of the eschatological Temple by comparing the use of צמח as a
messianic designation in the Qumran texts, other Targum passages and
rabbinic writings. The community at Qumran is using צמח as a messianic
name, as can be seen in the following texts:

> YHWH declares to you that he will build you a house. I will raise up your
> seed after you and establish the throne of his kingdom forever. I will be a
> father to him and he will be a son to me. This refers to the Branch of David
> (הואה צמח דויד)[37] (4QFlor col 1:11; commenting on 2 Sam 7:11).

> Until the messiah of justice comes, the branch of David (צמח דויד) (4QpGen
> col 5:3-4).

Even more striking is the pesher on Isa 11:1-5 where, following the
quotation from Isaiah, the text is given a sectarian explanation. (Is 11:1)
ויצא] חטר מגזע] ישי ונצר משד[ןשיו יפדה וגח]ה עלו ר[וח[38]. The quotation follows
the Hebrew text and uses נצר. In the commentary on this verse, the term
netzer is rendered "the shoot of David" but uses the expression צמח from
Zech 6:12, (צמח דויד).[39] These texts show that by the time of the Qumran
writings the two terms *tzamah* and *netzer* are synonymous and the roles of
both have become fused. The man named "Branch" who will build the
temple of the Lord, according to Zechariah 6, has been identified as the
messianic shoot of David, the *netzer*.

Because Qumran is already using the term צמח as an accepted messianic designation, Juel concludes that the term צמח was understood as a
messianic term prior to the Christian era.[40] This evidence shows that even
prior to the Johannine writings the role of Temple builder was being applied to the Messiah who has become identified with the 'Branch' of
Zechariah.

Is there evidence in the Fourth Gospel to show that this community
also saw the Messiah as the Temple builder? The oracle of Isaiah, looking
to a future Davidic Messiah, does not use צמח *(tzmh)*, but instead uses נצר
(ntzr), an equivalent term for branch or shoot. Recent excavations have
shown that the word "Nazareth" has its root meaning in the word נצר. From

[37] The English text taken from Garcia Martinez, *Dead Sea Scrolls,* 136; the Hebrew
from Lohse, *Die Texte aus Qumran,* 256.

[38] 4Q161 (4QpIsaᵃ line 11). Florentino Garcia Martinez and Eibert Tigchelaar, *The
Dead Sea Scrolls Study Edition*, 1Qq-4Q273. 2 vols. (New York: Brill, 1997) 1:316.

[39] 4Q161 (4QpIsaᵃ line 18). Garcia Martinez and Tigchelaar, *Dead Sea Scrolls
Study* Edition, 1:316.

[40] Juel, *Messiah and Temple,* 189–90.

the Greek, it was not clear if Nazareth would be spelt in Hebrew with a צ
(tz) or the simpler ז (z). Excavations at Caesarea in 1962 found a clear Hebrew inscription referring to a family from Nazareth using the letter צ,
thus clarifying that Nazareth is derived from נצר.[41] When Jesus is called
the "Nazarene," there is, therefore, the possibility that this means more
than the identity of his small village of origin, but that it is a messianic
title having its basis in נצר from the oracle of Isaiah (11:1).

Billerbeck associates the oracle of Isaiah with the Matthean statement that "Joseph settled in Nazareth in that there should be fulfilled what
was said by the prophet (in the words נצר and נצמח): he shall be called a
Nazarene."[42] While citing Billerbeck, Schaeder dismisses the argument
that Isa 11:1 lies behind the Matthean prophecy "since '*neser*' was not a
name borne by the Messiah. The equivalent "branch" of Isa 4:2; Jer 23:5;
33:15 and esp. Zech 3:8; 6:12 is certainly a name, but in this case the word
is *semah* rather than *neser,* and there is no link with Ναζαρέθ,
Ναζωραῖος."[43] However, as Schaeder also notes, there were rabbinic rules
of interpretation allowing for the substitution of equivalent words.[44] The
1962 excavations and the Qumran writings discussed above establish clearly
a first-century messianic understanding of the term "Branch" *netzer* and its
link to the word "Nazareth." The test would be how the word "Nazareth" is
used in the Gospels, simply as a place name, or as a messianic title.

In the Fourth Gospel Jesus is identified as the Nazarene only in his
"hour" (18:5,7; 19:19).[45] When the soldiers come to Gethsemane, they
ask for Jesus the Nazarene (τὸν Ναζωραῖον) (18:5). For emphasis this is
repeated (18:7). When Jesus is lifted up on the Cross, only in this Gospel
is he designated with two titles, "the Nazarene" and "the King of the Jews"
(Ἰησοῦς ὁ Ναζωραῖος ὁ βασιλεὺς τῶν Ἰουδαίων) (19:19). It must also
be noted that only this Gospel calls these words a title (τίτλος). In Mark
and Luke they are termed an inscription (ἐπιγραφή Luke 23:38; Mark
15:25), while in Matthew the words are called "the charge" (αἰτία Matt
27:37). In the Fourth Gospel, "Nazarene" is not a name derived from a
place, but a title that leads to Jesus' death and is written as part of the formal charge, followed immediately with its synonym, "King of the Jews."

[41] J. Strange, "Nazareth," *ABD* 4 (1992) 1050–51.
[42] Cited by H. H. Schaeder, "Ναζαρηνός, Ναζωραῖος," *TDNT 4* (1967) 878.
[43] Schaeder, "Ναζαρηνός," 878.
[44] Schaeder, "Ναζαρηνός," 878; also Manns, *L'Evangile,* 309–10.
[45] The only other reference to Nazareth in the Fourth Gospel is when Phillip invites
Nathanael to see Jesus, "son of Joseph from Nazareth" (1:45); and Nathanael's terse
reply, "can anything good come out of Nazareth?" (1:46). It is Joseph, not Jesus who is
directly associated with the place Nazareth.

This title, "the Nazarene, the King of the Jews," is the formal charge and final title applied to Jesus in the pre-Easter narrative. In chapter 2 Jesus had made the claim that he would raise up the destroyed Temple (2:19). In this prophecy he identifies himself as the future Temple builder, the one spoken of in Zechariah called "branch." In his "hour," in a manner still to be clarified, the narrative suggests that Jesus' claim, and the prophecy of Zechariah, will be fulfilled, when he, as the Nazarene, the Davidic Branch *(netzer/tzamah),* is raised on the cross, and in the hour of his departure, he prepares/builds the new Temple.

Eschatological Gift of the Spirit

With the closure of the age of prophecy, it seemed that God had withdrawn the Spirit from Israel.[46] The Spirit was understood as a gift reserved for the end of time, when God would pour out the Spirit in abundance (Isa 44:3; Joel 2:28; Ezek 11:19; 36:26-27; 39:29; Zech 12:10). The post-resurrection community experienced the gifts of the Spirit which they interpreted as the dawning of the *eschaton* (Acts 2:16-17). Bultmann and Dodd would see in the Fourth Gospel's treatment of "the hour" a fully realized eschatology. In this view, the "hour" is the *kairos* moment of death, glorification, Spirit-gift and parousia,[47] and the Johannine Gospel is the testimony of a community already experiencing the *parousian* return of Jesus. This approach overlooks the very real absence spoken of and prepared for throughout the last discourse. The whole purpose of the discourse is to prepare the disciples for the absence of Jesus and to offer them consolation. While the discourse does speak of Jesus' return (14:3, 18, 28) and does promise the disciples will not be orphaned (14:18), the tone and words of the discourse speak of a community still awaiting the parousia.

What can we make of the promise of a return, of the disciples being where Jesus is (14:3)? Is it the return in the post-resurrection appearances of Jesus? This solution is attractive but does not resolve the fact that these appearances come to an end; there is not a continuous vision of the Risen Jesus. This return is short-lived and still leaves the paradox of presence in absence, promised in Jesus' statements. The paradox is resolved in a unique way, in the Johannine writings, in the identity and function of the Paraclete, promised in chapter 14 after each explanatory dialogue. Through the Paraclete, the evangelist proposes a profound insight into the manner of Jesus' ongoing presence within the community, even as it awaits his final exaltation and return at the end of time.

---

[46] B. Sommer, "Did prophecy cease? Evaluating a reevaluation," *JBL* 115 (1996) 47.

[47] Bultmann, *Gospel,* 585-86; Dodd, *Interpretation,* 394–95.

The first mention of the Paraclete speaks of him as "another Paraclete" (ἄλλον παράκλητον) (14:16). Introduced in this way, the disciples (and readers) must surely wonder who is the first Paraclete. The Gospel describes the function of the Paraclete in almost identical words to the function of Jesus and thus identifies Jesus as the former Paraclete.[48] The Gospel is very careful to maintain the separate and distinct identity of both Jesus and Paraclete even as it establishes a very close relationship between both. Spirit-Paraclete and Jesus are not assimilated into each other. Their close relationship is very like the intimacy of *logos* and *theos*. The λόγος may be described as θεός, but is not called ὁ θεός (1:2). Jesus is the one on whom the Spirit descends and remains (1:32), but Jesus is not the Spirit. Jesus is the incarnate *logos,* the Father's gift already given to the world (3:16), whereas in the time of Jesus' ministry the Spirit has not yet been given for Jesus is not yet glorified (7:39). The Spirit is christic in its role (16:14, 15), but the Spirit is not Christ, since the risen and glorified Christ will send the Spirit (16:7). The distinctions between the Father, Jesus, and the Spirit-Paraclete are maintained even in the intimacy of their union.

Because Jesus is the bearer of the Spirit from the time of his Baptism (1:32), Jesus can say to the disciples that the Paraclete is now with (παρά) them (v. 17). Jesus himself mediates the presence of the Spirit-Paraclete to the disciples. But when Jesus returns to the Father, the mediating roles are reversed. Jesus' role as Spirit-bearer ends, and in his moment of return he gifts the disciples with the Spirit (19:30; 20:22). Within the discourse he can truly promise a future time when the Paraclete will be in (ἐν) the disciples (14:17). The Paraclete, dwelling in the disciples, will mediate a continuing presence of Jesus in the time-gap before the parousia. The immediate experience of the post-resurrection community is pneumatic, but the sole purpose of the gift of the Spirit is to mediate a presence of the now absent one. On this point of the presence and function of the Spirit, D. Moody Smith's comments indicate the experiential nature of the Fourth Gospel's pneumatology:

> The Spirit or Paraclete as the mode of Jesus' abiding with his disciples seems to be a *felt reality* [emphasis mine], a presence regarded as given rather than imagined. It is not, in other words, a mere theological idea of the Evangelist or of his community. Exactly how the Spirit-Paraclete makes the presence of Jesus known and felt in the community is never stated in so

---

[48] R. E. Brown, "The Paraclete in the Fourth Gospel," *NTS* 13 (1966–1967) 126–27; Burge, *The Anointed Community,* 140–43.

many words. That is, the exact mode of his activity, the phenomenology of his presence, is not described, although its function is clear enough.[49]

The Presence of the Absent One

How is the Spirit-Paraclete experienced in the Johannine community? When, through the mediation of the Spirit, does the community experience the "coming" of Jesus and his presence with them?

In looking at earlier references to the Spirit, there are clear associations with the community's worship and sacraments. John witnesses the descent of the Spirit upon Jesus (1:32-33), presumably at his baptism given the immediate context (v. 31), and Nicodemus was told of the necessity of birth by water and Spirit (3:5-6, 8). The Samaritan Woman was told of an hour that is both coming and is now present when worship will be ἐν πνεύματι καὶ ἀληθείᾳ (4:23-24). Reading the καὶ epexegetically, since the second noun has no definite article, this phrase about worship reads "a Spirit which is true" or "a true Spirit" or even "a Spirit of truth," which is very close to what is said in 14:17. Following the discourse on the bread from heaven and its eucharistic allusions (6:51c-58), Jesus affirmed the life-giving role of the Spirit, available in his words (6:63). At the feast of Tabernacles, within the context of the Jewish water rituals, Jesus promised to be the one who would quench thirst, then, immediately, he spoke of the Spirit still to be given (7:39).

These earlier references clearly link the Spirit-Paraclete with the community's sacramental celebrations of baptism and Eucharist. True worship can only occur in Spirit, a Spirit of truth. In the community's cultic *anamnesis,* the Spirit-Paraclete is present to ὑπομιμνῄσκειν and διδάσκειν (14:26). The Paraclete will mediate the presence of Jesus primarily through the function of teaching and reminding (14:26). This verse (v. 26) describes the key role of the Paraclete within the believer. The human faculties of memory and insight, and the activity of worship and prayer, are named as the primary moments when the community experiences the gift of the Spirit and, through the stirrings of the Spirit, these cultic moments become the special times of Jesus' presence. David Aune speaks of a "cultic vision" of Jesus, a *visio Christi.*[50] This may be so, but the Gospel gives

---

[49] D. M. Smith, "The Presentation of Jesus in the Fourth Gospel," *Int* 31 (1977) 375.

[50] "In our opinion, the "coming" of Jesus in the relevant passages under discussion from John 14 refers primarily to the recurring cultic "coming" of Jesus in the form of a pneumatic or prophetic *visio Christi* within the setting of worship 'in the Spirit' as celebrated by the Johannine community." See Aune, *Cultic Setting,* 89–135; the quotation is found on 129.

greater emphasis to remembering and understanding. Several times throughout the Gospel there are intrusions of post-resurrection insight or interpretation (2:21; 7:39; 11:51; 12:33) giving evidence of the teaching and reminding activity of the Spirit.

Each of these post-resurrection insights is related to the reinterpretation of the Temple. The body of Jesus is the Temple of God's dwelling (2:21). Jesus draws on the image of water flowing from the side of the Temple to reinterpret the meaning of the feast of Tabernacles and the evangelists links this with the future gift of the Spirit (7:39). Fearing Jesus will be the impetus for the destruction of the Jewish Temple, Caiaphas prophesied Jesus' death for the nation (11:51), ironically ensuring that the true Holy Place was destroyed by "the Jews." The "lifting-up" of Jesus in death (12:33) fulfills the prophecy that the eschatological Temple would be lifted-up and be a source of in-gathering for the nations (Isa 2:2-3).

The activity of the Spirit, mediating a presence of Jesus, enables the Johannine community to reinterpret Israel's Temple traditions and to see that Israel's hopes for an eschatological Temple have now been realized. During the time of Jesus' ministry, he was the new Temple. When this Temple was destroyed by the Jewish leaders, Jesus ushered in the messianic age when the Spirit was poured out on his community, and he became the Branch, the נצר (netzer), the Temple-builder, establishing a community in which God could continue to dwell. Just as the Spirit is a proleptic gift of the *eschaton,* so also the worshipping, remembering community is a proleptic experience of the eschatological House of God. Stibbe's conclusion is along similar lines when he comments, "The realized eschatology in the rest of John 14 suggests that this house is not so much an eternal home in heaven as a post-resurrection, empirical reality for the true disciples."[51] I add a qualifying note to Stibbe in presenting the role of the Paraclete as mediating this "empirical reality" and also in claiming that it is not so fully realized that there is no sense of a further "parousian" return.

Conclusion

In the context of a farewell meal, Jesus gathers his own and prepares them for his approaching "hour." His words speak of the reality of his departure, but at the same time they hold out a promise of consolation to disciples, who in the present time can only experience bewilderment and lack of comprehension (14:5, 8, 22). It is only when Jesus passes through his "hour" that the following promises can be understood.

[51] Stibbe, *John,* 160.

The death of Jesus will be a journey to the Father for Jesus (14:2), and at the same time will be the Spirit-gift of the Father and Jesus to the community (14:16, 26; 16:7; 19:30; 20:22). Through the indwelling Spirit, notably in their communal worship, the community will continue to experience the presence of Jesus abiding with them, even as they await his final coming in glory. Spirit-empowered memory and insight will recall the words of Jesus to the disciples. Because Jesus is the divine *logos,* the *anamnesis* of the community will not be an empty nostalgia for times past but a living encounter with the life-giving Word of God (Gen 1:3; Jn 1:3; 5:24).

In the departure and Spirit-gift of Jesus, those of his own who receive him and keep his word (14:23) will become children of God (1:12) and, as members of God's οἰκία, they will be the *household of the Father,* where the Father, Jesus and Paraclete will make their μονήν (14:23). With the departure of Jesus, the Christian community will still have access to God's Temple. These are the consoling promises given to a group of friends as Jesus prepares for the moment of his departure. In the approaching "hour" promises will become reality as one Temple is destroyed and a new Temple raised up.

Raising the New Temple

JOHN 18:1–19:42

By the time the Fourth Gospel was being developed into its final written form, a passion narrative was already well established in the Christian tradition. How does the Johannine community tell its story of Jesus' death, remaining true to the facts of the traditional narrative, and at the same time maintaining its own christological perspective that has been unfolding within the Gospel? Far from being a "mere postscript,"[1] the Passion brings to a climax many themes developed in the Gospel such as, the "lifting up" of the Son of Man (3:14, 15; 8:28; 12:32), the gathering of the flock belonging to the Shepherd King (10:15, 16; 11:52; 12:19, 32), and the theme to be further developed in this chapter, the destruction of the old Temple and the raising of the new Temple (2:19).

The Prologue announced that Jesus is the incarnate revealer of God, now tabernacling among us (1:14). His first public action in Judea, fulfilling the obligation to "go up" to Jerusalem for Passover, was to enter the Temple which he claimed as his "Father's House," and to speak of its future destruction and raising (2:19). The readers were then told, through the editorial comment, that the Temple he spoke of was the Temple of his own body (2:21). While many scholars see in the Johannine community the fulfillment of these words about a raised Temple, few attempt to show how the narrative actually depicts this. For the plot of this gospel, as announced in chapter 2, to be effective the reader must see in the death of Jesus the destruction and raising of a Temple.

---

[1] E. Käsemann, *The Testament of Jesus according to John 17* (Philadelphia: Fortress, 1968) 7.

The identification of Jesus as the living Temple of God's presence, with future implications for worship and for those who believe, continued throughout the Gospel in chapters 4, 7, 8, 10:22-42; 14:2-3. The Gospel drew upon the images of Israel's cult in its presentation of Jesus. During Passover, Jesus was the true bread from heaven (6:35, 48, 50, 51, 53). While celebrating Tabernacles, Jesus revealed himself as a source of water to quench thirst (7:37) and as the light of the world (8:12). Within the feast of Dedication, celebrating the reconsecration of the Temple in 164 B.C.E., Jesus spoke of himself as the "consecrated one" (10:36). Since Temple and cultic imagery have been so central to the christology of the Fourth Gospel, before addressing the final Passover it is important to briefly recall the function of Israel's Temple and its cultic activity.

The Temple, from the divine perspective, was the House of God, the בת יהוה. It was the sacred place of God's own choosing for a dwelling on earth, a temple/palace היכל mirroring God's royal dwelling in the heavens. The Temple in Jerusalem was the place of God's enthronement above the carved cherubim wings surrounding the Ark within the holy of holies:

> The LORD reigns; let the peoples tremble!
> He sits enthroned upon the cherubim; let the earth quake! (Ps 99:1)

From a human perspective, the Temple was the place where humanity, through its cultic activity, was deemed worthy to have access to the divine presence. The very design of the Temple stressed the utter holiness of God and the degrees of possibility of encountering God, depending on one's worthiness:

> Within the boundaries of the sanctuary, what was known to be pure was offered by personnel chosen for the purpose, in the presence of the people of God and of God himself. Nothing foreign, no one with a serious defect or impurity, nothing unclean was permitted. . . In no other place was Israel more Israel or God more God, than in the sanctuary.[2]

The most central act of Israel's cult was the twice daily sin offering, the *Tamid* (Num 28:4). Because God is holy, Israel must be holy: "You shall be holy, for I am holy" (Lev 11:45). The Temple's cult was a means of continual purification, thus enabling God to be present in Israel's midst.

If Jesus is the new Temple, how are the following aspects of Israel's Temple activity presented in the Johannine Passion?

---

[2] B. Chilton, *The Temple of Jesus: His Sacrificial Program within a Cultural History of Sacrifice* (University Park, Penn.: Pennsylvania State University, 1992) 106.

- In the portrayal of the crucified Jesus, where is the presence and enthronement of Israel's God whom they encountered in the Temple and whom their Temple liturgies praised as King?
- How does Jesus fulfill the prophecies concerning the building of the eschatological Temple (Zech 6:11-13)?
- In what way does Jesus meet the requirements of Israel's sacrificial system?

The particular way in which the evangelist presents the death of Jesus must address these questions if the promises given throughout the narrative are to be fulfilled and if the Gospel is to be a witness to the truth.

The Development of a Passion Narrative

The story of Jesus' death and its interpretation as fulfilling the plan of God revealed in the Scriptures seems to have been an essential part of the early Christian *kerygma* (1 Cor 1:21-23; 11:23-26; 15:3-5). Some suggest that an early form of passion narrative developed from the apostolic preaching. Other scholars point to the frequent citing of the psalms and scriptural references and suggest that a narrative may have arisen within a liturgical context.[3] With reference to either the liturgy or the *kerygma,* these scholars believe that there was an already developed account of the passion prior to Mark's Gospel.[4] Opposing this view is a group of scholars, strongly influenced by Norman Perrin, who argue that the Passion narrative is the creation of Mark and did not have an existence prior to this Gospel.[5]

I follow the arguments of Raymond Brown who proposes that "on the pre-Gospel level . . . there existed at least a sequence of the principal stages in the death of Jesus, along with some stories about episodes or figures connected with that death."[6] The following sequence would be part of any telling of the death of Jesus:

    i. a betrayal and arrest on the mount outside the city
   ii. a Jewish trial

---

[3] A brief discussion of theories of the development of the passion narrative can be found in D. Senior, *The Passion of Jesus in the Gospel of Mark* (Wilmington, Del.: Glazier, 1984) 9–11. A more detailed discussion of the issue of a pre-Marcan Passion can be found in R. Brown, *The Death of the Messiah: From Gethsemane to the Grave,* 2 vols (New York: Doubleday, 1994) 1:53–57; 2:1492–1524.

[4] A strong proponent of this view is R. Pesch, *Das Markusevangelium,* 3rd ed. 2 vols (Freiburg: Herder, 1980) 2:1–27.

[5] See the collection of essays in W. Kelber, ed. *The Passion in Mark* (Philadelphia: Fortress, 1976).

[6] Brown, *Death of the Messiah,* 1:92.

iii. a Roman trial
iv. death by crucifixion with two others at Golgotha
v. burial by disciples in a nearby tomb

These elements are generally used to form the structural divisions of the passion narrative. The Fourth Gospel will be faithful to the tradition and will present each incident through the lens of its own unique christology.

Structure Chapters 18–19[7]

Scene 1. 18:1-12
Jesus in a garden with his disciples (v. 1)
Confrontation with and Rejection by "his own" (συνέλαβον) (vv. 2-12)

Scene 2. 18:13-27
Taken to Annas/Caiaphas (vv. 13-14)
    Peter (vv. 15-18)
Interrogation by the High Priest (vv. 19-24)
    Peter (vv. 25-27)

Scene 3. 18:28-19:16a (Pilate)[8]
outside to "the Jews"—death penalty demanded (28-32)
    inside to Jesus—Kingdom not of this world (33-38a)
        outside to "the Jews"—Barabbas the law breaker (38b-40)
            inside to Jesus—dressed and hailed as king (19:1-3)
        outside to "the Jews"—Jesus the law breaker (4-8)
    inside to Jesus—"king" vs emperor (9-12)
outside to "the Jews"—death penalty granted (13-16a)

Scene 4. 19:16b-30
Crucifixion (vv. 16b-18)
    Final words of Pilate. The Nazarene/King (vv. 19-22)
Crucifixion (vv. 23-24)
    Final words of Jesus. The new Temple (vv. 25-30)

        Testimony of Death (vv. 31-37)

Scene 5. 19:38-42
Taken by "his own" (ἔλαβον) (vv. 38-40)
Jesus in a garden with his friends (vv. 41-42)

---

[7] While I follow a common structure of these chapters, I name each element in accordance with the emphasis of this thesis and these names will be clarified in the following discussion.

[8] The "outside—inside" design of this scene is noted by many. See D. Senior, *The Passion of Jesus in the Gospel of John* (Leominister, U.K.: Gracewing, 1991) 68; Schnackenburg, *Gospel,* 3:242; Brown, *Gospel,* 2:858–59.

Kingship and Temple

The voice of the LORD makes the oaks to whirl, and strips the forests bare;
  and in his temple all cry, "Glory!"
The LORD sits enthroned over the flood; the LORD sits enthroned as king for
  ever (Ps 29:9-10).

A consistent assertion throughout the Hebrew Scriptures is the Kingship of God. Even when a human king was anointed it was done with much
warning and reluctance (Jdg 9; 1 Sam 8:6). Israel's demand for a king was
in fact interpreted as a rejection of God. "And the LORD said to Samuel,
"Hearken to the voice of the people in all that they say to you; for they
have not rejected you, but they have rejected me from being king over
them." (1 Sam 8:7). Even after the time of David, who does find favor
with God, the prophets continue to remind Israel that YHWH is their true
King (e.g., Isa 33:22; 43:15; Jer 10:7, 10; Zeph 3:15; Zech 14:16; Mal
1:14). Kingship is an attribute of God's divinity so that to affirm one is to
affirm the other. "Thus says the LORD the King of Israel, and his Redeemer,
the LORD of hosts: I am the first and I am the last; besides me there is no
god" (Isa 44:6). The psalms of Israel's Temple liturgy abound in praise of
God's kingship (e.g., Pss 29:10; 47:6; 93:1; 97:1; 98:6; 145:1). The
Temple itself is God's earthly palace (היכל) and in the Holy of Holies God
is enthroned upon the cherubim (Ps 99:1). The Temple therefore is the
place where God's Kingship is most manifest and where Israel celebrates
her acceptance of God's absolute sovereignty.

The Arrest of a King 18:1-12

Throughout the Gospel Jesus has made claims about his relationship
with Israel's God. As Son, he is one with the Father (10:30) and in his humanity personifies YHWH's self manifestation as "I Am" (Isa 41:4). When
the arresting officers come seeking Jesus the Nazarene (18:5, 7), Jesus'
double affirmation ἐγώ εἰμι (vv. 5, 8) shifts the encounter from an arrest
to a divine theophany, and sets the revelatory character of the Johannine
Passion.[9] Jesus' actions testify to the truth of his words as, throughout the
narrative, Jesus is the sovereign master. The arresting party do not enter

---

[9] A number of scholars see the reaction of the soldiers in falling to the ground as a
sign of a divine manifestation. See Talbert, *Reading John,* 233; Barrett, *Gospel,* 520;
Brown, *Death of the Messiah,* 1:260-62; Bultmann, *Gospel,* 639. Carson, *Gospel,*
578–79, rejects the theophanic interpretation and reads the ἐγώ εἰμι as a simple statement of identification.

the garden, Jesus "went out" to them (v. 4).[10] The group with Judas need to carry lanterns and torches for they are associated with the powers of darkness (cf. 13:2, 30) and in the face of Jesus' self-identification they fall impotently to the ground, a normal human response to a theophany (cf. Dan 10:9). The powers of darkness have no sway over one named in this Gospel as the light of life (1:4-5). Jesus displays his control of the situation when his command stays Peter's hand (v. 11) and he arranges the release of his disciples (v. 8), fulfilling the words he had spoken, "While I was with them, I kept them in thy name, which thou hast given me; I have guarded them, and none of them is lost but the son of perdition, that the scripture might be fulfilled" (17:12).[11]

The arresting party are a most unlikely group to be associated in any way: soldiers, officers of the priests, and Pharisees who are part of the Passion story only in the Fourth Gospel. In fact they are more representative than historical figures.[12] "The line-up of adversaries represents a wide spectrum of those who have been or will prove to be hostile to Jesus."[13] The moment in the garden brings to conclusion a series of confrontations between Jesus and "the Jews." Jesus' self-revelatory words, the images of a garden, darkness and light, give to this final confrontation with his enemies a cosmic significance typical of apocalyptic writings.[14] In chapter 12 Jesus had entered Jerusalem to royal acclamations (12:13-14) and with the coming of the Greeks to see him, Jesus recognized that his "Hour" had now arrived (12:23). His "Hour" is the definitive moment of judgment when "the ruler of this world will be driven out" (12:31). After Judas' departure into the night (14:30), Jesus knew that the betrayal was taking place, and warned that "the ruler of this world is coming," and he added, "he has no power over me" (14:30). The Hour, when the presence of the

---

[10] Manns, *L'Evangile,* 421; C. H. Giblin, "Confrontations in John 18,1-27," *Bib* 65 (1984) 218.

[11] Stibbe sees in this episode allusions to Jesus as the Good Shepherd who lays down his life for his sheep (10:11). See *John as Storyteller,* 96–105 where he develops the imagery of the Shepherd King.

[12] Barrett, *Gospel,* 516, notes that the composition of the arresting party is "historically improbable." Schnackenburg, *Gospel,* 3:223, speaks of this incident as a "theological representation" in which Jesus confronts the "whole unbelieving cosmos."

[13] Giblin, *Confrontations,* 216.

[14] Kovacs elaborates on the cosmic mythology within the Fourth Gospel and argues for its basis within Jewish apocalyptic literature rather than Hellenistic Gnosticism. The Cross is not simply a point of departure but it is "the locus of a cosmic battle, in which Jesus achieves a decisive victory over Satan." See J. Kovacs, "'Now shall the ruler of this world be driven out': Jesus' Death as Cosmic Battle in John 12:20-36," *JBL* 114 (1995) 227–47, especially 246 for the quotation.

true King is to be revealed, at the same time breaks the power of the world's ruler. Jesus' sovereignty during the scene of his "arrest" dramatizes the powerlessness of this world's ruler.[15]

The Trial of a King 18:28–19:16a

With great irony Jesus' sovereignty is most clearly asserted through the secular ruler, Pilate. Pilate's backwards and forwards movements between "the Jews" and Jesus indicate his vacillation between the kingship claims of Jesus, which he recognizes (18:35, 39; 19:14), and the claims of his Roman emperor (v. 12). He moves outside his Roman world view and into the Jewish world in giving Jesus the title "the King" (ὁ βασιλεύς).[16] In the mocking insults of the soldiers, Jesus is dressed in a royal purple robe and crowned (19:2). Displayed as a King, Jesus is presented to his people (19:5, 14) who vociferously reject him (vv. 6, 15). "The Jews'" response aligns them with the powers of this world over and against the Kingship of God. Their cry, "We have no king but Caesar (Καίσαρα)" (19:15), is idolatrous. It is a choice to reject God's divine sovereignty now manifest before them in Jesus, who alone, and not the emperor, can identify himself as "I am." As earlier Pilate moved into the Jewish world view in calling Jesus "King," now "the Jews" move across into the world of Rome to name their ruler as Καίσαρα. "In denying all claims to kingship save that of the Roman Emperor Israel abdicated its own unique position under the immediate sovereignty of God."[17]

The Execution of a King 19:16b-30

It is Pilate who insists on the title—"Jesus the Nazarene, the King of the Jews" (Ἰησοῦς ὁ Ναζωραῖος ὁ βασιλεὺς τῶν Ἰουδαίων) (19:19). In fact two titles are used synonymously "the Nazarene" and "the King of the Jews." The Fourth Gospel does not emphasize Jesus' upbringing or ministry in Nazareth;[18] The lack of emphasis accorded to a Nazareth

---

[15] It is possible that the naming of the "Kedron" is a deliberate allusion to David's flight from Jerusalem where he too crossed the Kedron (2 Sam 15:23). Jesus would be thereby given a Davidic royal status.

[16] F. Genuyt, "La Comparution de Jésus devant Pilate: Analyse sémiotique de Jean 18, 28–19, 16," *RSR* 17 (1985) 144–46.

[17] Barrett, *Gospel*, 546.

[18] As noted in the previous chapter, the Greek word order links Joseph with Nazareth more clearly than Jesus, Ἰησοῦν υἱὸν τοῦ Ἰωσὴφ τὸν ἀπο Ναζαρέτ (John 1:45).

tradition enables the evangelist to use "Nazarene" as a unique and emphatic messianic title where it occurs only in the Passion narrative (18:5, 7; 19:19).

In the previous chapter the following points were made about the title, "the Nazarene," as a messianic designation, and as a name for the builder of the eschatological Temple:

- In the messianic oracle of chapter 11, Isaiah speaks of the future spirit-endowed ruler as a shoot (נצר—*ntzr*) and a branch. "There shall come forth a shoot from the stump of Jesse, and a branch shall grow out of his roots" (Isa 11:1).[19] The "branch" imagery is taken up in later prophets with a similar messianic thrust (Jer 23:5; 33:15). The word "Nazareth" comes from the Hebrew stem *ntzr.*

- The prophet Zechariah states that the future Temple builder will be a man named Branch (צמח tzamah). "Thus says the LORD of hosts, "Behold, the man whose name is the Branch: for he shall grow up in his place, and he shall build the temple of the LORD" (Zech 6:12 cf. 3:8).[20]

- The Targums and Qumran use the expression צמח as a messianic name thus establishing that, by the first century, the two terms נצר and צמח are equivalent messianic terms and that one of the tasks of the Messiah was to build the eschatological Temple.

The Royal Temple Builder

Zechariah explicitly states that the eschatological Temple will be built by the person named "Branch" who combines both royal and High Priestly functions:

Take from the exiles Heldai, Tobi'jah, and Jedai'ah, who have arrived from Babylon; and go the same day to the house of Josi'ah, the son of Zephani'ah. Take from them silver and gold, and make a crown, and set it upon the head of Joshua, the son of Jehoz'adak, the high priest; and say to him, "Thus says the LORD of hosts, 'Behold, the man whose name is the Branch: for he shall grow up in his place, and he shall build the temple of

[19] The poetic parallelism establishes that *shoot* and *branch* are equivalent terms.

[20] Barrett, *Gospel,* 541, notes this passage from Zech as a possible background to Pilate's declaration, "Behold the man" (ἰδοὺ ὁ ἄνωροπος 19:5); compare Zech 6:12 "Behold a man" (Ἰδοὺ ἀνήρ). Senior, *Passion in John,* 88, also makes this association. These comments strengthen my claim that Zechariah 6:11-12 provides a major interpretive key for the understanding of Jesus' death within this Gospel.

the LORD. It is he who shall build the temple of the LORD, and shall bear royal honor, and shall sit and rule upon his throne'" (Zech 6:10-13a).

In the Passion narrative the process of Temple-building begins with Jesus' death. As he dies, he changes the relationships between the Beloved Disciple and his mother, and in so doing constitutes the new Temple/ Household of God, a new *locus* wherein the Spirit may continue to dwell.

The close relationship between Jesus and the Beloved Disciple has already been described with words echoing the intimacy of Son and Father (cf. 13:23; 1:18). The expressions εἰς τὸν κόλπον and ἐν τῷ κόλπῳ are used in the LXX primarily to express familial relationships, either the relationship between husband and wife (Gen 16:5; Deut 13:7; 28:56; 2 Sam 12:8; Sir 9:1) or the relationship between mother and child (Num 11:12; 1 Kgs 3:20; 17:19; Ruth 4:16; Isa 49:22).[21] So this phrase expresses extraordinary closeness while maintaining a distinct identity.

In the Fourth Gospel Jesus' mother is not given a personal name; she is always named in terms of her function and relationship as "the mother of Jesus." Nor does the Fourth Gospel contain a scene where the title "mother" is extended to all believers as in the Synoptics (Mark 3:35; Luke 8:21; Matt 12:50). Although called "mother," her physical maternity has had no function in the narrative so far. Her motherhood is to function in a different symbolic way. When she is introduced by the narrator she is called ἡ μήτηρ αὐτου (19:25, cf. 2:1). When the narrator changes to give us Jesus' perspective, she is not called his mother but the mother (τὴν μητέρα). Jesus speaks to the mother (19:26). The use of the definite article gives this title a universal significance.

The double use of the term ἴδε informs the reader that Jesus' words are prophetic revelations.[22] "Woman, behold your son. . . behold your mother" (vv. 26-27). Jesus' proclamation is far more than that of a dying son making provision for the future care of his mother.[23] It is a statement that brings the mission of Jesus to its completion (v. 28). In these words Jesus establishes a new relationship between "the mother" and the Beloved Disciple and thereby new relationships between himself and the

[21] R. Meyer, "κόλπος," *TDNT* 3 (1965) 824–26.

[22] de Goedt proposes that ἴδε introduces a revelatory formula. See M. de Goedt, "Un schème de révélation dans la quatrième évangile," *NTS* 8 (1961–62) 142–50. Brown, (*Death of the Messiah,* 1021) takes this concept further and speaks of this expression as not just revelatory but as an "act of empowerment that both reveals and makes come about a new relationship."

[23] Similarly Senior, *Passion in John,* 113: "It is more than the gracious act of a dutiful son."

community of believers. The actual form of the words is similar to the formula of adoption.[24]

In the Fourth Gospel, the term "Son" has been consistently used as a title of Jesus: Son of God (1:34, 49; 3:18; 5:25; 10:36; 11:4, 27; 19:7), Son of Man (1:51; 3:13, 14; 5:27; 6:27, 53, 62; 8:28; 9:35; 12:23, 34; 13:31), only Son (1:14, 18; 3:16) and simply "Son" (3:17, 35, 36; 5:19, 20, 21, 22, 23, 26; 6:40; 8:36; 14:13; 17:1). The reader's first association when hearing the phrase "Behold your son," would be that it refers to Jesus. But there is a jarring note—**your** son. Jesus has never been called son of Mary. By giving his mother the title "Woman" in her relationship to himself, both in this scene and earlier at Cana (2:4), Jesus directs her maternal role elsewhere, to another son who is being born in this Hour. These two statements, "Behold your son," and "Behold your mother," establish a new relationship between the disciple and the mother of Jesus, and in so doing they establish a new relationship between the disciple and Jesus.

Most commentators emphasize the expansion of Mary's motherhood indicated by these words. But this is only possible if sonship is also expanded. If the woman always called "the mother of Jesus" is presented now as the mother of the Beloved Disciple, then Jesus' sonship is extended to embrace others.[25] This scene depicts the promise of divine filiation when believers, represented by the Beloved Disciple,[26] will be incorporated, through the Spirit, into the sonship of Jesus.[27] This divine filiation is the ultimate revelation of the Hour and brings Jesus' mission to its completion. Following this scene, Jesus knows that all things have been finished (v. 28). The declaration that Jesus knew "all was now finished" (v. 28) makes verses 26 and 27 the climax and fulfillment of Jesus' mission.

According to Stibbe, this scene "really constitutes the climactic work in his ministry. John 19:25-27 is therefore a crucial narrative episode in the Johannine passion account."[28] Those who believe, who receive the incarnate *logos,* are drawn into the intimate relationship between Father and Son. "But to all who received him, who believed in his name, he gave power to become children of God" (1:12; cf. 17:24, 26). While "the Jews"

[24] Barrett, *Gospel,* 552, states that the words are both revelatory and adoptive.

[25] de Goedt, "Un scheme de revelation," 145: " . . . le disciple bien-aimé est adopté par Jésus comme frère."

[26] Collins, *These things have been written,* 1–45.

[27] Following the gift of the Spirit (19:30), the Father of Jesus is called the Father of the disciples, "Go to my brothers and sisters and say to them, I am ascending to my Father and your Father, to my God and your God" (20:17) [author translation].

[28] Stibbe, *John as Storyteller,* 154.

may claim "Abraham is our Father" (8:39), the Christian disciples can claim an even greater paternity in being a child of God.[29]

After Jesus' word of completion τετέλεσται, he performs his final sovereign act as he bows his head and hands down (παρέδωκεν) upon the nascent Christian community the promised gift of the Spirit (v. 30).[30] The phrase παρέδωκεν τὸ πνεῦμα is frequently seen through a synoptic interpretative model. Jesus gives up his spirit (i.e., his life). This is not what the Johannine text says. The term παραδίδωμι is not a euphemism for death;[31] it refers to the handing on or bequest of something to a successor.[32] Nor is the Spirit presented as a possession of Jesus; it is not "his" spirit or "my" spirit (cf. Luke 23:46); it is the Spirit (τὸ πνεῦμα).[33] This final παραδίδωμι is the conclusion of a number of "handing overs" within the Passion (18:2, 5, 35, 36; 19:11, 16). From the cross Jesus gives down to the seminal Christian community the eschatological gift of the Spirit, constituting the believers into a new household of God.[34] At this moment Jesus' words to Nicodemus are realized as a disciple experiences being "born from above" (3:3, 5).

In the previous chapter on "My Father's House" (14:2), I discussed the term μοναὶ and its cognate μένω, and a series of Divine Dwellings described in chapter 14:

- the Father dwelling in Jesus (14:10)
- the future dwelling of the Spirit/Paraclete in the believers (14:17)
- the dwelling of both Jesus and the Father with the believer (14:23)

Jesus is able to be called the "Temple" precisely because of the mutual indwelling of Father and Son. As God's glory once resided in Israel's Temple, now it is manifest in Jesus. Chapter 14 widened the sense of Temple to include the future community of believers. The many dwellings (μοναὶ) of the Father's household (οἰκία) are a series of interpersonal relationships between the Father, Jesus, Paraclete, and believer. The divine

---

[29] Recall the earlier discussion between Jesus and "the Jews" within the feast of Tabernacles, 8:31–58.

[30] The role of the Spirit will be developed below.

[31] F. J. Moloney, "The Johannine Passion and the Christian Community," *Salesianum* 57 (1995) 43–44.

[32] Burge, *The Anointed Community*, 134; also M. Vellanickal, *Studies in the Gospel of John* (Bangalore: Asian Trading Corporation, 1982) 151.

[33] Against Carson, *John*, 353, who writes "τὸ πνεῦμα clearly means the spirit of Jesus himself."

[34] Hoskyns, *The Fourth Gospel*, 532; Brown, *Gospel*, 2:931; *idem, Death of the Messiah*, 2:1082; Barrett, *Gospel*, 554.

indwellings in the midst of a believing community enables the community to be the new Temple raised up in Jesus' Hour. The community, participating in Jesus' divine filiation, is the house (household) of God. The prologue had already stated that the ones who did receive Jesus would become children of God (1:12). Just as Jesus could be described as Temple and Son because of his intimate union with God, so too these images of Temple and divine filiation can be applied to the Christian believer. In his Hour, the familial imagery is given a new depth of reality as Jesus' words and the gift of the Spirit constitute a new household of God which can rightly be depicted as the new Temple.

The Johannine crucifixion adds significantly to the synoptic presentation. The words ὁ Ναζωραῖος are added to the *titulus* placed above the head of Jesus. This additional title alludes to the נצר *(ntzr)* messianic shoot (Isa 11:1) who is identified by the prophet Zechariah as the builder of the eschatological Temple (Zech 6:12). The additional words to his mother and the Beloved Disciple expand the maternal function of his mother and the sonship of Jesus. Jesus' words establish a new relationship between the believer and Jesus, and the believer and the Father. The handing down of the Spirit completes the scene and clarifies the new relationship established through Jesus' words. From this moment, through the indwelling Spirit, the believer is drawn into the οἰκία τοῦ πατρός μου (14:2). Even as the soldiers set about the task of crucifying Jesus, the Nazarene is building a new Temple/household of God. With skilled artistry the evangelist structures the crucifixion in two interwoven parallel scenes.

Temple destroying	Temple building
Crucifixion (16b-18)	Pilate's words. The Nazarene (19-22)
Crucifixion (23-24)	Jesus' words. A new Temple/household (25-30)

Testimony of Death (vv. 31-37)

As the soldiers destroy the 'body/Temple' of Jesus on behalf of "the Jews," the Nazarene Temple builder is in the process of raising up a new Temple thus fulfilling Jesus' words to "the Jews": "Destroy this temple and in three days I will raise it up" (2:19).

The Passover Lamb

In examining the feasts of Tabernacles (John 7–8) and Dedication (John 10:22-42), I showed the close relationship between Johannine chris-

tology and the feasts' significance and liturgical symbols. The Johannine
Passion narrative is situated in the feast of the Passover (18:28, 39) specifically on the Day of Preparation (19:14, 31, 42).

The Fourth Gospel adds to the synoptic accounts certain details to
bring out the association between Jesus and the Passover festival. On two
occasions the text notes that Jesus is bound (18:12, 24). In Matthew and
Mark, Jesus is bound after his examination by the Jewish authorities and
before he is handed over to Pilate (Matt 27:2; Mark 15:1). Luke has no
reference to Jesus being bound at all. It is possible that through the double
reference to Jesus' bonds (18:12, 24), the Fourth Evangelist is drawing on
the story of Isaac who is the bound sacrificial victim in Genesis 22. The
binding of Isaac became a highly developed theological motif called the
Aqedah in rabbinic writings. Attempts have been made to give a pre-
Christian date to the *Aqedah* theology wherein Isaac is an adult who willingly moves to his death.[35] The actual term *Aqedah* comes from the act of
binding the *Tamid* lamb (the daily whole offering) and first appears in the
Mishnah.[36] More recently the pre-Christian dating of the *Aqedah* tradition
has been challenged.[37]

Even without presuming an *Aqedah* tradition, the Isaac motif of
Genesis 22 is still part of the biblical tradition and it recurs again in John
19:17 when, like Isaac, Jesus carries for himself (βαστάζων ἑατῷ) the
wood of his own death (Gen 22:6). Support for the Isaac typology is
strengthened by the book of Jubilees (ca. 160 B.C.E.),[38] which portrays the
sacrifice of Isaac as the origin of Passover observance (Jub. 18:17-19).[39]
"His blood, not the Paschal Lamb's, was regarded by Yahweh on the first
Passover night."[40] By the time the book of Jubilees is written, Passover is
linked with the tradition of Isaac's sacrifice. Even though it is difficult to

[35] R. Le Déaut, *La Nuit Pascale: Essai sur la signification de la Pâque juive à partir du Targum d'Exode XII 42,* Analecta Biblica 22 (Rome: Biblical Institute Press,
1963) 133–212; R. J. Daly, "The Soteriological Significance of the Sacrifice of Isaac,"
CBQ 39 (1977) 45–75.

[36] P. R. Davies and B. D. Chilton, "The Aqedah: A Revised Tradition History,"
CBQ 40 (1978) 515. The description of the binding of the lamb is in *m. Tamid* 4.1.

[37] Davies and Chilton, *The Aqedah,* 514–46.

[38] Charlesworth, *Pseudepigrapha,* 2:43.

[39] Jubilees 17:15 dates the sacrifice of Isaac in the first month and from the information in 17:15 and 18:3 it took place on the fourteen day of the first month. "Nous
croyons pouvoir affirmer que, pout l'auteur des *Jubilées,* l'Aqéda est le *premier sacrifice pascal,* et qu'Abraham est considéré comme une sorte de *fondateur* de la fête de la
Pâque," R. Le Déaut, *La Nuit Pascale,* 180.

[40] B. Grigsby, "The Cross as an Expiatory Sacrifice in the Fourth Gospel," *JSNT* 15
(1982) 59.

be entirely sure of an *Aqedah* tradition prior to the first century, there are sufficient parallels with Genesis 22 and Jubilees 18 to see an Isaac motif in the Johannine presentation of Jesus.

Through Isaac typology an important transition takes place. The Temple metaphorically moves a few hundred meters west. In the Genesis account, the sacrifice of Isaac is to take place in the land of Moriah which the chronicler associates with the Temple Mount (Gen 22:2; 2 Chr 3:1). The place of Isaac's sacrifice is therefore the place of the future Temple. By associating Jesus' death with the Isaac story, Golgotha becomes a new Moriah, the place where a new Temple is to be built, a new Passover Lamb is to be sacrificed, and a Father willingly surrenders his beloved Son.[41]

At the beginning and the conclusion of the trial before Pilate, the narrator adds details that emphasize the Passover context. When Jesus is handed over to Pilate, "the Jews" do not go inside the praetorium to ensure that they are not defiled and unable to eat the Passover meal (18:28). At the end of Pilate's inquisition, the evangelist adds the following detail, "Now it was the day of Preparation for the Passover; and it was about noon" (19:14). This detail of day and time gives a sacrificial significance to what is occurring:

> At the time of Jesus, this was the hour when the priests in the Temple would begin the slaughter of the lambs to be used in the Passover meal later that evening. Exodus 12:6 required that the lambs had to be killed "in the evening" of the preparation day. In the first century, the large number of pilgrims meant that tens of thousands of lambs needed to be slaughtered; rabbinic law, therefore, interpreted "evening" to begin at noon so that the necessary work could be completed before the Passover feast began at sundown.[42]

At the same time that the lambs are being handed over to the priests for the Passover sacrifice in the Temple, Pilate is handing over Jesus to "the Jews" who are demanding his death.

Another reminder of the Day of Preparation comes immediately after the death of Jesus (19:31). Because of the approaching Sabbath and Passover, the bodies are removed from public display and the soldiers verify that death has occurred. Unlike the other criminals, Jesus does not have

---

[41] "Both the Jewish and the Christian systems of sacrifice come to be seen as founded upon a father's willingness to surrender his beloved son and the son's unstinting acceptance of the sacrificial role he has been assigned in the great drama of redemption." See J. Levenson, *The Death and Resurrection of the Beloved Son: The Transformation of Child Sacrifice in Judaism and Christianity* (New Haven: Yale University Press, 1993) 175.

[42] Senior, *Passion in John,* 96; also Brown, *The Death of the Messiah,* 1:847; Barrett, *Gospel,* 545.

his legs broken, rather his side is pierced, causing a flow of blood and water. This incident is then followed by two scriptural quotations that are given as a means of interpreting the meaning of the blood and water.[43] "For these things took place that the scripture might be fulfilled, 'Not a bone of him shall be broken'" (v. 36).

There are several views as to which biblical verse is being referred to. Some scholars argue for Ps 34:20 with its description of the suffering of the just one, "He keeps all their bones; not one of them shall be broken" (NRSV).[44] Others see a pentateuchal reference to the Passover lamb.[45] The Passover lamb, killed on this day, is to be a perfect victim without blemish (Exod 12:5) and "you shall not break a bone of it" (Exod 12:46, cf. Num 9:12). A third view attempts to harmonize the depiction of the Just Man in Psalm 34 and the Paschal lamb in the Pentateuch texts.

A further association with the Passover lamb is found in verse 29 when the soldiers use a hyssop branch to pass a sponge of vinegar to Jesus. The hyssop is the branch used to smear the blood of the first Passover lamb on the doorposts of the Israelite houses (Exod 12:22). Only the Fourth Gospel mentions the hyssop branch. The synchronization of the "handing over to death," mention of the hyssop, the biblical citation, and the Isaac typology are subtle suggestions, rather than overt statements that Jesus is the true Passover lamb, but such subtle and unobtrusive means have been characteristic of the Fourth Gospel's symbolism. The readers

---

[43] In keeping with the artistry of the Gospel I look for a theological meaning in the action rather than a simple physiological description. For a discussion on the anatomical causes for blood and water to flow see A. F. Sava, "The Wound in the Side of Christ," *CBQ* 19 (1957) 343–47; J. Wilkinson, "The Incident of the Blood and Water in John 19.34," *SJT* 28 (1975) 149–72.

[44] Dodd, *Interpretation,* 230–38; Bultmann, *Gospel,* 677 n. 1; Schnackenburg, *Gospel,* 3:191–92; Haenchen, *John* 2:200.

[45] Carson, *Gospel,* 627; Morris, *Gospel,* 727; S. Porter, "Can Traditional Exegesis Enlighten Literary Analysis of the Fourth Gospel? An examination of the Old Testament Fulfillment Motif and the Passover Theme," *The Gospels and the Scriptures of Israel,* ed. Craig Evans and W. R. Stegner, Journal for the Study of the New Testament Supplement Series 104 (Sheffield: Sheffield Academic Press, 1994) 404–5. Moloney, *Reading John,* 72; Brown, *Death of the Messiah,* 2:1184–88; Schwank, *Evangelium,* 466; de la Potterie, *The Hour,* 169; B. Longenecker, "The Unbroken Messiah: A Johannine Feature and its Social Function," *NTS* 41 (1995) 437. Grigsby cites three reasons for reading the quotation as a reference to the Paschal lamb. Linguistically it stands closest to Num 9:12 (MT). The Paschal context and the haste to remove the bodies is similar to the requirement that the slain lamb must not remain into the following day. Finally, he follows Guilding's thesis that Exod 12:46 and Num 9:12 were read during Nissan. See "The Cross as an Expiatory Sacrifice," 58.

have followed Johannine symbolization through two earlier Passovers, the Sabbath, Tabernacles, and Dedication. Following such an educative narrative, the subtle allusions to the Passover lamb would not be lost on the Johannine readers.

Jesus' Death as a New Passover

By presenting Jesus as the new Paschal lamb, the evangelist is giving the Christian community a symbolic interpretation of Jesus' death and testifying that this death has already been attested to by the Scriptures.[46] The Johannine emphasis is not primarily a death to atone for sin, or a sacrifice of expiation, because the Passover lamb was not expiatory but a replacement: "Its purpose was not sacrificial but apotropaic."[47] Later in the tradition, a further sacrifice was added within the Passover as a sin offering, but this was not the Passover lamb (Num 28:22; Ezek 45:21-25). The primary purpose of the blood of the Passover lamb is to provide a salvific sign marking the households of the Israelites:

> Tell all the congregation of Israel that on the tenth day of this month they shall take every man [sic] a lamb according to **their fathers' houses,** a lamb for a household (emphasis added). Then they shall take some of the blood, and put it on the two doorposts and the lintel of the houses in which they eat them. The blood shall be a sign for you, upon the houses where you are; and when I see the blood, I will pass over you, and no plague shall fall upon you to destroy you, when I smite the land of Egypt (Exod 12:3, 7, 13).

The Johannine model of salvation is, in the light of the Exodus, an act of liberation from the dominion of slavery to the freedom of children within the household/Temple of God, "By strength of hand the LORD brought us out of Egypt, from the house of bondage" (Exod 13:14). In this model there is a liberation from sin, where sin is perceived as a power which enslaves humanity to "the ruler of this word," just as Israel was once held captive within the house of slavery.[48] But with the incarnation of Jesus,

---

[46] Obermann, *Die christologische Erfüllung,* 309–10.

[47] Ashton, *Understanding,* 491.

[48] In Deuteronomy, the "house of slavery" image is used in contexts of a warning not to follow other gods. A contrast is set up between belonging to the Lord and belonging to other gods. Having been brought out of the house of slavery, Israel must not return to it by falling into idolatry. "Take care that you do not forget the LORD, who brought you out of the Land of Egypt, out of the house of slavery. The LORD your God you shall fear; him you shall serve and by his name alone shall you swear. Do not follow other gods. . ." (Deut 6:12-14a. cf. 5:6; 13:10).

the true king has come, offering life (John 10:10) and freedom. "Truly truly I say to you everyone who commits sin is a slave to sin. The slave does not remain in the household forever; the son/daughter remains forever. If therefore the son sets you free you will be free indeed" (8:34-36 my translation). The contrast between slave and child is yet another way of expressing the idea of belonging to the ruler of this world or belonging to the household/Temple of the true king.

The liberation model of salvation is very different from Israel's sacrificial system. Jesus' death, although presented as a Paschal sacrifice, is never described as a "laying down of life" **for sin,** where sin is the cause or reason for his death. All the expressions describing Jesus' death are couched in terms of the people who will benefit by his death:

> ". . . the bread which I shall give **for the life of** the world is my flesh" (6:51).
> "The good shepherd lays down his life **for the sheep**" (10:11 also v. 15).
> "It is expedient for you that one man should die **for the people**" (11:50 cf. 51, 52; 18:14).
> "No-one has greater love than this, to lay down one's life for one's friends" (15:13 NRSV).

In the Fourth Gospel Jesus' death is a free laying down of life for those whom he loves, and in this consummate act of love Jesus offers liberation from the slavery of sin. It is love rather than sin which is the dominant power leading to Jesus' death:

> No-one has greater love than this, to lay down one's life for one's friends. You are my friends if you do what I command you. I do not call you servants any longer, because the servant does not know what the master is doing; but I have called you friends, because I have made known to you everything that I have heard from my Father (15:13-15 NRSV).

The liberation Jesus offers is only possible to those who recognize who Jesus is, and the Father whom he makes known. "The Jews, "who are described in this narrative as those children of Abraham who are slaves to sin (8:34) and children of the devil (8:44), do not recognize Jesus and his word finds no room in them (8:37).[49] The disciples, by contrast, are those in whom Jesus' words abide (15:7), who abide in Jesus' love (15:9, 10) and Jesus' love means they are no longer slaves (15:15). The disciple

---

[49] A very clear discussion on "Sin" and "Paternity" can be found in J. T. Forestell, *The Word of the Cross: Salvation as Revelation in the Fourth Gospel,* Analecta Biblica 57 (Rome: Biblical Institute Press, 1974) 148–55.

recognizes the Father in Jesus (14:10) and is called to live as a son/daughter of this Father by doing the same works as Jesus, the son (14:12).

In his entire life Jesus was God's gift to the world, given in love for salvation (3:16). God's love, expressed in Jesus, achieves what Israel's sacrificial system could never achieve, a way of being one with God. No longer does humanity need to do **cultic acts** to remove the barrier which sin creates between humanity and God. For love of humanity God has crossed the barrier (3:16). God has come to the world through the incarnate Son (1:14). In the Son, those who choose to believe this gift of love have a way of access to the Father (14:6). The way of the Son is utter gift from God, and not a human cultic action. In the Hour, the fullness of this gift of love is revealed as Jesus' gives himself over to death as a new Passover lamb, whose death creates a new household/Temple of God, and whose blood is the sign of those belonging to this household. In belonging to the household of God, the believer is freed from the household of slavery, the dominion of sin. The "doing" now required of the believer is to do as Jesus, the Son, did (13:15), to love "as I have loved" (15:12). Living in a communion of love is the way of manifesting the ongoing presence of God in the world (17:23), the only way of being a free son/daughter of the household/Temple of God (8:35; 14:23).

The Spirit

In the discussion above I have interpreted Jesus' death through the lens of the first biblical quotation, "Not one of his legs shall be broken." There is a second biblical passage which is also cited in relation to 'these things' which occurred, i.e., the piercing of Jesus' side and the flow of blood and water. The second quotation, "And again another scripture says, 'They shall look on him whom they have pierced'" (v. 37), finds greater agreement from scholars as having its source in the prophet Zechariah:[50]

> And I will pour out on the house of David and the inhabitants of Jerusalem a spirit of compassion and supplication, so that, when they look on him whom they have pierced, they shall mourn for him, as one mourns for an only child, and weep bitterly over him, as one weeps over a first-born (Zech 12:10).

While only one phrase of the entire verse is quoted, this phrase serves as a reminder of the whole context of the passage which speaks of a spirit

---

[50] See Menken, *Old Testament Quotations,* 168–78, for a detailed discussion on the form of this quotation and its possible pre-Johannine existence as an early Christian *testimonium.*

of compassion and supplication being poured out, followed by a cleansing stream of water. "On that day there shall be a fountain opened for the house of David and the inhabitants of Jerusalem to cleanse them from sin and uncleanness." (Zech 13:1). As with the first quotation, this second biblical reference provides insight into the Johannine interpretation of Jesus' death.

In the Hour Jesus brings the work he was sent to accomplish to its conclusion. His final τετέλεσται (v. 30) echoes the judgment of Genesis when God finished (using a form of τελέω) the work of creation (Gen 2:1).[51] Throughout the Gospel Jesus had claimed that God in fact was still working (5:17), that the creative work of God had not yet been completed, and that he has been sent to complete (τελέω) this work (4:34; 5:36; 17:4). In the Hour, as the sixth day comes to an end, Jesus announces the completion of God's creative work so the Sabbath can truly begin (19:31). As one creative act draws to its end, the new eschatological age is ushered in and its first gift is the Spirit.

When Jesus dies, he inclines his head and gives down the Spirit to the small group of believers gathered at the foot of his cross. They are symbolically "reborn" from above, as children of God (cf. 3:3). Here at the cross, where God's Kingship is powerfully emphasized, Jesus' strange words to Nicodemus are fulfilled, "No-one can enter the Kingdom of God without being born of water and Spirit" (3:5 NRSV).

This is a constitutive gift of the Spirit, drawing believers into Jesus' own divine sonship. Later in "the Hour," the ministerial function of the Spirit will be emphasized. There are not two bestowals of the Spirit. I would rather speak of two moments within the one Hour,[52] one moment where the focus is on the believer's relationship to Jesus, and a second moment where the focus is on the believer's relationship to the world, as the agent of Jesus in the world.[53] A parallel can be made with Jesus' own life. The start of Jesus' ministry is preceded by the descent of the Spirit upon him (1:32-34). Immediately after John's testimony about the Spirit

---

[51] M. Hengel, "The Old Testament in the Fourth Gospel," *The Gospels and the Scriptures of Israel,* ed. Craig Evans and W. Richard Stegner, Journal for the study of the New Testament Supplement Series 104 (Sheffield: Sheffield Press, 1994) 393–94.

[52] The unity in the hour of the crucifixion (chs. 18–19) and the resurrection (ch. 20) is evident in the Johannine insistence that the day of death is a day of "Preparation." Death is not the end, but is the essential preparatory stage leading to the dawn of the eschatological "eighth day," the "great day," (cf. 8:12). See the earlier discussion on the "great day" within the feast of Tabernacles.

[53] For clear discussion on the use of ἀποστέλλειν and πέμπειν as they apply to Jesus and the disciples, see Burge, *Anointed Community,* 200–4.

coming down and remaining on him, Jesus begins to gather the community of disciples (1:35-51).

This presence of the Spirit is therefore associated with ministry. However, Jesus is the incarnation of the *logos* who was with God in the beginning (1:1). Since the relationship between *logos* and God has no beginning point, there is no description of a "first" descent of the Spirit constituting Jesus as Son. The sonship of the divine *logos* is eternal. The believer on the other hand must first be drawn into the divine filiation and then, like the Son, be sent on mission into the world. "As the Father has sent me, even so I send you" (20:21).[54] For this reason the narrative describes two moments in the giving of the Spirit to the believers, a moment of birth at the Cross (19:30) and a moment of mission (20:21-23).[55]

The ministerial gift of the Spirit is linked with the cleansing, purifying Spirit evidenced in the Scriptures (Jer 31:34; Ezek 36:26, 29, 33) and Qumran (1QS, IV:20-23).[56] John's designation of Jesus as "the Lamb of God who takes away the sin of the world" (1:29) is also linked to the Spirit since it follows his observing the Spirit descending upon him (1:32). The title "Lamb of God" as used by the Baptist is not a reference to a sacrificial sin-offering, or the Paschal lamb, but a messianic title which has its background in Jewish apocalyptic literature.[57] Some commentators relate the Baptist's recognition of Jesus as "the Lamb of God who takes away the sin of the world" (1:29) to the Passover lamb, but as I noted above, the Passover lamb was not directly expiatory nor is Jesus' death presented as an expiatory sacrifice. The Baptist's comment is not a proleptic reference to Jesus' death for such prolepses are quite explicit (cf. 2:21, 22; 6:71; 12:33). At this early stage in the narrative the "Lamb of God" title is but one of a series of Jewish titles found in this first chapter: Rabbi (1:38), Messiah (1:41) he of whom Moses and the prophets wrote (1:45), Son of God, King of Israel (1:49).

---

[54] Burge, *Anointed Community,* 199 n. 6, notes that although two different words are used for "sent," ἀπέσταλκεν, πέμπω, they are used synonymously.

[55] In the missioning moment the creation theme is still present in the N. T. *hapax legomenon,* ἐνεφύσησεν. Hengel sees in this choice of word a direct reference back to Gen 2:7 where this is the LXX trans. describing God breathing into the nostrils of Adam to bring the inanimate clay-creature to life. See Hengel, "Old Testament," 391.

[56] S. Lyonnet and L. Sabourin, *Sin, Redemption, and Sacrifice: A Biblical and Patristic Study,* Analecta Biblica 48 (Rome: Biblical Institute Press, 1970) 30.

[57] See Dodd, *Interpretation,* 230–38. A more thorough examination of this title within the Gospel and Apocalypse can be found in J. D'Souza, *The Lamb of God in the Johannine Writings* (Allahabad: St. Paul, 1968) 140–43. See also the discussion in Lyonnet, *Sin, Redemption and Sacrifice,* 39–41.

With the ministerial gift of the Spirit (1:33) Jesus is the agent/ Lamb of God in the world. Because Jesus is "of God" he acts as God who alone can take away sin. Within this Gospel the ministry of "taking away sin" does not look like the exorcisms of the Synoptics. Taking away the power of sin, for John, is revealing the power of God's love in giving Jesus, the true sovereign of the world, who has come to humanity and in so doing has taken away the barriers between God and humanity, and destroyed the enslaving power of the false "ruler of this world"[58]:

> The death of Christ in Jn is the fullest expression of God's love for men [sic] and the communication of eternal life to those who believe in this love. The manifestation of divine love destroys the power of the devil in the world and rescues mankind [sic] from Satan's thraldom of hatred, lying, murder and self-glorification.[59]

Jesus is one who baptizes ἐν πνεύματι ἁγίῳ, with a Spirit of holiness (1:33). His baptizing activity is recorded only once when the disciples receive a πνεῦμα ἅγιον (20:22). The disciples then continue Jesus' own mission and act as his agents in continuing God's activity of destroying sin's power. Forestell argues that 20:23 is a foreign addition to the narrative made in order to deal with later pastoral problems in the Church.[60] While the vocabulary of *forgiveness* is not usual in the Fourth Gospel, the theology itself is not foreign. By revealing the true Father, Jesus has been engaged in the work of taking away the power of sin and drawing humanity into the household of God:

> *The meaning of the cross in the Fourth Gospel is the completion of revelation and revelation is atoning* (that is, it brings humans into a friendly relationship with God). The revelation of God's true self has within it power to overcome the alienation of humans from God.[61]

The prophets described this in terms of cleansing and purifying (Ezek 36:25-27; Zech 13:1). As the Temple waters brought life and healing to the arid wasteland (Ezek 47:9-12), so Jesus came offering waters of eternal life (4:14) and rebirth (3:3, 5). Through the gift of the Spirit at the Cross (19:30), they are constituted as the new Temple of God's presence, so

---

[58] For a discussion on sin as a power than separates the world from God, see Lyonnet, *Sin, Redemption and Sacrifice,* 39–42.

[59] Forestell, *The Word of the Cross,* 166.

[60] Forestell, *The Word of the Cross,* 157.

[61] Kysar, *The Maverick Gospel,* 54. On this same page he speaks of the Cross as creating a new family of God.

they too can offer the world the waters of life and healing. On the first day of the week, through the power of the Spirit (20:21-23), Jesus' ministry is to continue through the ministry of the disciples. There is no suggestion in the text as to what forgiveness of sin looks like. The community is simply told that sins will be forgiven through them. It would be quite wrong to read back into these words later Christian rituals and specific words of forgiveness. Forgiveness of sin could simply be the love displayed within the community, a love that reveals and calls sin into judgment, the same loving and judgmental presence operative in Jesus' person.

Presence in Absence—Johannine Sacramentality

The issue of the blood and the water is followed by a most emphatic testimony of a witness (v. 35). This scene, more than any other moment within the crucifixion, is singled out "so that you also may believe."[62] The blood and water must have had particular significance for the Johannine community to be given such emphasis by the narrator who self-consciously reaches out across space and time to "you," the later readers. The first-person testimony indicates that the blood and water is the link between the events narrated and the community of believers of later generation.[63] Here we glimpse the sacramental life of the Johannine community. When Jesus is no longer a physical presence with them, the community can still be drawn into his filial relationship with God and participate in the sacrificial gift of his life in their sacraments of baptism and Eucharist.[64]

---

[62] So striking is this first-person testimony, that some commentators believe it is a secondary addition; so Bultmann, *Gospel,* 678; Brown, *Gospel,* 2:945; Beasley-Murray, *John,* 354. Against such opinions it is worth noting that first-person testimony was present in the Prologue (1:14, 16) and narrative comments are not unusual in this Gospel (e.g., 2:17; 21-22; 12:16; 20:30-31).

[63] Obermann states that the link is made in the Scripture quotation from Zechariah when the subject of the verb "look" is not identified: "Der universale Charakter wird durch das unbestimmte Subjekt in ὄψονται erreicht, mit dem alle unter dem Kreuz Stehenden (Soldaten, 'Juden' und Gläubige) gemeint sind." See *Die christologische Erfüllung,* 324).

[64] The controversial issue of Johannine Sacramentality is treated more fully in F. J. Moloney, "When is John talking about Sacraments?," *ABR* 30 (1982) 10–33. Moloney presents Johannine sacramentality within its historical context, in the absence of Jesus and in the community's conflict with the synagogue; also J. P. Heil, *Blood and Water: The Death and Resurrection of Jesus in John 18–21,* Catholic Biblical Quarterly Monograph Series 27 (Washington, D.C.: Catholic Bible Association of America, 1995) 105–9. Barrett, *Gospel,* 556–57, notes a possible Sacramental interpretation but sees this as secondary; the primary importance of the blood and water was to testify to the death. Schnackenburg, *Gospel,* 3:291, and Brown, *Gospel,* 2:952, also see the

During the first Passover in Jerusalem (2:23) Jesus encountered Nicodemus (3:1).[65] Jesus spoke to him of being born "from above" (ἄνοθεν) (3:3) of a birth through water and the Spirit (3:5) and of "entering the Kingdom of God" (3:5). From the cross the Spirit is given and water flows from the pierced side of Christ. These images emerge from the baptismal practices of the early community, previously recorded at the end of Matthew's Gospel (28:19).

Within the second Passover, Jesus offered his own life as a new bread from heaven and promised life only to those who would eat his flesh and drink his blood (6:51, 53, 54). On the cross a new Passover lamb is slain, and blood flows as Jesus surrenders his life for others, giving his blood as the sign for the new household of God freed from slavery to sin's power. In the eucharistic practice of the early Church, the household of believers can continue to participate in the salvific activity of Jesus. The third and final Passover encapsulates the teaching and motifs of the earlier Passovers through the image of the pierced side, the sign of the blood, and the accompanying biblical passages. The community of believers are to look to their baptismal waters, and their eucharistic bread and see in and through the symbols the ongoing presence of Jesus in their midst.

The High Priest

For centuries there has been an interpretation of the seamless robe as a symbol of Jesus' sacerdotal role. In recent years scholars have moved away from this interpretation to seeing, in the undivided tunic, a symbol of church unity. In what follows I wish to examine again the possibility of Jesus as the High Priest, as the offerer, as well as the offering, i.e., the Paschal lamb.[66]

The symbolism within the Gospel is primarily directed to the person of Jesus, he is the lamb of God (1:29, 36), the bridegroom (3:29), the source of living water (4:10), bread from heaven (6:50), light (8:12), good shepherd (10:14), vine (15:1). Where the Gospel directs the symbolism away

---

sacramental meaning as secondary. Carson, *Gospel,* 624, totally rules out any sacramental reference.

[65] There is nothing in the text to indicate any change of place or time from the Passover in v. 23 to the dialogue with Nicodemus. The ἦν beginning 3:1 is a connective, linking the introductory verses to the conclusion of ch 2. See Brown, *Gospel,* 1:129. Léon-Dufour, *Lecture* 1:282, notes also the use of the pronoun αὐτὸν to refer to Jesus who was last named in 2:24.

[66] For discussions on the tunic as a symbol of unity, see Schuchard, *Scripture Within Scripture,* 125–132; I. de la Potterie, "La tunique sans couture, symbole du Christ grand prêtre?," *Bib* 60 (1979) 255–69.

from Jesus this is clearly indicated in the texts: "I am the vine, **you** are the branches" (15:5), "Who ever believes in me, as Scripture said, 'out of his side shall flow rivers of living water.' Now this he said **about the Spirit.** . ." (7:38, 39);[67] or is to be understood from the context, ". . . he who enters by the door is the shepherd of the sheep. . . the sheep hear his voice, and he calls his own sheep by name and leads them out . . . and the sheep follow him for they know his voice" (10:2-4). Because the Gospel symbolism is primarily christological, the division of Jesus' garments should first be approached as a possible illustration of some aspect of Jesus' mission and/or identity. There are three emphases in the Passion narrative that taken together lend support to the notion of Jesus' priesthood.

At the close of the Farewell Discourse, Jesus prays " For their sake I consecrate myself . . ." (ὑπὲρ αὐτῶν [ἐγὼ] ἁγιάζω ἐμαυτόν) (17:19). In the immediate context of his returning to the Father, and the earlier use of ὑπὲρ in association with death for the nation (ὑπὲρ τοῦ ἔθνους) as prophesied by Caiaphas (11:51), the shepherd laying down life for his sheep (ὑπὲρ τῶν προβάτων) (10:11), and Jesus' laying down life for his friends (ὑπὲρ τῶν φίλων) (15:13), Jesus' prayer of self-consecration suggests a sacrificial understanding of his death, for in the LXX ἁγιάζω usually means to set apart for God, and is used of animals who are killed for cultic purposes (Exod 13:2; 28:41; 29:1; 40:9; Lev 16:4).[68] In his coming to the Father, Jesus passes his life over, into the realm of the sacred. Jesus consecrates himself, as a priest consecrates the victim to be consumed upon the altar:

> Thus it is plausible that, when in xvii 19 Jesus speaks of self-consecration, we are to think of him not only as the incarnation of God's word consecrated by the Father but also as a priest offering himself as a victim for those whom God has given him.[69]

The crucifixion may be a Roman execution, but it is also Jesus' self-offering for others. The notion of one death for the nation, spoken by Caiaphas (11:50), "accords with the sacrificial nature of the Jewish high

---

[67] See also the image of the woman in labor and its reference to the disciples (16:21-22).

[68] Carson, *Gospel,* 567, notes that this passage evokes the biblical language where consecration becomes synonymous with sacrificial death (Deut 15:19, 21); also Talbert, *Reading John,* 227.

[69] Brown, *Gospel,* 2:766–67; note also the comment by Barrett, *Gospel,* 511, "The language is equally appropriate to the preparation of a priest and the preparation of a sacrifice."

priesthood."[70] While it may appear that this priestly function is carried out by Caiaphas, Annas, and the other Jewish priests, who offer Jesus to the Romans (18:35) in order to save the nation and the "Holy Place" (Temple) (11:48), in fact Jesus, by his self-surrender, and dedicatory prayer, is the true offerer, and Caiaphas unwittingly participates in the destruction of the true Temple.

Second, in the Jewish interrogations (19:13-27), there are eight references to the High Priest (vv. 13, 15 x2, 16, 19, 22, 24, 25). There is also confusion about who is meant by this title; in verses 19 and 22 it appears that Jesus is being questioned by the High Priest, but in verse 24 he is sent from Annas to the Caiaphas.[71] This confusion about the identity of the high priest raises the question, who is the real High Priest? Several times in the Gospel narrative there has been a similar question put to the readers, demanding a choice between Jesus and another character or even a Jewish cultic symbol. In chapter 4, the reader and the Samaritan woman are asked to choose between two water-givers, Jacob or Jesus. In chapter 6 two breads are contrasted, the Manna and Jesus. At the feast of Tabernacles, Jesus is the true source of water and light. Given the consistency of this Johannine technique of contrasts to reveal the identity of Jesus, it is possible that the main function of the Jewish "Trial," is to point to Jesus' high priestly identity since it does not bring the issue to a resolution with a judgment. The only genuine trial in this narrative is Pilate's.

The most significant indicator that Jesus has a high priestly role is linked to his "Nazarene" task as the builder of the eschatological Temple. I have already discussed the kingly function of the title "Nazarene" but it also has a priestly function. According to Zechariah the Temple builder combines both royal and sacerdotal roles. The man named "Branch" is Joshua/Jesus the son of the High Priest (Zech 6:11-12):

Take from them silver and gold, and make a crown, and set it upon the head of Joshua, the son of Jehoz'adak, the high priest; and say to him, "Thus says the LORD of hosts, 'Behold, the man whose name is the Branch: for he shall grow up in his place, and he shall build the temple of the LORD'" (Zech 6:11-12).

[70] J. P. Heil, "Jesus as the Unique High Priest in the Gospel of John," *CBQ* 57 (1995) 731.
[71] Staley treats this confusion about the High Priest in some detail as a deliberate rhetorical devise that forces the reader into an interpretive dilemma, a dilemma I pose in the question: "Who is the real High Priest?" J. Staley, *Reading with a Passion: Rhetoric, Autobiography, and the American West in the Gospel of John* (New York: Continuum, 1995) 98–109.

The crown Jesus wears not only indicates his royalty but also signifies his priesthood for it is the sign of both King (2 Sam 12:30; 2 Kgs 11:12) and High Priest (Lev 8:9). There is no indication that the crown is removed from Jesus' head. On the cross he is therefore wearing royal and sacerdotal symbols.

Apart from these three general indicators of a priestly theme, the scene at the foot of the cross, with its uniquely Johannine emphases, indicates this interpretation through the particular words used. The tunic is described carefully; it is seamless, woven from above (ἄνωθεν), and woven entirely (ὅλου) (19:23). De la Potterie is correct in stating that the seamless garment of the High Priest is not the inner tunic (χιτών), but the outer robe of the ephod,[72] "It shall have in it an opening for the head, with a woven binding around the opening, like the opening in a garment, that it may not be torn" (Exod 28:32). However, both garments are similar in being seamlessly woven and the soldiers' words, like the words of Exodus, show a concern not to tear the garment. This is sufficient to establish a degree of correspondence between the seamless garment of the High Priest and that worn by Jesus, so that the symbolism of priesthood applies to Jesus.[73] Symbolism does not require exact correspondence. Earlier, the soldiers had arrayed him in a crown of thorns and a purple robe (19:2), these were not identical with the crown and robe of a king, but they were sufficient to suggest kingship. The undivided seamless garment of Jesus in this context is suggestive of priesthood.

The action of the soldiers in casting lots is the very action used to decide who among the priests will be the one to make the offering. In fact the usual sense of λαγχάνω (v. 24) is in terms of priestly duties (Luke 1:9), and in John 19:24 it has the **unusual** sense "to cast lots."[74] Heil adds that as Jesus' authority comes "from above" so too his tunic is woven "ἄνωθεν." In the description of the High Priest's robes they are clearly designed by God's command (Exod 36:12, 14, 28, 33, 36, 38), their origin comes "from above."[75] Jesus' tunic, like the garments of the High Priest is woven (ὑφαντός Exod 28:6, 28; 36:10, 11, 15, 29, 35 LXX) and is whole (δι ὅλου).[76] Taken in isolation none of these terms—ἄνωθεν, ὑφαντός, δι

---

[72] de la Potterie, *The Hour,* 126; de la Potterie, *La tunique,* 260.

[73] There is no need to refer to the confusing statement about the High Priest's garments found in Josephus (*Ant* iii.161). The Exodus description of a seamless robe that cannot be torn provides the analogy.

[74] H. Hanse, "λαγχάνω," *TDNT* 4 (1967) 1. In the Scripture quotation (19:24), the phrase used is ἔβαλον κλῆρον.

[75] Heil, *Jesus as the Unique High Priest,* 742.

[76] The robe of the ephod was similarly entirely (ὅλον) and of blue (Exod 28:27; 36:30 LXX).

ὅλου, λαγχάνω—are conclusive indicators of priesthood, but taken together, in the context of Jesus' self-giving sacrifice, his Nazarene title and its links to Zechariah, they can indicate Jesus' High Priestly function.

One reason why some commentators cannot accept any possible allusions to priesthood in this scene is because they do not accept that there is any "priestly" christology within the Fourth Gospel. "The Theology of the priesthood of Jesus is not Johannine. . . ."[77] Is this an accurate assessment? Or can a concept of priesthood fit within the christology of the Fourth Gospel?

In terms of a "doing of cultic actions," the answer must be "No." During the first Passover Jesus expressed a prophetic critique of such cultic activity in driving out of the Temple the sacrificial animals that were essential for Israel's cult. However, other aspects of priesthood can be applied appropriately to Jesus. Although not of a Levitical line, he is the "first born son," the only son (1:18; cf. Num 3:12-13). He is the Consecrated One (10:36; cf. Exod 28:41), and he is the only one who enters the presence of God (1:18; cf. Lev 16:2). In the Gospel he functions as priest when he makes intercessory prayer for his disciples (17:10-26), when he reveals God in the world (17:6, 8, 26), and when he gives his own life for the sake of others (11:50; 15:30; 17:19). In his own person and activity there are parallels with some aspects of Jewish priesthood.

A consistent Johannine theme has been the presentation of Jesus as the one who brings to completion the rituals and symbols of Israel's cult. In his role of Priest and unbroken lamb, Jesus brings to completion and transcends Israel's sacrificial cult. The cultic activity of Israel was understood as a means of overcoming the barriers between God and the people caused by sin. The forgiveness of sin was God's action, and the expiatory sacrifices were seen as God's gift to the people to achieve covenantal communion (Lev 17:11):

> According to the theory of expiatory sacrifice for sin, the efficacy of the sacrifice does not lie in the offering of the victim, spotless though it must be, but in the rites performed with the blood released by the immolation of the victim. Since blood is the divine element and contains the life, it restores community of life with god and the people. Such sacrifices do not have satisfactory value but are provided by a gracious God for the restoration of union between himself and his people.[78]

Now a new gift has been given. The gift of the Torah, and the cultic activity associated with the Mosaic covenant, have been brought to per-

---

[77] de la Potterie, *The Hour,* 126. Similarly, Schuchard, *Scripture within Scripture,* 128.
[78] Forestell, *The Word of the Cross,* 164–65.

fection in God's gift of Jesus (1:17), who is the new Temple (2:21) offering a new means of communion with God. The former cultic acts and the priesthood they required are transcended in Jesus' priesthood. The Son, given in love to the world (3:16), reveals to his disciples a new commandment of love (13:34), and demonstrates to them the utmost depths of his love, and the Father's love, in the gift of his life for them. Cultic sacrificial activity will no longer be the means of communion of life between humanity and God. This activity is now transcended by the loving union among disciples which will draw believers into union with God (14:23; 15:12; 17:20-26). Jesus is the definitive Passover lamb and definitive High Priest. From this time on there is no further need of cultic sacrificial rituals.

Pierced Side and Temple

The piercing of the side of Jesus and the flow of blood and water provide a very graphic final depiction of the crucifixion, and a number of scholars look to passages in the Scriptures as background to this scene. The passage many scholars refer to is Ezekiel 47[79] and the waters flowing from the Temple.[80]

The Temple is part of the eschatological program in the closing chapters of Ezekiel. There is no description of its being built which suggests that this Temple comes from God. The water flows down from the side of the Temple (Ezek 47:1-2), as the blood and water issue from the side of Jesus (John 19:34). Although John adds a flow of blood where Ezekiel has only water, this may well be influenced by the sacrificial interpretation of the death just witnessed, where blood is so important. The word used for side (πλευρά) does not occur in Ezekiel 47, but it is the word consistently used to describe the inner chambers at the side of the Temple (1 Kgs 6:5, 6, 8, 15, 16; Ezek 41:5, 6, 7, 8, 9, 26).

---

[79] X. Léon-Dufour, *Lecture,* 4:163; Manns, *L'Evangile,* 426–27; de la Potterie, *The Hour,* 175.

[80] An alternative image is that of the water from the rock at Meribah (Num 20:9-13), especially the Targumic version which reads "And Moses raised his hand and smote the rock with this staff twice: the first time blood dripped, but the second time much water came forth, and he gave the congregation and their livestock (water) to drink" (*Tg. Ps.-Jon.* Num 20:11). Attractive though this is, the image of the rock in the wilderness has not been a prominent christological symbol throughout the Gospel, whereas the symbol of the Temple has been. The context of the miracle at Meribah is one of quarrel and discord within the congregation which seems an unlikely theme to introduce at this moment of "the hour" when Jesus is gathering disciples to himself (12:32). The symbol of the rock is not significant enough to carry the theology of the "hour."

In Jesus' death, the "inner chamber" of his body/Temple is opened, releasing the waters of the Spirit. One Temple is in the process of being destroyed, even as a new Temple is being raised. Architectural imagery is employed to convey a theology of the Spirit who dwells within Jesus and will now dwell within the disciples. The waters of Ezekiel's Temple issued forth into the land vivifying (Ezek 47:9), nourishing, and healing (Ezek 47:12). The new Temple, endowed with the Spirit, will be an ongoing source within the world of life-giving waters (John 4:14, 7:38) and cleansing from sin (John 20:23).

The image of the pierced side may also draw on another aspect of Temple architecture, namely the altar. In the Mishnah the following description is given of the altar of burnt-offerings:

> And at the south-western corner there were two holes like two narrow nostrils by which the blood that was poured over the western base and the southern base used to run down and mingle in the water channel and flow out into the brook Kidron (*m. Mid.* 3:2).

Ezekiel's description of the altar in the Temple also refers to a gutter cavity around the altar in which the water and blood flow down to be drained. The term for this gutter is חיק (Ezek 43:13). This is an unusual architectural term and seems to have developed from an analogy with the human body where it usually means the "lap" or "bosom."[81] A writer familiar with the Jerusalem Temple and its altar, who has already brought together architecture and anatomy, in speaking of Jesus' body as the Temple (2:21), may here be further exploiting the rich symbolism of Jewish sacrifice. Christians need no longer look to the blood and water in the חיק (cavity) of a pierced altar, for the blood and water have now been released from the side (πλευρά) of Jesus.

The choice of the term πλευρά to describe the side of Jesus, where earlier the evangelist had used κόλπος (13:23), as well as alluding to the description of the inner chambers of the Temple, may also be a deliberate allusion to God's work of creation. In the Yahwist's description of God's first creative activity, he describes the birth of the woman, later called the mother of life (Gen 3:21), as a birth from the side (τῶν πλευρῶν) (Gen 2:21). The flow of blood and water from the side of Jesus, seen against the Genesis background, may symbolize a moment of birth, a moment when a new life comes into being.[82] The concept of birth is not foreign to the

---

[81] M. Dijkstra, "The Altar of Ezekiel: Fact or Fiction?," *VT* 42 (1992) 27–28.

[82] A wide range of interpretations of the blood and water, as well as a list of Patristic associations, can be found in E. Malatesta, "Blood and water from the pierced side

Gospel. The gift of the Spirit has been described to Nicodemus as being born from above (3:3, 5, 7). Jesus hands down the Spirit to the mother and 'son' who stand at the foot of the cross. The words to the mother of Jesus, who like Eve is called woman (19:26, cf. Gen 2:23) and mother (19:27, cf. Gen 3:21), and the beloved disciple, create a new set of familial relationships and constitute a new household of God.

Jesus' words and the accompanying gift of the Spirit can be understood as a birth "from above," thus fulfilling the words to Nicodemus. Those who accept Jesus and receive the gift of the Spirit can now be called "children of God" (1:12). The first creative activity of God is brought to completion in Jesus' death, and the release of the Spirit ushers in the dawn of a new creation.[83] An action that appears to be a confirmation of death, is, from the Johannine perspective, a moment of birth.

7:38 and 19:34

The graphic image of the pierced side and the flow of water (and blood) tempts scholars to see this moment as the fulfillment of the passage during the earlier Feast of Tabernacles (7:38). This is particularly so if one reads the christological sense in the punctuation and translation. When discussing this passage I argued that it is not a christological image, but looks ahead to the Christian community as the new Temple and source of the living waters of the Spirit. There are no verbal associations between 7:38 and 19:34 such as using the identical word for side, by repeating κολίας in 19:34 or using πλευρά in 7:38. Elsewhere the evangelist does use such intertextual associations through verbal links (i.e., κόλπος 1:18; 13:23; τὰ ἴδια 1:11; 19:37, τοὺς ἰδίους 13:1). The lack of clear verbal associations allows both passages to be treated as independent units, which are not to be read over and against each other.

The one point of similarity is that both passages draw on the symbolism of water from the side of the eschatological Temple. While Jesus is in the world, his body is the Temple of God's presence and so he can offer living water (4:10). But there will come a time when the Temple of his

---

of Christ (Jn 19, 34)," *Segni E Sacramenti Nel Vangelo Di Giovanni,* ed. Pius-Ramon Tragan, Studia Anselmiana 67 (Rome: Editrice Anselmiana, 1977) 165–81.

[83] The theme of creation is very richly developed by Manns, *L'Evangile,* 401–29. He draws attention to many other Genesis motifs within the Johannine Passion: the garden, the Kedron torrent (18:1), the tree of life in the middle of the garden (cf. 19:18), the rabbinic location of Eden beside the Jerusalem Temple. See Barker, *The Gate of Heaven,* 57–95. On the Kedron as a seasonally flowing river, see Barrett, *Gospel,* 517.

physical body is no longer present. I have argued that Jesus is the Nazarene builder of the new Temple. The flow of blood and water (19:34) symbolizes the initiating moment when Jesus, as he dies, gives over the Spirit to the embryonic community (19:30). "John 19:34b, in short, makes the death (the flow of blood) the moment when the life-giving Spirit (the flow of water) streams forth."[84] In the earlier feast of Tabernacles Jesus' words point ahead to the believers, who, having received the Spirit, have been constituted as the new Temple/household of God and can continue to provide access to a source of living water (20:22).[85] In the absence of Jesus, the world still has a life-giving Temple of God's dwelling, in the community of disciples. The two passages are related but their Temple imagery points in different directions—to the future Temple/community (7:38)—to the Temple of Jesus in its moment of transformation (19:34).

Burial as a King 19:38-42

In the scenes of the arrest and burial Jesus is in a garden with his friends. As Manns comments, "Le symbol du jardin encadre la section."[86] In the scene of the arrest Jesus' sovereign control was much in evidence. In his burial, Jesus is treated as a King:

> And this is no burial like that in the Synoptic tradition, without anointing and aromatic oils (cf. Mark 16:1; Luke 23:55-56). Rather Jesus is buried as befits a king, with a staggering amount of myrrh and aloes, bound in cloth wrappings impregnated with aromatic oils.[87]

The garden, with its evocation of the creation story, also links Jesus' death with his resurrection. For when Mary Magdalen encounters the Risen Jesus she supposes that he is a gardener (20:15).

Conclusion

Familial and architectural imagery are drawn on to express the richness of the Johannine interpretation of Jesus' death. Jesus is the true Temple of God's presence (1:14). "The Jews," through their priesthood, hand him over to Pilate and so carry out the destruction of the Temple which Jesus had prophesied (2:19) and they had tried to avoid (11:50). At the same

---

[84] M. C. de Boer, *Johannine Perspectives on the Death of Jesus,* Contributions to Biblical Exegesis & Theology 17 (Kampen: Kok Pharos, 1996) 295.

[85] Lindars, *Gospel,* 587, correctly relates 7:39 and 20:22.

[86] Manns, *L'Evangile,* 409.

[87] R. Brown, *A Crucified Christ in Holy Week: Essays on the Four Gospel Passion Narratives* (Collegeville: The Liturgical Press, 1986) 67.

time as the Passover lambs are being sacrificed in the Temple on Mount Moriah, Jesus is being handed over to death as the new Passover lamb on a new Moriah (19:14). In the Hour of his death Jesus is manifest as the royal and sacerdotal Temple builder, the "Nazarene" (19:19), fulfilling the prophecy of Zechariah (Zech 6:11-12). The new Temple is born through the creative Spirit released upon the nascent community by Jesus in his last breath (19:30). A new "household of God" (οἰκία τοῦ Θεοῦ cf. 14:2) comes into being at the foot of the cross when believers are drawn into Jesus' own filial relationship with the Father (19:26, 27). Endowed with the Spirit, the new household of God enables an ongoing presence of God in the world.

The two functions of Israel's Temple have now been subsumed by the Christian community. In the Christian community, God has a new dwelling place. A Temple building is no longer required, for God's dwelling is still being enfleshed in the household of the believers, as it had once been enfleshed in the body of Jesus. The Temple-as-building no longer needs to function as a place to achieve cultic purity through animal sacrifices, for God's own Son and the Spirit have been given, to achieve the "taking away" of sin which the human cult could never do. The mediating dispensation of Israel, her worship and rituals, are no longer necessary, for God has come into the human story in Jesus, and remains within the story through the community of those who believe.

When the Temple no longer exists, and Israel's sacrificial cult no longer functions, the rabbis turn to the law to find in *Torah* a replacement for all they have lost. In this situation the author of 2 Baruch offers these words of consolation to Israel:

> The whole people answered and they said to me:
> ". . . For the shepherds of Israel have perished, and the lamps which gave light are extinguished, and the fountains from which we used to drink have withheld their streams. Now we have been left in the darkness and in the thick forest and in the aridness of the desert."

> And I answered and said to them:
> "Shepherds and lanterns and fountains came from the Law and when we go away, the Law will abide. If you, therefore, look upon the Law and are intent upon wisdom, then the lamp will not be wanting and the shepherd will not give way and the fountain will not dry up" (2 Bar 77:11, 13-16).[88]

Around the same time as the author of 2 Baruch,[89] the fourth evangelist presents Jesus, not the Torah, as the true shepherd, light, fountain, and

---

[88] Charlesworth, *Pseudepigrapha,* 1:647.

[89] Charlesworth, *Pseudepigrapha,* 1:617: "The Apocalypse of Baruch seems to come from the first or second decade of the second century."

most importantly, as the new Temple. "'Holy space' has been 'christified,' and the category of place replaced by that of person."[90] But if that were the only transformation, the Christian community would be as desolate and bereft in the departure of Jesus, as the community of Israel was in the loss of their Temple. The Gospel narrative doubly transforms the heritage of Israel, transferring the christological image of the Temple to the Christian community which remains in the world, under the guidance of the Spirit-Paraclete. Christians of all time have access to the Father. Geographical and temporal distance from the historical events of the Gospel is no disadvantage. In fact, those who believe without seeing, are counted as "blessed" (20:29).

[90] Walker, *Jesus and the Holy City,* 191.

The Dwelling Place of God

The destruction of the Jerusalem Temple brought about radical changes to first-century Judaism. No longer able to satisfy sacrificial cultic requirements, rabbinic Judaism turned to the Torah as the central focus of the covenantal relationship with God. Fulfillment of Torah replaced Temple sacrifices as a means of atonement:

> To Yohanan ben Zakkai, preserving the Temple was not an end in itself. He taught that there was another means of reconciliation between God and Israel, so that the Temple and its cult were not decisive. What really counted in the life of the Jewish people? Torah piety.[1]

A religious group which had its origins in Judaism saw in Jesus the presence and activity of Israel's God. They found in his person and word a new revelation that, while in continuity with their traditions, far surpassed them. As Judaism looked to Torah, this Christian group turned to Jesus. Though sharing common roots, the two groups separated on the issue of Jesus' identity:

> To point to Jesus the Christ as the replacement of the fallen Temple and of the sacred holy places (like Bethel), as John does at a time when the war against Rome had deprived Jews of their Land and Temple and had desecrated their holy places so that their loss was constantly and painfully present, was to touch a most raw nerve. . . His theme of "replacement" was, therefore, peculiarly sensitive and challenging and could not but provoke resentment.[2]

---

[1] Neusner, *Judaism in a Time of Crisis,* 321–24; J. Dutheil, "L'évangile de Jean et le Judaïsme: le Temple et la Torah," *Origine et Postérité de l'Evangile de Jean,* ed. Alain Marchadour, Lectio Divina 143 (Paris: Cerf, 1990) 71–85

[2] Davies, "Aspects of the Jewish Background," 56.

The Fourth Gospel articulates the faith of one late first-century Christian community. This community, now cast out of the synagogue (9:22; 12:42; 16:2), tells the story of Jesus in such as way as to reassure its Jewish members that they have not lost their heritage. On the contrary, they are the real inheritors of all that Judaism promised. In the person, words and ministry of Jesus, God's former gifts to Israel are brought to their perfection (1:17). Jesus is the one and only revealer of God (1:18; 3:13); Jesus is the one and only way to the Father who can offer truth and life (14:6).

Review

At a time when the Temple no longer existed, and Judaism was redefining itself because of that loss, the Fourth Gospel presents the Temple as the major, consistent, and pervasive symbol of Jesus' identity and mission. Judaism had once looked to the Ark, the Tabernacle, and especially the Temple as the visible point of contact between God and humanity. Through the processes of their history, especially with the loss of the Solomonic Temple, Israel moved away from emphasizing the cultic presence of God, towards a more personal and covenant-based presence of God's Spirit placed within (Ezek 36:26; 37:12). In the later Wisdom tradition, God's presence in Israel was personified in Lady Wisdom and embodied in the Torah. Sinai and Wisdom traditions came together in a reformulation of Israel's claim to possess divine revelation. In the aftermath of the destruction of Jerusalem, under the leadership of the rabbis, synagogue worship, with its emphasis on Torah, replaced the Temple and its sacrificial cult.[3]

Drawing on these same Sinai and Wisdom traditions, the Fourth Gospel proclaims that the Word, who participates in the very nature of God (1:1), has now entered the human story in the flesh of Jesus (1:14). The locus of divine revelation is a human person. When Jewish Christians could no longer join in synagogue worship or participate in the great festivals of their faith and history, the Fourth Gospel affirms a new place of worship made possible because, in Jesus, God dwells in the midst of humanity. The Temple provided a striking symbol for the Johannine community's presentation of Jesus' identity. As once God had dwelt in Israel through her holy places, the Ark, Tabernacle, and Temple, God has given all people a new holy dwelling place in the living flesh of Jesus.

The hermeneutical key identifying Jesus as the Temple of God occurs in the narrative at the start of Jesus' ministry in Jerusalem. The Pro-

---

[3] The focus on Torah led to the rich rabbinic traditions expressed in the later commentaries such as the Mishnah, the Tosefta, and the dual Talmuds.

logue prepared the reader for this claim when, through the use of the verb "dwell" (σκηνόω), it described the incarnation of the Word in terms of Israel's Tent and Tabernacle traditions (1:14). During the "First Days" (1:19-59), a further indication was given when Nathanael was promised sight of a new House of God (Bethel), and the location of this new Bethel would be a person, the Son of Man (1:51).[4] The full revelation of Jesus as the new "house of God" (בֵּית־אֵל) is situated, with great dramatic irony, within Israel's Temple (בֵּית־יהוה) at the Passover feast in Jerusalem (John 2:13-25). Jesus' actions in the Temple are presented, not as a mere cleansing, but as an action specifically directed at Israel's sacrificial cult. When he expels from the Temple the animals and money-traders essential to Israel's cult, Jesus effectively demonstrates that such cultic actions are no longer required.

His words to "the Jews" interpret his deeds, indicating a future time when *they* would destroy the Temple and *he* would raise it up (2:19). "The Jews" respond by throwing his words back at him (2:20). Their rejection of the words of the *logos* (cf. 1:1-2, 14), is the first of a series of rejections that leads ultimately to the destruction of the Temple of his body on Golgotha. In this scene, placed so early in the narrative, the reader is given an explicit statement of Jesus' identity and his mission. His body is a living Temple, a house wherein his Father dwells and although this Temple will be destroyed, he will raise it up. His mission is to be a Temple-builder, to create a new holy place wherein God may be worshipped and be in communion with humanity.

The "Temple" scene displays a Johannine narrative technique which will recur throughout the Gospel. By situating Jesus' self-designation as the Temple within the Temple itself, the evangelist heightens the sense of dramatic irony. The knowing reader registers the impact of word, actions, and location. The cultic setting of a Temple building is superimposed upon the body of a human being. The reader, like "the Jews" within the scene, is challenged to integrate two seemingly different realities—building stones and human flesh. No explanation is given as to how this integration can be accomplished. It is up to the narrative itself to guide the reader in making sense of the symbol.

In Jerusalem, Jesus' actions and words declare that he himself is the new "holy place" of Israel, bringing to completion a long tradition of cultic dwellings—the Ark, the Tabernacle, and ultimately the Temple. In the dialogue with the Samaritan woman, Jesus reveals himself as the

---

[4] The promise to Nathanael of a vision of angels recalls Jacob's dream at Bethel (Gen 28:12). This "House of God" allusion was not explored in this study as the scene in the Gospel does not suggest a cultic context, nor is the symbolism given further development as it is in the passages chosen.

culmination of Samaritan cultic traditions. It is Jesus, not "our father Jacob" (4:12) who can offer a welling up of living waters lasting forever (4:14). The sacred place of Samaritan worship, like the sacred place of Jewish worship is already being replaced by Jesus' presence. True worship happens neither ἐν this mountain nor ἐν Jerusalem (4:21) but ἐν Spirit (4:23). In the narrative so far, Jesus is the only one who has received the Spirit (1:33-34), but as the Gospel story develops it will be clear that the Spirit is to be given to believers (7:39) so that there will come a time when others will also be able to offer true worship of the Father.

Jesus' claims in Jerusalem and in Samaria derive from his identity as the enfleshed Word who has a unique abiding relationship with God (1:1, 14). Jesus goes beyond the Samaritan expectations of a prophet (4:19), and the Jewish expectations of a Messiah (4:25). At the conclusion of the dialogue with the woman, Jesus reveals himself as "I am" (4:26). Jesus is the self-manifestation of God now dwelling in human history. God's gift of salvation is not restricted to one people but is an expression of God's love for the world (3:16). Through the woman, the Samaritans come to Jesus and receive him as the savior of the world (4:42). National boundaries are broken down; local cultic sites are replaced by a new Temple which can be called "a house of prayer for all peoples" (Isa 56:7).

Thus far in the Gospel the focus has been on the person of Jesus as the new Temple and new sacred place where God and humanity meet. The symbolism of Temple has shifted from a building to a single person. In the feast of Tabernacles a further shift of meaning is indicated. While Jesus is physically present, his body is the *locus* of God's dwelling, but the members of the Johannine community live in a time when Jesus is no longer physically in their midst. If the Temple has its *sole* meaning expressed in the *sarx* of Jesus, then the Johannine community is in the same position as its Jewish contemporaries who have lost their Temple. The absence of Jesus, the Tabernacle/Temple of God (1:14; 2:21) could leave the believers lamenting the loss of God's presence dwelling among them. The Temple requires a further shift of meaning if the disciples are not to be left orphans (14:18).

In the feast of Tabernacles, there is an indication that there will be a time in the future, related to a future gift of the Spirit, when believers will also be a source of "Temple waters." The Gospel makes the promise that the Christian community will still have the presence of a Temple, will still have God's presence dwelling in its midst. During this feast, Jesus' words move beyond the narrative time to a future time when the Spirit will be given to the believers (7:39). The last day of Tabernacles (7:37), the "eighth day," looks ahead to a future "eighth day" when the Risen Jesus breathes the Spirit onto the disciples and missions them to continue his work (20:21-23). With the eschatological gift of the Spirit dwelling in the disciples, they will become the new Temple envisaged by the prophet Ezekiel (47:1-12). They will become a source of living water (7:37; 4:7-15) able to continue the mission the Father entrusted to Jesus (20:21). The future Christian community will be a *locus* for God's continued dwelling in the world. This is the promise indicated at Tabernacles when the symbolism of water is first applied to Jesus: "If anyone thirst, let him come to me and drink" (7:37)—and then to the believer—"Whoever believes in me, as Scripture has said, 'out of his heart shall flow rivers of living water'" (7:38).

The final feast of the Jews is the culmination of Jesus' self revelation to his own people. At the feast of Dedication, while celebrating a feast when the altar was reconsecrated to God, Jesus speaks of himself as "the Consecrated One" (10:36). Such a self-designation continues the symbolic trajectory flowing through the narrative. Jesus is God's glory tabernacling with us (1:14), the Temple of God's presence (2:21), the new cultic site of true worship for all people (4:21, 23); the true life giving water and light of the world (7:37; 8:12). All of these claims stem from Jesus' identity. They are only true because of his unique oneness with the Father. In the person of Jesus, Israel encounters God's presence dwelling in their midst. Jesus' climactic affirmation of union with the Father (10:30, 38) meets a final rejection by "the Jews" who seek once more to arrest him (10:39).

One of the major themes of the Last Discourse (chs. 13–17) is the preparation of the disciples for the future absence of Jesus. This theme of departure is dominant in chapter 14 and is introduced using the image of "my Father's house" (14:2). This chapter develops even further the promise indicated in chapter 7 that in the future the believers themselves would be a living Temple of God's presence (7:38). The terminology "my Father's house" was used in chapter 2 to mean the Temple building in Jerusalem (2:16) before the word "Temple" was given a symbolic sense in referring to Jesus' body (2:21). I argued that in the Scriptures the term "my Father's house" is used most frequently to mean those who belong within the household. It has a personal and relational sense rather than a physical building. The personal and relational sense is given further emphasis in the Gospel by the use of "household" (οἰκία) rather than house (οἶκος) to speak of the Father's house(hold). οἰκία has a wider range of meaning than οἶκος and when used, even on its own, it can mean the household, the people who are in some way bound to the master of the house. The use of οἰκία within the phrase "in my Father's house(hold)" continues to move the symbolism of Temple away from a building towards a quality of personal relationships.

The expression "many dwellings" (μοναὶ πολλάι) does not mean, in this context, many physical rooms. Throughout chapters 14 and 15 the verb μένω is used many times to speak of the "dwelling" of the Father, Paraclete, and Jesus with the believer (14:10, 17, 23), and the "dwelling" of the believer in Jesus (15:4, 5, 6, 7, 9, 10). Within the Temple (household of the Father), there is a series of interpersonal relationships described as the dwelling of the Father, Jesus, and the Paraclete within the believer. Although Jesus will no longer be a physical presence with the disciples, the promised gift of the Paraclete will ensure that his presence remains among them and ensure that they will still have God's Temple in their midst (14:16-17). The community of believers will be drawn into God's own household when the Paraclete comes. The Paraclete, dwelling in the disciples, will mediate a continuing presence of Jesus.

In the Discourse the description of the believers as the living Temple (household) of God, is a matter of promise. In Jesus' Hour the promise becomes a reality for the small group gathered at the foot of the cross. In his final Hour, the imagery of Temple and family are drawn together as Jesus fulfills the title he is given in this Gospel as "the Nazarene."

The title "Nazarene" has its origins in the messianic oracle found in Isa 11:1. This passage speaks of a shoot נצר (ntzr) and a branch growing out of the stump/roots of Jesse. In the Fourth Gospel there is no emphasis on Nazareth as the hometown of Jesus and when it is used in Jesus' "hour." It is given a definite article, giving it the sense of a title (18:5, 7; 19:19). Jesus is "the Nazarene," the one who fulfils the image found in Isaiah, the one who is the shoot and branch growing from Jesse's roots. The image of a branch is used by the prophet Zechariah where it is the name of one who will build the Temple (Zech 6:12). While Zechariah does not use the Hebrew *netzer* (נצר) but *tzamah* (צמח) the two terms have similar meanings. At Qumran the two terms are used synonymously (4QpIsa[a] line 11), and in the Targums צמח is clearly a messianic title like נצר for it is translated as "Messiah" (משיחא). The traditional knowledge that Jesus came from Nazareth, against the background of a messianic Temple builder (Branch) in Zechariah, and the Davidic Branch (נצר) in Isaiah, may have influenced the evangelist to give a special meaning to the term "Nazarene."

Jesus is arrested as "the Nazarene" (18:5, 7) and is crucified under this title (19:19). At the cross, through the Roman soldiers, "the Jews" destroy the one revealed in this Gospel as the Temple of God. In their rejection of Jesus, they bring about the words Jesus spoke to them in the Temple, "Destroy this Temple" (2:19). From the cross Jesus begins the process of building the new Temple (household) of God when he creates a new series of relationships for the Beloved Disciple. This disciple, representative of all believers in Jesus, becomes "son" to the mother of Jesus, and with this change of relationship the disciple is drawn into Jesus' own sonship. Participating in Jesus' sonship, the disciple is enabled to be "son/daughter" of the Father: "I am ascending to my Father and your Father" (20:17). The promise introduced in the Prologue is realized as the believer become a child of God (1:12). Here at the cross as Jesus' dies and hands down the Spirit, the Beloved Disciple, representative of all disciples, is reborn into a new familial relationship with the Father, drawing him into the "household" of the Father. As one Temple is raised up on the cross, a new Temple is being raised up at the foot of the cross.

At this final Passover, Jesus brings to completion Israel's Passover rituals. Jesus is the Passover victim and the Priest. The sacrificial functions once carried out within the Temple are transferred to Golgotha. As we have seen within the cycle of Israel's great feasts (John 5, 7, and 10), the Johannine community, although separated from their Jewish synagogue community, have not lost their traditions and festivals. Passover, Sabbath, Tabernacles, Dedication have now been given their most complete meaning in Jesus.

Conclusion

In the introductory pages I articulated two questions:

- in what way does the Temple reveal the identity and mission of Jesus?

- in the absence of the historical Jesus of Nazareth, what is the significance of the Temple for the Christian community?

In this study I have argued that the narrative in the Fourth Gospel is skillfully structured to highlight that the human flesh of Jesus fulfils and replaces Israel's Temple traditions. The incarnate Son, in his very being, is God's gift of love for the world (3:16). In Jesus God dwells and achieves a communion of life with us that Israel had sought through cultic rituals.

Within the community's ongoing sacramental worship and loving relationships, they experienced a continuing presence of Jesus now mediated through the Spirit-Paraclete. While they had lost the sight of Jesus, their Temple, they had not lost the experience of his Temple presence. It is not possible to reconstruct the nature of this experience with guaranteed certainty. But the experience has shaped a text from which we can draw some conclusions—tentative though they must be. The work of Sandra Schneiders reminds us that theology emerges from experience:

> It is crucial to recognise that the theology of the Gospel arises from, rather than generates, the spirituality of the Gospel. It is the theology, however,

that gives us access to the spirituality. In other words, it was a particular *lived experience* of union with God in the risen Jesus through his gift of the Spirit/Paraclete within the believing community (spirituality) that gave rise gradually to a particular *articulated understanding* of Christian faith (theology). This theology was encoded in the Gospel text, and through it we gain access to the experience, the spirituality, that gives this Gospel its unique character.[5]

At some point in their experience of Jesus still with them, the community must have come to a realization that now *their* humanity was the locus of God's ongoing presence in the world; that they were participating in Jesus' own experience of God, the intimacy between Son and Father. They discovered that in their union with Jesus, the Son they too were sons/daughters of the Father, now drawn into the household of the Father. This experience is not unique to the Johannine community, indeed it seems to have been part of the earlier experience of the Pauline communities. Paul too speaks of Temple (1 Cor 3:16, 17; 6:19; 2 Cor 6:16), of being part of God's household (Eph 2:19; 2 Cor 5:1) of being sons/daughters of God (Gal 4:6, 7) and of the Spirit living in us (Gal 4:6; Rom 8:9, 15, 26) enabling us to say "Abba" (Rom 8:15; Gal 4:6).

It is the genius of John that he is able to give this Christian experience and language a narrative shape; to draw on a pre-existing seminal theology and use this to tell the story of Jesus. In so doing the Fourth Evangelist establishes a continuity between the remembered life of Jesus, and the ongoing life of the Risen Lord experienced in the community. Temple provides a bridging metaphor.[6] As the Temple symbolizes the nature and mission of Jesus, so too it symbolizes the nature and mission of the Johannine community. When the Temple Mount has become rubble, and the synagogue is no longer accessible, a Christian community finds it has lost nothing. Their traditions can still be celebrated; celebrated now in their fulfillment and no longer as promise. They still have communion with God for a new Temple has been raised up in their midst.

God dwells with us (1:14). This is the Good News proclaimed within the Johannine community and announced that readers may believe and

---

[5] S. Schneiders, *Written that you may believe: Encountering Jesus in the Fourth Gospel* (New York: Crossroad, 1999) 48.

[6] Cullman expressed the link between worship and history in the following way: ". . . the Gospel of John regards it as one of its chief concerns to set forth the connection between the contemporary christian worship and the historical life of Jesus. . . It traces the line from the Christ of history to Christ the Lord of the community, in which the Word continually becomes flesh." See O. Cullman, *Early Christian Worship,* Studies in Biblical Theology 10 (London: SCM, 1953) 37–38.

have life (20:31). No longer need Christians look back with longing to the past, to the traditions of Israel's tabernacle or Temple, nor to the experience of the historical Jesus. God dwells with us **now,** in the living Temple of the Christian community. Believers, drawn into the community through water and the Spirit, are drawn into Jesus' own relationship with God. In the Son, we are sons/daughters, becoming the new household/Temple of the Father (14:2). St. Augustine's comments on this verse succinctly express the arguments of this thesis:

> "In my Father's house are many dwellings," what else can we suppose the house of God to mean but the temple of God? And what that is, ask the apostle, and he will reply, "For the temple of God is holy, which [temple] ye are."[7]

---

[7] The Gospel of John. Tractate 68. John 14:1-3.

Bibliography

Reference works and sources

Aland, K., M. Black, C. M. Martini, B. M. Metzger, and A. Wikgren, Eds. *The Greek New Testament*. 3rd ed. Stuttgart: United Bible Societies, 1983.

Balz, H., and G. Schneider, Eds. *Exegetical Dictionary of the New Testament*. 3 vols. Grand Rapids, Mich.: Eerdmans, 1990–1993.

Botterweck, G. J., and H. Ringgren, eds. *Theological Dictionary of the Old Testament*. 6 vols. Grand Rapids, Mich.: Eerdmans, 1974—.

Brenton, L. *The Septuagint with Apocrypha: Greek and English*. Peabody, Mass.: Hendrickson, 1986.

Brown, R. E., J. A. Fitzmyer, and R. E. Murphy, Eds. *The New Jerome Biblical Commentary*. Englewood Cliffs, N.J.: Prentice Hall, 1989.

Buttrick, G. A., ed. *The Interpreter's Dictionary of the Bible*. 5 vols. Nashville: Abingdon, 1962.

Charlesworth, J., ed. *The Old Testament Pseudepigrapha*. 2 vols. London: Darton, Longman & Todd, 1985.

Chilton, B. *The Isaiah Targum*. The Aramaic Bible 11. Edinburgh: T. & T. Clark, 1987.

Danby, H. *The Mishnah*. Oxford: Oxford University Press, 1933.

Elliger, K., and K. Rudolph. *Biblia Hebraica Stuttgartensia*. Stuttgart: Deutsche Bibelgesellschaft, 1983.

Freedman, D. M., ed. *Anchor Bible Dictionary*. 6 vols. New York: Doubleday, 1992.

Freedman, H., and M. Simon, eds. *Midrash Rabbah*. 5 vols. London: Soncino, 1977.

Garcia Martinez, Florentino. *The Dead Sea Scrolls Translated: The Qumran Texts in English*. Leiden: E. J. Brill, 1994.

223

Garcia Martinez, Florentino, and Eibert Tigchelaar. *The Dead Sea Scrolls Study Edition, 1Qq-4Q273.* 2 vols. New York: Brill, 1997.

Gordon, R. P., and K. J. Cathcart. *The Targum of the Minor Prophets.* The Aramaic Bible 14. Edinburgh: T. & T. Clark, 1989.

Greenup, A. W. *Sukkah, Mishna and Tosefta: With introduction, translation and short notes.* Translations of Early Documents. Series 3. Rabbinic Texts. New York: Macmillan, 1925.

Kittel, G., and G. Friedrich, eds. *Theological Dictionary of the New Testament.* 10 vols. Grand Rapids, Mich.: Eerdmans, 1964–1976.

Liddell, H. R., and R. Scott. *Greek - English Lexicon.* Oxford: Clarendon, 1971.

Lohse, E. *Die Texte aus Qumran: Hebräisch und Deutsch.* Munich: Kösel-Verlag, 1971.

Malatesta, E. *St. John's Gospel: 1920–1965.* Analecta Biblica 32. Rome: Pontifical Biblical Institute, 1967.

McNamara, M., *Targum Neofiti 1: Genesis.* The Aramaic Bible 1A. Edinburgh: T & T Clark, 1992.

McNamara, M., and E. Clarke. *Targum Neofiti 1: Numbers. Targum Pseudo-Jonathan: Numbers.* The Aramaic Bible 4. Edinburgh: T & T Clark, 1995.

McNamara, M., and M. Maher. *Targum Neofiti 1: Exodus; Targum Pseudo-Jonathan: Exodus.* The Aramaic Bible 2. Edinburgh: T & T Clark, 1994.

Metzger, B. *The Text of the New Testament: Its Transmission, Corruption, and Restoration.* 3rd ed., New York: Oxford University Press, 1992.

Schaff, P., ed. *Augustin [e sic] : Homilies on the Gospel of John, Homilies on the First Epistle of John, Soliloquies.* Nicene and Post-Nicene Fathers 7. Peabody, Mass.: Hendrickson, 1995.

Van Belle, G. *Johannine Bibliography 1966–1985.* Leuven: Leuven University Press, 1988.

Vermes, G. *The Dead Sea Scrolls in English.* 3rd. ed. Sheffield: JSOT Press, 1987.

The Works of Josephus: Complete and Unabridged. Trans. William Whiston. Peabody, Mass.: Hendrickson, 1987.

Zerwick, M. *An Analysis of the Greek New Testament. Vol. 1. Gospels—Acts.* Rome: Biblical Institute Press, 1974.

Commentaries on the Fourth Gospel

Barrett, C. K. *The Gospel According to St. John.* 2nd ed., London: SPCK, 1978.

Beasley-Murray, G. R. *John*. Word Biblical Commentary 36. Waco: Word Books, 1987.

Brown, R. E. *The Gospel According to John*. Anchor Bible 29–29a. 2 vols. New York: Doubleday, 1966, 1970.

Bultmann, R. *The Gospel of John: A Commentary*. Trans. G. R. Beasley Murray et al. Oxford: Blackwell, 1971.

Carson, D. A. *The Gospel According to John*. Grand Rapids, Mich.: Eerdmans, 1991.

Dodd, C. H. *The Interpretation of the Fourth Gospel*. Cambridge: Cambridge University Press, 1953.

Ellis, P. *The Genius of John: A Composition-Critical Commentary on the Fourth Gospel*. Collegeville: The Liturgical Press, 1984.

Haenchen, E. *John 1–2*. Trans. R. W. Funk. Hermeneia. 2 vols. Philadelphia: Fortress, 1984.

Hoskyns, E. C. *The Fourth Gospel*. Ed. F. N. Davey. London: Faber & Faber, 1947.

Kysar, R. *John*. Augsburg Commentary on the New Testament. Minneapolis: Augsburg, 1986.

Léon-Dufour, X. *Lecture de l'Évangile selon Jean*. 4 vols. Parole de Dieu. Paris: Seuil, 1988, 1990, 1993, 1996.

Lightfoot, R. H. *St. John's Gospel: A Commentary*. London: Oxford University Press, 1956.

Lindars, B. *The Gospel of John*. New Century Bible. London: Oliphants, 1972.

Moloney, F. J. *Belief in the Word: Reading John 1–4*. Minneapolis: Fortress, 1993.

_____. *Signs and Shadows: Reading John 5–12*. Minneapolis: Fortress, 1996.

_____. *Glory not Dishonour: Reading John 13–21*. Minneapolis: Fortress, 1998.

_____. *John,* Sacra Pagina 4. Collegeville: The Liturgical Press, 1998.

Morris, L. *The Gospel According to John,* rev. ed. New International Commentary on the New Testament. Grand Rapids, Mich.: Eerdmans, 1995.

Pfitzner, V. *The Gospel According to St. John*. ChiRho Commentary Series. Adelaide: Lutheran Publishing House, 1988.

Schnackenburg, R. *The Gospel according to St. John*. Trans. K. Smyth et al. 3 vols. Herder's Theological Commentary on the New Testament. London: Burns & Oates, 1968–1982.

Schwank, B. *Evangelium nach Johannes*. Ottilien: EOS, 1996.

Stibbe, M. *John*. Readings: A New Bible Commentary. Sheffield: JSOT Press, 1993.

Talbert, C. H. *Reading John: A Literary and Theological Commentary on the Fourth Gospel and the Johannine Epistles.* London: SPCK, 1992.

General references

Alexander, P. "Targum." *ABD* 6 (1992) 320–31.

Alter, R. *The Art of Biblical Narrative.* New York: Basic Books, 1981.

Anderson, A. A. *2 Samuel.* Word Biblical Commentary 11. Dallas: Word Books, 1989.

Antwi, D. J. "Did Jesus Consider His Death to be an Atoning Sacrifice?" *Int* 45 (1991) 17–28.

Ashton, J. "The Identity and Function of the *Ioudaioi* in the Fourth Gospel." *NovT* 27 (1985) 40–75.

_____. "The Transformation of Wisdom: A Study of the Prologue of John's Gospel." *NTS* 32 (1986) 161–86.

_____. *Understanding the Fourth Gospel.* Oxford: Clarendon Press, 1993.

Aune, D. E. *The Cultic Setting of Realized Eschatology in Early Christianity.* Supplements to Novum Testamentum 28. Leiden: E. J. Brill, 1972.

Ball, D. *"I Am" in John's Gospel: Literary Function, Background and Theological Implications.* Journal for the Study of the New Testament Supplement Series 124. Sheffield: Sheffield Academic Press, 1996.

Barker, M. *The Gate of Heaven: The history and Symbolism of the Temple in Jerusalem.* London: SPCK, 1991.

_____. *On Earth as it is in Heaven: Temple Symbolism in the New Testament.* Edinburgh: T & T Clark, 1995.

Barrett, C. K. *New Testament Essays.* London: SPCK, 1971.

Bauer, J. B. "Drei Tage." *Bib* 39 (1958) 354–58.

Beasley-Murray, G. R. *Baptism in the New Testament.* Grand Rapids, Mich.: Eerdmans, 1962.

Behm, J. "ἐκχέω." *TDNT* 2 (1964) 467–69.

Bertram, G. "ὑψόω." *TDNT* 7 (1971) 606–13.

Bienaimé, G. *Moïse et le don de l'eau dans la tradition juive ancienne: Targum et Midrash.* Analecta Biblica 98. Rome: Biblical Institute Press, 1984.

Blenkinsopp, J. "Deuteronomy." *NJBC* (1989) 94–109.

Bligh, J. "Jesus in Samaria." *Heythrop Journal* 3 (1964) 329–46.

Bodi, D. "Der altorientalische Hintergrund des Themas der "Ströme lebendigen Wassers" in Joh 7,38," *Johannes-Studien*, Ed. Martin Rose. 137–58. Zurich: TVZ, 1991.

Boers, H. *Neither on this Mountain nor in Jerusalem.* Society of Biblical Literature Monograph Series 35. Atlanta: Scholars Press, 1988.

Boismard, M.-É. *St. John's Prologue*. London: Blackfriars, 1957.

_____. *Moses or Jesus: An essay in Johannine Christology*. Trans. B. T. Viviano. Minneapolis: Fortress, 1993.

Borse, U. " ἱερόν." *EDNT* 2 (1991) 175–76.

Botha, J. E. *Jesus and the Samaritan Woman: A Speech Act Reading of John 4:1-42*. Supplements to Novum Testamentum 65. Leiden: E. J. Brill, 1991.

Brown, R. E. *A Crucified Christ in Holy Week: Essays on the Four Gospel Passion Narratives*. Collegeville: The Liturgical Press, 1986.

_____. *The Death of the Messiah: From Gethsemane to the Grave*. 2 vols. New York: Doubleday, 1994.

_____. "The Paraclete in the Fourth Gospel." *NTS* 13 (1966–1967) 113–32.

_____. *The Community of the Beloved Disciple*. New York: Paulist, 1979.

_____. "Not Jewish Christianity or Gentile Christianity but Types of Jewish/ Gentile Christianity." *CBQ* 45 (1983) 74–79.

Brown, R. E., P. Perkins, and A. Saldarini. "Apocrypha; Dead Sea Scrolls; Other Jewish Literature." *NJBC* (1989) 1055–82.

Buchanan, G. W. "Symbolic Money-changers in the Temple?" *NTS* 37 (1991) 280–90.

Bull, R. J. "An Archaeological Footnote to 'Our Fathers Worshiped on this Mountain,' Jn 4:20." *NTS* 23 (1976-77) 460–62.

Burge, G. H. *The Anointed Community: The Holy Spirit in the Johannine Community*. Grand Rapids, Mich.: Eerdmans, 1987.

Busse, U. "Open Questions on John 10," *The Shepherd Discourse of John 10 and Its Context*, Eds. Johannes Beutler and Robert Fortna. 1–17. Society for New Testament Studies Monograph Series 67. Cambridge: Cambridge University Press, 1991.

Byrne, B. *'Building' and 'Temple' imagery in the Qumran Texts*. Unpublished M.A. Thesis; Dept. of Middle Eastern Studies, University of Melbourne, 1971.

Campbell, A. F. *The Study Companion To Old Testament Literature: An Approach to the Writings of Pre-Exilic and Exilic Israel*. Old Testament Studies 2. Wilmington, Del.: Michael Glazier, 1989.

Campbell, A. F. and M. A. O'Brien. *Sources of the Pentateuch: Texts, Introductions, Annotations*. Minneapolis: Fortress, 1993.

Carmichael, C. "Marriage and the Samaritan Woman." *NTS* 26 (1979–1980) 332–46.

Carroll, J., and J. Green. *The Death of Jesus in Early Christianity*. Peabody, Mass.: Hendrickson, 1995.

Carter, W. "The Prologue and John's Gospel: Function, Symbol and the Definitive Word." JSNT 39 (1990) 35–58.

Charlesworth, J. H., ed. *John and the Dead Sea Scrolls.* Christian Origins Library. New York: Crossroad, 1990.

Chilton, B. *The Temple of Jesus: His Sacrificial Program within a Cultural History of Sacrifice.* University Park, Penn.: Pennsylvania State University, 1992.

Clements, R. E. *God and Temple.* Philadelphia: Fortress, 1965.

Collins, R. F. *These things have been written: Studies on the Fourth Gospel.* Louvain Theological and Pastoral Monographs, 2. Louvain: Peeters Press, 1990.

Coloe, M. "The Structure of the Johannine Prologue and Genesis 1." *ABR* 45 (1997) 40–55.

Coloe, M. "Like Father, Like Son: The Role of Abraham in Tabernacles—John 8:31-59." *Pacifica* 12 (1999) 1–11.

Congar, Y. *Le Mystère de Temple: L'Economie de la Présence de Dieu a sa Créature de la Genèse a l'Apocalypse.* Paris: Les Éditions du Cerf, 1958.

Cortés, J. "Yet another look at Jn 7,37-38." *CBQ* 29 (1967) 75–86.

Cross, F. M. "The Tabernacle." *Biblical Archaeologist* 10 (1947) 45–68.

Cross, F. M. *Canaanite Myth and Hebrew Epic: Essays in the History of the Religion of Israel.* Cambridge: Harvard University Press, 1973.

Cullman, O. *Early Christian Worship.* Studies in Biblical Theology 10. London: SCM, 1953.

_____. "L'opposition contre le temple de Jérusalem, motif commun de la théologie johannique et du monde ambiant." *NTS* 5 (1958–1959) 157–73.

Culpepper, R. A. "The Pivot of John's Prologue." *NTS* 27 (1980–1981) 1–31.

_____. *Anatomy of the Fourth Gospel: A Study in Literary Design.* Philadelphia: Fortress, 1983.

D'Souza, J. *The Lamb of God in the Johannine Writings.* Allahabad: St. Paul, 1968.

Dacy, M. "Sukkot: Origins to 500 C.E." Unpublished M. Phil. thesis; Dept. of Semitic Studies, University of Sydney, 1992.

Dahms, J. "The Johannine use of MONOΓENHΣ reconsidered." *NTS* 29 (1983) 222–32.

Dahood, M. *Psalms 1:1-50.* Anchor Bible 16. New York: Doubleday, 1966.

_____. *Psalms 11:51-100.* Anchor Bible 17. New York: Doubleday, 1968.

_____. *Psalms 111:101-150.* Anchor Bible 17A. New York: Doubleday, 1970.

Daly, R. J. "The Soteriological Significance of the Sacrifice of Isaac." *CBQ* 39 (1977) 45–75.

Daniélou, J. *The Presence of God.* Trans. W. Roberts. London: A. R. Mowbray, 1958.

Davies, G. H. "Ark of the Covenant." *IDB* 1 (1962a) 222–26.

_____. "Tabernacle." *IDB* 4 (1962b) 498–506.

Davies, P. R., and B. D. Chilton. "The Aqedah: A Revised Tradition History." *CBQ* 40 (1978) 514–46.

Davies, W. D. *The Gospel and the Land.* Sheffield: JSOT, 1974.

_____. "Reflections on Aspects of the Jewish Background of the Gospel of John," *Exploring the Gospel of John: In Honor of D. Moody Smith*, Eds. R. Alan Culpepper and C. Clifton Black. Louisville: Westminster John Knox Press, 1996.

de Boer, M. C. *Johannine Perspectives on the Death of Jesus.* Contributions to Biblical Exegesis & Theology 17. Kampen: Kok Pharos, 1996.

de Goedt, M. "Un Schème de révélation dans le quatrième évangile." *NTS* 8 (1961–1962) 142–50.

de la Potterie, I. "La tunique sans couture, symbole du Christ grand prêtre?" *Bib* 60 (1979) 255–69.

_____. "'Nous adorons, nous, ce que nous connaissons, car le salut vient des Juifs.' Histoire de l'exégèse et interprétation de Jn 4:22." *Bib* 64 (1983) 74–115.

_____. "Structure du Prologue de saint Jean." *NTS* 30 (1984) 354–81.

_____. *The Hour of Jesus.* Middlegreen, U.K.: St. Paul, 1989.

Dettwiler, A. *Die Gegenwart des Erhöhten: Eine exegetische Studie zu den johanneischen Abschiedsreden (Joh 13,31–16,33) unter besonderer Berücksichtigung ihres Relecture-Charakters.* Göttingen: Vandenhoeck & Ruprecht, 1995.

Dijkstra, M. "The Altar of Ezekiel: Fact or Fiction?" *VT* 42 (1992) 22–36.

Dodd, C. H. "A Hidden Parable in the Fourth Gospel," *More New Testament Studies*, 30–40. Manchester: Manchester University Press, 1968.

Donin, H. H., ed. *Sukkot.* Popular Judaica Library. Jerusalem: Keter Books, 1974.

Dschulnigg, P. "Die Zerstörung des Tempels in den syn. Evangelien," *Tempelkult und Tempelzerstörung (70 n. Chr.) Festschrift für Clemens Thoma zum 60. Geburtstag.*, Eds. Simon Lauer and Hanspeter Ernst. 167–87. Bern: Peter Lang, 1995.

Duke, P. *Irony in the Fourth Gospel.* Atlanta: John Knox Press, 1985.

Dutheil, J. "L'évangile de Jean et le Judaïsme: le Temple et la Torah," *Origine et Postérité de l'Evangile de Jean,* Ed. Alain Marchadour. 71–85. Paris: Cerf, 1990.

Edwards, R. "ΧΑΡΙΝ ΑΝΤΙ ΧΑΡΙΤΟΣ (John 1:16): Grace and the Law in the Johannine Prologue." *JSNT* 32 (1988) 3–15.

Evans, C. A. "Jesus' Action in the Temple: Cleansing or Portent of Destruction." *CBQ* 51 (1989) 237–70.

_____. *Word and Glory: On the Exegetical and Theological Background of John's Gospel*. Journal for the Study of the New Testament Supplement Series 89. Sheffield: JSOT Press, 1993.

_____. "On the Prologue of John and the *Trimorphic Protennoia*." *NTS* 27 (1981) 395–401.

Fee, Gordan D. "Once More—John 7:37-39." *ExpT 89* (1978) 116–18.

Fennema, D. A. "John 1:18: 'God the Only Son.'" *NTS* 31 (1985) 121–35.

Fiorenza, E. S. "Cultic Language in Qumran and in the NT." *CBQ* 38 (1976) 159–77.

Fitzmyer, J. *The Gospel according to Luke: A New Translation with Introduction and Commentary*. Anchor Bible 28, 28A. New York: Doubleday, 1985.

Forestell, J. T. *The Word of the Cross: Salvation as Revelation in the Fourth Gospel*. Analecta Biblica 57. Rome: Biblical Institute Press, 1974.

Freed, E. D. "Who or what was before Abraham in John 8:58?" *JSNT* 17 (1983) 52–59.

Gärtner, B. *The Temple and the Community in Qumran and the New Testament*. Society for New Testament Studies Monograph Series 1. Cambridge: Cambridge University Press, 1965.

Genuyt, F. "La Comparution de Jésus devant Pilate: Analyse sémiotique de Jean 18,28–19,16." *RSR* 17 (1985) 133–46.

Giblin, C. H. "Confrontations in John 18,1-27." *Bib* 65 (1984) 210–31.

Grelot, P. "Jean, VII, 38: Eau du rocher ou source du Temple?" *RB* 70 (1963) 43–51.

_____. *Les Juifs dans L'Evangile selon Jean: Enquête historique et réflexion théologique*. Cahiers de la Revue Biblique 34. Paris: Gabalda, 1995.

Grigsby, B. "The Cross as an Expiatory Sacrifice in the Fourth Gospel." *JSNT* 15 (1982) 51–80.

_____. "'If Any Man Thirsts. . .': Observations on the Rabbinic Background of John 7,37-39." *Bib* 67 (1986) 101–8.

Guilding, A. *The Fourth Gospel and Jewish Worship*. Oxford: Clarendon Press, 1960.

Gundry, R. H. "'In my Father's House are many Μοναί' (John 14:2)." *ZNW* 58 (1967) 68–72.

Gutbrod, W. Ἰσραήλ - Ἰουδαῖος." *TDNT* 3 (1965) 356–91.

Hanse, H. "λαγχάνω." *TDNT* 4 (1967) 1–2.

Haran, M. "The Divine Presence in the Israelite Cult and the Cultic Institutions." *Bib* 50 (1969) 251–67.

_____. *Temples and Temple Service in Ancient Israel: An Inquiry into the Character of Cult Phenomena and the Historical Setting of the Priestly School*. Oxford: Clarendon, 1978.

Harner, P. B. *The "I Am" of the Fourth Gospel: A Study in Johannine Usage and Thought*. Facet Books. Philadelphia: Fortress, 1970.

_____. "Qualitative Anarthrous Predicate Nouns: Mark 15,39 and John 1,1." *JBL* 92 (1973) 75–87.

Harrington, D. J. *The Gospel of Matthew.* Sacra Pagina 1. Collegeville: The Liturgical Press, 1991.

Harris, E. *Prologue and Gospel: The Theology of the Fourth Evangelist.* Journal for the Study of the New Testament Supplement Series 107. Sheffield: JSOT Press, 1994.

Harvey, A. E. *Jesus on Trial: A Study in the Fourth Gospel.* London: SPCK, 1976.

Hayward, C. T. R. *The Jewish Temple: A non-biblical sourcebook.* London: Routledge, 1996.

Heil, J. P. *Blood and Water: The Death and Resurrection of Jesus in John 18–21.* Catholic Biblical Quarterly Monograph Series 27. Washington, D.C.: Catholic Bible Association of America, 1995a.

_____. "Jesus as the Unique High Priest in the Gospel of John." *CBQ* 57 (1995b) 729–745.

_____. "The Narrative Strategy and Pragmatics of the Temple Theme in Mark." *CBQ* 59 (1997) 76–100.

Hengel, M. "The Old Testament in the Fourth Gospel," *The Gospels and the Scriptures of Israel,* Eds. Craig Evans and W. Richard Stegner, 380–95. Journal for the Study of the New Testament Supplement Series. 104. Sheffield: Sheffield Press, 1994.

Himmelfarb, M. "From Prophecy to Apocalypse: The *Book of the Watchers* and Tours of Heaven," *Jewish Spirituality from the Bible through the Middle Ages,* ed. Arthur Green. 145–65. London: SCM, 1985.

Hodges, Z. "Rivers of Living Water - John 7:37-39." *Bibliotheca Sacra* 136 (1979) 239–48.

Hooke, S. H. "'The Spirit was not yet'." *NTS* 9 (1962–1963) 372–80.

Jaubert, A. "L'Image de la Vigne (Jean 15)," *Oikonomia. Heilsgeschichte als Thema der Theologie. Oscar Cullmann zum 65. Geburtstag gewidmet.,* ed. F. Christ. 93–99. Hamburg-Bergstedt: H. Reich Verlag, 1967.

Johns, L and D Miller. "The Signs as Witnesses in the Fourth Gospel: Re-examining the Evidence." *CBQ* 54 (1994) 519–35.

Johnson, L. T. *The Gospel of Luke.* Sacra Pagina 3. Collegeville: The Liturgical Press, 1991.

Jones, G. H. "The concept of holy war," *The World of Ancient Israel: Sociological, Anthropological and Political Perspectives,* ed. R. E. Clements. 299-321. Cambridge: Cambridge University Press, 1989.

Jones, L. P. *The Symbol of Water in the Gospel of John.* Journal for the Study of the New Testament Supplement Series 145. Sheffield: Sheffield Academic Press, 1997.

Juel, D. *Messiah and Temple*. Society of Biblical Literature Dissertation Series 31. Missoula, Mont.: Scholars Press, 1977.

Kalimi, I. and J. Purvis. "The Hiding of the Temple Vessels in Jewish and Samaritan Literature." *CBQ* 56 (1994) 679–85.

Käsemann, E. *The Testament of Jesus according to John 17*. Philadelphia: Fortress, 1968.

_____. *New Testament Questions of Today*. New Testament Library 41. London: SCM, 1969.

Kelber, W., ed. *The Passion in Mark*. Philadelphia: Fortress, 1976.

Koester, C. R. "Hearing, Seeing, and Believing in the Gospel of John." *Bib* 70 (1989a) 327–48.

_____. "The Saviour of the World (John 4:42)." *JBL* 109 (1990) 665–80.

_____. *Symbolism in the Fourth Gospel: Meaning, Mystery, Community*. Minneapolis: Fortress, 1995.

_____. *The Dwelling of God: The Tabernacle in the Old Testament, Intertestamental Jewish Literature, and the New Testament*. Catholic Biblical Quarterly Monograph Series 22. Washington, D. C.: Catholic Biblical Association of America, 1989b.

Köhler, W. "ἐπί." *EDNT* 2 (1991) 21–23.

_____. "παρά." *EDNT* 3 (1993) 12–13.

Kovacs, J. "'Now shall the ruler of this world be driven out': Jesus' Death as Cosmic Battle in John 12:20-36." *JBL* 114 (1995) 227–47.

Kraus, H-J. *Theology of the Psalms*. Minneapolis: Augsburg, 1979.

_____. *Psalms 1–59: A Commentary*. Minneapolis: Augsburg, 1988.

_____. *Psalms 60–150: A Commentary*. Minneapolis: Augsburg, 1989.

Kysar, R. *John, the Maverick Gospel*. Atlanta: John Knox Press, 1976.

_____. "John 10:22-30." *Int* 43 (1989) 66–70.

L'Heureux, C. E. "Numbers." *NJBC* (1989) 80–93.

Lamarche, P. "Le Prologue de Jean." *RSR* 52 (1964) 497–537.

Le Déaut, R. *La Nuit Pascale: Essai sur la signification de la Pâque juive à partir du Targum d'Exode XII 42*. Analecta Biblica 22. Rome: Biblical Institute Press, 1963.

_____. *The Message of the New Testament and the Aramaic Bible (Targum)*. Subsidia Biblica 5. Rome: Biblical Institute Press, 1982.

Lee, D. A. *The Symbolic Narratives of the Fourth Gospel: The Interplay of Form and Meaning*. Journal for the Study of the New Testament Supplement Series 95. Sheffield: JSOT Press, 1994.

_____. "Beyond Suspicion? The Fatherhood of God in the Fourth Gospel." *Pacifica* 8 (1995) 140–54.

_____. "Abiding in the Fourth Gospel: A Case-study in Feminist Biblical Theology." *Pacifica* 10 (1997) 123–36.

Léon-Dufour, X. "Le signe du temple selon saint Jean." *RSR* 39 (1951) 155–75.

_____. "Towards a Symbolic Reading of the Fourth Gospel." *NTS* 27 (1981) 439–56.

Levenson, J. *The Death and Resurrection of the Beloved Son: The Transformation of Child Sacrifice in Judaism and Christianity.* New Haven: Yale University Press, 1993.

Levine, E. *The Aramaic Version of the Bible: Contents and Context.* Berlin: Walter de Gruyter, 1988.

Longenecker, B. "The Unbroken Messiah: A Johannine Feature and Its Social Function." *NTS* 41 (1995) 428–441.

Lowe, M. "Who were the ΙΟΥΔΑΙΟΙ?" *NovT* 18 (1976) 101–30.

Lowe, R. "'Salvation' is not of the Jews." *JTS* 32 (1981) 341–68.

Lüdemann, G. "ὑψόω." *EDNT 3* (1993) 410.

Lyonnet, S., and L. Sabourin. *Sin, Redemption, and Sacrifice: A Biblical and Patristic Study.* Analecta Biblica 48. Rome: Biblical Institute Press, 1970.

Maccini, R. G. "A Reassessment of the Woman at the Well in John 4 in light of the Samaritan Context." *JSNT* 53 (1994) 35–46.

_____. *Her Testimony is True: Women as Witnesses according to John.* Journal for the Study of the New Testament Supplement Series 125. Sheffield: Sheffield Academic Press, 1996.

MacRae, G. "The meaning and evolution of the Feast of Tabernacles." *CBQ* 22 (1960) 251–76.

Malatesta, E. "Blood and water from the pierced side of Christ (Jn 19,34)," *Segni E Sacramenti Nel Vangelo Di Giovanni,* Ed. Pius-Ramon Tragan. 165–81. Rome: Editrice Anselmiana, 1977.

Manns, F. *Le Symbole Eau-Esprit dans le Judaisme Ancien.* Studium Biblicum Franciscanum Analecta 19. Jerusalem: Franciscan Printing Press, 1983.

_____. *John and Jamnia: How the Break Occurred between Jews and Christians c. 80–100 A.D.* Jerusalem: Franciscan Printing Press, 1988.

_____. *L'Evangile de Jean à la lumière du Judaïsme.* Studium Biblicum Franciscanum Analecta 33. Jerusalem: Franciscan Printing Press, 1991.

_____. *Jewish Prayer in the time of Jesus.* Studium Biblicum Franciscanum Analecta 22. Jerusalem: Franciscan Printing Press, 1994.

Martyn, J. L. "Glimpses into the History of the Johannine Community," *L'Évangile de Jean: Sources, rédaction, théologie,* Ed. M. de Jonge. 149–75. Gembloux: Duculot, 1977.

McCaffrey, J. *The House With Many Rooms: The Temple Theme of Jn 14, 2-3.* Rome: Biblical Institute Press, 1988.

McCarter Jr., P. K. *11 Samuel: A New Translation with Introduction, Notes and Commentary.* Anchor Bible 9. New York: Doubleday, 1984.

McCreesh, T. "Proverbs." *NJBC,* 453–61. 1989.

McKelvey, J. *The New Temple: The Church in the New Testament.* Oxford Theological Monographs. Oxford: Oxford University Press, 1969.

McNamara, M. "Targumic Studies." *CBQ* 28 (1966) 1–19.

_____. *Targum and Testament: Aramaic Paraphrases of the Hebrew Bible: A Light on the New Testament.* Grand Rapids, Mich.: Eerdmans, 1972.

_____. "'To prepare a resting-place for you.' A Targumic expression and John 14:2f." *Milltown Studies* 3 (1979) 100–7.

Meagher, J. C. "John 1:14 and the New Temple." *JBL* 88 (1969) 57–68.

Meeks, W. A. "Breaking Away: Three New Testament Pictures of Christianity's Separation from the Jewish Communities," *"To See Ourselves As Others See Us": Christians, Jews, "Others" in Late Antiquity,* Eds. Jacob Neusner and Ernest Frerichs. 93–115. Chico, Calif.: Scholars Press, 1985.

_____. *The Prophet-King: Moses Traditions and the Johannine Christology.* Supplements to Novum Testamentum 14. Leiden: Brill, 1967.

Menken, M. *Old Testament Quotations in the Fourth Gospel: Studies in Textual Form.* Contributions to Biblical Exegesis and Theology 15. Kampen: Kok Pharos, 1996.

Meyer, P. "'The Father': The Presentation of God in the Fourth Gospel," *Exploring the Gospel of John: In Honour of D. Moody Smith,* Eds. R. A. Culpepper and C. C. Black. 255–73. Louisville: Westminster John Knox, 1996.

Meyer, R. "κόλπος." *TDNT* 3 (1965) 824–26.

Meyers, C. "Temple, Jerusalem." *ABD* 6 (1992) 350–69.

Michaelis, W. "σκηνή." *TDNT* 7 (1971) 368–94.

Michel, O. "οἶκος, οἰκία." *TDNT* 5 (1964–76) 119–34.

_____. "ἱερόν." *TDNT* 3 (1965) 231–47.

_____. "ναός." *TDNT* 4 (1967) 880–90.

Minear, P. S. "The audience of the Fourth Gospel." *Int* 31 (1977) 339–54.

Moloney, F. J. "Narrative Criticism of the Gospels." *Pacifica* 4 (June 1991) 181–201.

_____. "The Johannine Son of God." *Salesianum* 38 (1976) 71–86.

_____. *The Word Became Flesh.* Theology Today Series 14. Dublin/Cork: Mercier Press, 1977.

_____. "From Cana to Cana (Jn. 2:1–4:54) and the Fourth Evangelist's Concept of Correct (and Incorrect) Faith." *Salesianum* 40 (1978a) 817–43.

_____. "The Fulness of a Gift which is Truth." *Catholic Theological Review* 1 (1978b) 30–33.

_____. *The Johannine Son of Man.* 2nd ed., Biblioteca di Scienze Religiose 14. Rome: LAS, 1978c.

_____. "When is John talking about Sacraments?" *ABR* 30 (1982) 10–33.

_____. "Reading John 2:13-22: The Purification of the Temple." *RB* 97 (1990) 432–52.

_____. "The Johannine Passion and the Christian Community." *Salesianum* 57 (1995) 25–61.

_____. *Reading John: Introducing the Johannine Gospel and Letters.* Blackburn: Dove, 1995.

_____. "Who is 'The Reader' in/of the Fourth Gospel," *The Interpretation of John,* Ed. John Ashton. 219–33. 2nd ed. Edinburgh: T & T Clark, 1997.

Montefiore, C. G., and H. Loewe. *A Rabbinic Anthology.* New York: Schocken, 1974.

Moore, G. F. *Judaism in the First Centuries of the Christian Era: The Age of the Tannaim.* 3 vols. Cambridge: Harvard University Press, 1927–30.

Mowinckel, S. *The Psalms In Israel's Worship.* 2 vols. Oxford: Basil Blackwell, 1967.

Murphy, R. E. *The Tree of Life: An Exploration of Biblical Wisdom Literature.* Anchor Bible Reference Library. New York: Doubleday, 1990.

_____. "Wisdom in the OT." *ABD* 6 (1992) 920–31.

Navone, J. J. "*Glory* in Pauline and Johannine Thought." *Wor* 42 (1968) 48–52.

Nereparampil, L. *Destroy this Temple: An Exegetico-Theological study on the meaning of Jesus' Temple-Logion in Jn 2:19.* Bangalore: Dharmaram College, 1978.

Neusner, J. "Judaism in a Time of Crisis: Four Responses to the Destruction of the Second Temple." *Judaism* 21 (1972) 313–27.

_____. "Varieties of Judaism in the Formative Age," *Jewish Spirituality from the Bible through the Middle Ages,* Ed. Arthur Green. 171–97. London: SCM, 1985.

_____. "The Absoluteness of Christianity and the Uniqueness of Judaism." *Int* 43 (1989a) 18–31.

_____. "Money-Changers in the Temple: The Mishnah's Explanation." *NTS* 35 (1989b) 287–90.

_____. *The Classics of Judaism: A textbook and reader.* Louisville: Westminster John Knox, 1995.

Neusner, J., and C. Thoma. "Die Pharisäer vor und nach der Tempelzerstörung des Jahres 70 n. Chr.," *Tempelkult und Tempelzerstörung (70 n. Chr.) Festschrift für Clemens Thoma zum 60. Geburtstag,* eds. Simon Lauer and Hanspeter Ernst. 189–230. Bern: Peter Lang, 1995.

Neyrey, J. H. "Jacob Traditions and the Interpretation of John 4:10-26." *CBQ* 41 (1979) 419–37.

_____. "The Jacob Allusions in John 1:51." *CBQ* 44 (1982) 596–605.

_____. "The Trials (Forensic) and Tribulations (Honor Challenges) of Jesus: John 7 in Social Science Perspective." *BTB* 26 (1996) 107–24.

Nicholson, G. C. *Death as Departure: The Johannine Descent-Ascent Schema.* Society of Biblical Literature Dissertation Series 63. Chico, Calif.: Scholars Press, 1983.

Nodet, É. "La Dédicace, les Maccabées et le Messie." *RB* 93 (1986) 321–75.

Noth, M. *A History of Pentateuchal Traditions.* Englewood Cliffs, N.J.: Prentice-Hall, 1972.

O'Day, G. R. "John," *The Women's Bible Commentary,* eds. Carol A. Newsom and Sharon H. Ringe. 293–304. Louisville: Westminster/John Knox, 1992.

Obermann, A. *Die christologische Erfüllung der Schrift im Johannesevangelium.* Wissenschaftliche Untersuchungen zum Neuen Testament 83. Tübingen: J.C.B. Mohr, 1996.

Okure, T. *The Johannine Approach to Mission: A Contextual Study of John 4:1-42.* Wissenschaftliche Untersuchungen zum Neuen Testament 2, Reihe 32. Tübingen: J.C.B. Mohr [Paul Siebeck], 1988.

Olsson, B. *Structure and Meaning in the Fourth Gospel: A Text-Linguistic Analysis of John 2:1-11 and 4:1-42.* Coniectanea Biblica, New Testament Series 6. Lund: Gleerup, 1974.

Ottosson, M. " הֵיכָל." *TDOT* 3 (1978) 382–88.

Painter, J. "The Church and Israel in the Gospel of John: A Response." *NTS* 25 (1978–1979) 103–112.

_____. "Johannine symbols: A Case Study in Epistemology." *Journal of Theology for Southern Africa* 27 (1979) 26–41.

_____. "John 9 and the Interpretation of the Fourth Gospel." JSNT 28 (1986) 31–61.

_____. "Tradition, history and interpretation in John 10," *The Shepherd Discourse of John 10 and its Context,* Eds. Johannes Beutler and Robert Fortna. 53–74. Cambridge: Cambridge University Press, 1991.

Pancaro, S. "The relationship of the Church to Israel in the Gospel of St. John." *NTS* 21 (1974–1975) 396–405.

_____. *The Law in the Fourth Gospel: The Torah and the Gospel, Moses and Jesus, Judaism and Christianity according to John.* Supplements to Novum Testamentum 42. Leiden: Brill, 1975.

Pesch, R. *Das Markusevangelium.* 3rd ed., 2 vols. Freiburg: Herder, 1980.

Pollard, T. E. "The Father-Son and God-Believer Relationships according to St. John: A brief study of John's use of Prepositions," *L'Évangile de Jean: Sources, rédaction, théologie,* ed. M. de Jonge. 363–69. Bibliotheca Ephemeridum Theologicae Lovaniensis. Gembloux: Duculot, 1977.

Porter, S. "Can Traditional Exegesis Enlighten Literary Analysis of the Fourth Gospel? An examination of the Old Testament Fulfillment Motif and the Passover Theme," *The Gospels and the Scriptures of Israel,* Eds. Craig Evans and W. R. Stegner. 396–428. Journal for the Study of the New Testament Supplement Series 104. Sheffield: Sheffield Academic Press, 1994.

Pridik, K.-H. "καί." *EDNT* 2 (1990–1993) 227–28.

Reim, G. *Studien Zum Alttestamentlichen Hintergrund des Johannesevangeliums.* Cambridge: Cambridge University Press, 1974.

Reinhartz, A. "The Gospel of John," *Searching the Scriptures,* ed. Elisabeth Schüssler-Fiorenza. 561–600. New York: Crossroad, 1994.

_____. *The Word in the World: The Cosmological Tale in the Fourth Gospel.* Society of Biblical Literature Monograph Series 45. vols. Atlanta: Scholars Press, 1992.

Richardson, P. "Why Turn the Tables? Jesus' Protest in the Temple Precincts." *Society of Biblical Literature Seminar Papers* 31 (1992) 507–23.

Ricoeur, P. *Interpretation Theory: Discourse and the Surplus of Meaning.* Fort Worth: Texas Christian University Press, 1976.

_____. *The Rule of Metaphor: Multidisciplinary studies of the creation of meaning in language.* London: Routledge & Kegan Paul, 1977.

Rubenstein, J. "Sukkot, Eschatology and Zechariah 14." *RB* 103 (1996) 161–95.

Rylaarsdam, J. C. "Booths, Feast of." *IDB* 1 (1962) 455–58.

_____. "Dedication, Feast of." *IDB* 1 (1962) 812–13.

Sanders, E. P. *Jesus and Judaism.* London: SCM, 1985.

Sava, A. F. "The Wound in the Side of Christ." *CBQ* 19 (1957) 343–46.

Schaeder, H. H. "Ναζαρηνός, Ναζωραῖος." *TDNT* 4 (1967) 874–79.

Schneiders, S. M. "History and Symbolism in the Fourth Gospel," *L'Évangile de Jean: Sources, rédaction, théologie,* ed. M. de Jonge. 371–76. Bibliotheca Ephemeridum Theologicae Lovaniensis. Louvain: Louvain University Press, 1977a.

_____. "Symbolism and the sacramental principle in the Fourth Gospel," *Segni E Sacramenti Nel Vangelo Di Giovanni,* Ed. Pius-Ramon Tragan. 221–35. Rome: Editrice Anselmiana, 1977b.

_____. *The Revelatory Text: Interpreting the New Testament as Sacred Scripture.* San Francisco: Harper Collins, 1991; 2nd ed. Collegeville: The Liturgical Press, 1999.

_____. *Written that you may believe: Encountering Jesus in the Fourth Gospel.* New York: Crossroad, 1999.

Schnelle, U. "Die Tempelreinigung und die Christologie des Johannesevangeliums." *NTS* 42 (1996) 359–73.

Schuchard, B. G. *Scripture Within Scripture: The Interrelationship of Form and Function in the Explicit Old Testament Citations in the Gospel of John.* Society of Biblical Literature Dissertation Series 133. Atlanta: Scholars Press, 1992.

Scott, M. *Sophia and the Johannine Jesus.* Journal for the Study of the New Testament Supplement Series 71. Sheffield: JSOT Press, 1992.

Scullion, J. "The God of the Patriarchs." *Pacifica* 1 (1988) 141–56.

Seeley, D. "Jesus' Temple Act." *CBQ* 55 (1993) 263–83.

Segovia, F. F. *The Farewell of the Word: The Johannine Call to Abide.* Minneapolis: Fortress, 1991.

Senior, D. *The Passion of Jesus in the Gospel of Mark.* Wilmington, Del.: Glazier, 1984.

_____. *The Passion of Jesus in the Gospel of John.* Leominister, U.K.: Gracewing, 1991.

Siegler, J., ed. *Sapientia Iesu Filii Sirach.* Vol. X11, 2. Septuaginta VT Graecum. Göttingen: Vandenhoeck & Ruprecht, 1980.

Smith, D. M. "The Presentation of Jesus in the Fourth Gospel." *Int* 31 (1977) 367–78.

Sommer, B. "Did prophecy cease? Evaluating a reevaluation." *JBL* 115 (1996) 31–47.

Staley, J. L. "The Structure of John's Prologue: Its implication for the Gospel's narrative structure." *CBQ* 48 (1986) 241–64.

_____. *Reading with a Passion: Rhetoric, Autobiography, and the American West in the Gospel of John.* New York: Continuum, 1995.

_____. *The Print's First Kiss: A Rhetorical Investigation of the Implied Reader in the Fourth Gospel.* Society of Biblical Literature Dissertation Series, 82. Atlanta: Scholars Press, 1988.

Stibbe, M. *John as storyteller: Narrative criticism and the fourth gospel.* Society for New Testament Studies Monograph Series 73. Cambridge: Cambridge University Press, 1992.

Strange, J. "Nazareth." *ABD* 4 (1992) 1050–51.

Talbert, C. H. *Reading John: A Literary and Theological Commentary on the Fourth Gospel and the Johannine Epistles.* London: SPCK, 1992.

Tolmie, D. F. *Jesus' Farewell to the Disciples: John 13:1–17:26 in Narratological Perspective.* Biblical Interpretation Series 12. Leiden: E. J. Brill, 1995.

Tragan, P-R. "Le discours sur le pain de Vie: Jean 6, 26-71. Remarques sur sa composition littéraire," *Segni E Sacramenti Nel Vangelo Di Giovanni,* Ed. Pius-Ramon Tragan. 89–119. Rome: Editrice Anselmiana, 1977.

Ulfgard, H. *Feast and Future: Revelation 7:9-17 and the Feast of Tabernacles.* Stockholm: Almqvist & Wiksell, 1989.

Unterman, A. "Shekinah." *Encyclopedia Judaica* 14 (1971) 1350–52.

Van der Horst, P. "The Birkat ha-minim in Recent Research." *ExpT* 105 (1994) 363–68.

Vellanickal, M. *Studies in the Gospel of John.* Bangalore: Asian Trading Corporation, 1982.

Vermes, G. *Jesus and the World of Judaism.* London: SCM, 1983.

von Rad, G. *Wisdom in Israel.* London: SCM, 1972.

von Rad, G. and G. Kittel. "δόξα." *TDNT* 2 (1964) 233–55.

Von Wahlde, U. "Literary Structure and Theological Argument in Three Discourses with the Jews in the Fourth Gospel." *JBL* 103 (1984) 575–84.

Walker, P. *Jesus and the Holy City: New Testament Perspectives on Jerusalem.* Grand Rapids, Mich.: Eerdmans, 1996.

Westermann, C. *Genesis 1–11: A Commentary.* Trans. John Scullion. London: SPCK, 1984.

Wilkinson, J. "The Incident of the Blood and Water in John 19.34." *Scottish Journal of Theology* 28 (1975) 149–72.

Yee, G. A. *Jewish Feasts and the Gospel of John.* Wilmington, Del.: Michael Glazier, 1989.

Index of Authors

Talbert, C. H., 72, 97, 183, 202

Ulfgard, H., 120, 135, 137
Unterman, A., 60

Van der Horst, P., 60
Vellanickal, M., 189
Vermes, G., 21, 56

von Rad, G., 52, 53, 54, 55, 59
von Wahlde, U., 146

Walker, P., 4, 66, 67, 68
Westermann, C., 55
Wilkinson, J., 193

Yee, G. A., 120, 121, 148, 149, 152

Index of Biblical References

OTHER ANCIENT SOURCES

Made in the USA
Middletown, DE
28 October 2021

51207814R00150